MW01025720

RUMOR, FEAR
AND THE
MADNESS OF CROWDS

J. P. CHAPLIN

DOVER PUBLICATIONS, INC.
MINEOLA, NEW YORK

For Paul

Copyright

Copyright © 1959, 1987 by J. P. Chaplin
All rights reserved.

Bibliographical Note

This Dover edition, first published in 2015, is an unabridged republication of
the work originally published by Ballantine Books, New York, in 1959.

Library of Congress Cataloging-in-Publication Data

Chaplin, James Patrick, 1919–
    Rumor, fear and the madness of crowds / J.P. Chaplin.
        pages cm
    "Originally published by Ballantine Books, New York, in 1959."
    ISBN-13: 978-0-486-79545-4
    ISBN-10: 0-486-79545-4
    1. Hysteria (Social psychology)—Case studies. I. Title.
HM871.C43 2015
302'.17—dc23

                                                              2015015979

Manufactured in the United States by RR Donnelley
79545401   2015
www.doverpublications.com

CONTENTS

CONTENTS

FOREWORD

About Hysteria

To DELVE INTO MASS HYSTERIA is to encounter the strange, the bizarre, the incredible. Among our subjects are Martians, a reincarnated Irish woman, a dead movie star, a crazed anesthetist, an obsessed Attorney General of the United States—characters as different as one could hope to find, yet all drawn together by the madness that surrounded them, by hysteria. Some, like the mad anesthetist, had no reality save in the minds of the hysterical people who created them. Some, like the dead movie actor, were real enough. But whether real or imaginary, the almost unbelievable outbreaks of mass madness for which they were responsible are far stranger than anything deliberately contrived by man's fertile imagination. As viewed through the mellowing perspective of time, some of the events are comic, others tragic—all blending into the warp and woof of the great human comedy.

Some of the best known instances of mass hysteria can hardly be classified as comic. Take, for example, the Children's Crusade of 1213, in which mass hysteria generated by religious fanaticism sent over 30,000 European children on the long march to Palestine to assist in capturing the Holy City after five previous unsuccessful attempts by their elders. Many of the children perished along the way; many were turned back from Italian seaports; and those who eventually reached the Middle East were captured and sold into slavery by the Saracens.

Or consider the South Sea Company of England in 1711. Inflamed by tales of great wealth in South America and Mexico brought back by merchant seamen, men notoriously elastic in their veracity, a group of visionaries organized the Company to engage in trade with the Latins at odds of a hundred to one in favor of the British. The get-rich-quick mania spread through the upper classes in England with the rapacity of the Black Death, and eventually, when the bubble burst, lost fortunes for thousands.

Little different was the famous "Mississippi Scheme" a

decade later, which nearly wrecked the credit of France. Stories of the great wealth of the territories that are now the states of Mississippi and Lousiana trickled back to France and led to the organization of stock companies whose purpose was to finance gold-mining operations in the territory. Nearly six thousand Parisians were pressed into labor squadrons, outfitted at public expense, and held in readiness to be embarked for America. Most of them eventually deserted, sold their government-issue tools and clothes, and took up their former lives. As was true across the Channel during the South Sea madness, many personal fortunes were lost, and because of heavy governmental investment in the enterprise, France was on the verge of bankruptcy.

But the mass madness that is of greatest interest to Americans is the celebrated Salem witchcraft of colonial days. The delusion was triggered by a group of Puritan bobby-soxers who had been listening to too many tales of West Indies sorcery, voodoo rites, witchery and other such black and un-Christian arts. They had heard the stories from Tituba, a kitchen slave who, ironically enough, was employed in the rectory of the village minister, the Rev. Parris. Tituba, with the innocence of the savage, undertook to entertain the young ladies during the long winter evenings with tales from her childhood. But the girls, finding that they could attract considerable attention by having hysterical fits which they attributed to the work of witches, succeeded in deluding their more credulous elders. Their winter voodoo sessions served them in good stead; they put on a performance that would have done credit to Prince Beelzebub himself. They screamed they were being bitten, choked, pricked, strangled and stabbed. They rolled their eyeballs and were convulsed with racking pains. Or, if the evil spirits moved them otherwise, they became pale as death, with muscles relaxed, as though victims of catalepsy. They conversed with unseen apparitions—presumably those of their tormentors—they smelled brimstone, they saw "familiars" or witches' imps. The effect of this on a community which believed implicitly in Satan, witchcraft, and the imminence of Doomsday can readily be imagined. Farmers left their fields and housewives their kitchens to stand appalled at this work of Satan. Only a few doubted the reality of what they saw.

Eventually the madness spread to surrounding villages and, as a consequence, dozens of citizens, mostly elderly women, were thrown into jails, tried as witches, and twenty were eventually hanged. While the hysteria lasted, the girls acted in a role similar to that of a modern congressional investigating committee of the worst sort. They succeeded in getting in-

8

nocent persons "identified" as witches by confessed ex-witches who, of course, found it expedient to get on the side of the angels. They made their accusations stick by employing the Big Lie and by putting on fearful courtroom demonstrations of bewitchment for the benefit of the credulous judges. Eventually their accusations became so fantastic that they ceased to be credible even to the most hell-and-brimstone Puritan Divines, but not until incalculable damage had already been done.

Lest we take comfort in the fact that these strange events took place in the distant past when the human mind was ridden by superstitions and under the domination of religious fanatics, the studies in the chapters to follow will afford abundant proof that mass hysteria and crowd madness can still inspire the modern mind to heights of folly unsurpassed by any outbreaks from the pages of history.

It is not surprising, in view of the prevalence of hysteria, that it has been a subject of study long before our day. Its history is a fascinating story in itself. Recognized as a disease by the ancient Greeks, it was mistakenly attributed to a derangement of the uterus and called "hysteria," from the Greek word for uterus. It is odd that the Greeks, with all their wisdom and knowledge, should so limit the disease to women, for it is readily observable that the male half of the population is also subject to the disorder. Nevertheless, the classic misconception finds sanction in contemporary speech, for such exhibitions of wild excitement and mental disturbance are still, in the popular mind, considered a prerogative of the weaker sex.

The modern study of hysteria began in France shortly after the mid-point of the nineteenth century with the work of Charcot and his famous pupil, Janet. Charcot was a distinguished neurologist who held an appointment as visiting physician at the Salpetriere, a large Parisian hospital for the insane. The master and his pupils became interested in the practice of hypnotism, which at that time was considered in a class with black magic and other such dubious arts. Charcot, however, was a flamboyant personality as well as a rugged individualist, and he persisted in his investigations of the mental state of his disturbed patients by means of hypnosis despite adverse criticism from his more conservative colleagues.

To his surprise, Charcot discovered that a perfectly healthy arm could be rendered paralyzed or anesthetic by means of suggestions given during the hypnotic sleep. But of even greater importance was the finding that many of the hospitalized patients' symptoms could be temporarily alleviated by the same method. Occasionally a "paralyzed" arm or an "anesthetic" leg could be permanently cured by an intensive series of hypnotic treatments.

However, the deeper significance of his discoveries escaped Charcot. Without knowing, he had stumbled upon one of the greatest medical discoveries of all time, namely, that *physical symptoms and organic disorders can be caused by psychological factors*. Charcot maintained that there must be a somatic or nervous basis for the hysteric's symptoms, but it remained for his pupil, Janet, to recognize the essentially psychological nature of the disturbance.

Janet greatly extended Charcot's studies of the hysteric personality and published a number of technical books on the subject which are still considered basic texts in the field. Of greatest contemporary interest is Janet's concept of the state of dissociation which led to many famous studies of dissociated personalities—the Drs. Jekyll and Messrs. Hyde of abnormal psychology. As the recent popular book on the subject, *The Three Faces of Eve*, has so dramatically demonstrated, the human personality in hysterical states is capable of splitting or fragmenting into two or more separate selves, each of which may be totally unaware of what the other is doing.

Janet also described a number of other highly significant, if less dramatic, manifestations of hysteria. Among the more common are the paralyses and anesthesias already alluded to—blindness, deafness, compulsive vomiting, respiratory disorders, and the hysterical *fugue* or flight. The latter, incidentally, is frequently found in newspaper stories as "amnesia" or "loss of memory." Nevertheless, it is one of the many forms that this Janus-faced mental disorder may take.

While Charcot, Janet and their associates were delving into these fascinating abnormalities, an as yet unknown Viennese physician, Dr. Sigmund Freud, was struggling with the difficulty that many of his patients who complained of organic illnesses were, in reality, perfectly healthy physical specimens. Freud was both puzzled and helpless in the face of this difficult problem. Obviously, treating the patient's symptoms with conventional drugs was not the answer. Then the work of Charcot and the French school came to his attention. Following this promising lead, Freud made an extensive visit to Paris, where he learned the art of hypnotism and heard Charcot's views on hysteria. When he returned to Vienna, he began to apply his newly won knowledge to his neurotic patients. However, he soon discovered that suggesting away symptoms by hypnosis was, in effect, no different from dosing the patient with palliative drugs. Neither form of therapy got at the heart of the problem, which was psychological rather than physical. But in the course of his unsuccessful excursion into hypnotherapy, Freud also discovered something of far greater importance. If the patient could be induced to talk about his past experiences while under the hypnotic trance, he frequently relived highly emotional and traumatic repressed experiences which Freud came to recognize as the heart of the patient's mental difficulties. The resulting mental catharsis often gave the patient a relatively long-lasting measure of relief from his symptoms. Freud's genius lay in recognizing the fact that the curative agent was allowing his patients to reveal their unconscious during hypnosis. The verbal suggestions on the part of the therapist played only a minor role. Freud's discovery ultimately led to the psychoanalytic couch and the free-association technique, which he found to be more satisfactory for exploring the mind's underground than hypnosis. But that is another story. Let us return to hysteria, attempting to relate these individual clinical studies to mass hysteria.

Mass hysteria is a loosely used term which may refer to anything from mere excitement brought about by a disturbing rumor to true mass outbreaks of individual hysteria such as those which took place in Salem at the witch trials or those which occurred during the episode of the Mad Gasser to be described in a subsequent chapter. In cases of true mass hysteria, individuals become so disturbed that they may see or hear things that do not exist or suffer severe bodily disturbances such as choking, vomiting, convulsions, and the like. In the present book, the term is used in its broadest sense. That is, we shall find all degrees of hysterical manifestations, ranging from transitory instances of wild excitement to severe delusions accompanied by violent mental and bodily disturbances. However, irrespective of the form of the outbreak, *all* hysterical manifestations have one outstanding characteristic which links them together—they occur as the result of suggestion in highly suggestible individuals. Just as Janet could suggest an anesthesia in his patients, so can a sincere but credulous bearer of tales, a faith healer, a propagandist or a rumor-monger implant strange beliefs or generate wild excitement in the hypersuggestible.

Finally, before we delve into these curious byways of

human behavior, it should be emphasized that the hysteric, whether individual or *en masse*, is not a fraud or malingerer. The hysterically blind, deaf or paralyzed are truly incapacitated by their disorders and only a physician skilled in the intricacies of the unconscious can distinguish the organically ill from the hysterically disordered. Similarly, those who "see" flying saucers or Martian invaders do see something and are honestly convinced of the authenticity of their observations. What is real psychologically is real to the observer. By bearing this principle in mind, our laughter at the antics of our fellow men who are in the grip of mass hysteria will be tempered with sympathy as we read of those all too human individuals who people the pages to follow.

1: The "Secrets" of the Nunnery

THE RIGHT REVEREND BENEDICT J. FENWICK, D. D., eased his three hundred pounds of solid flesh into the massive leather chair he usually reserved for visitors. He sighed, partly with contentment and partly because he was bone-tired. It had been a strenuous day—a day that frequently taxed the Bishop's cheerful, vigorous disposition but never found him wanting. He reflected for a few moments on the ceremonies of his consecration that morning as Bishop of Boston, and allowed himself the luxury of a glow of pride. His new appointment was the culmination of years of strenuous work devoted to the interests of his Church. He could look back with satisfaction to the very beginning of his priestly career in New York City following his ordination at twenty-six. During his eight years in the metropolitan area, he had helped draw the plans for St. Patrick's Cathedral, had acted as a trouble-shooter in a southern diocese where a serious rift threatened to develop between two foreign-born factions, and had taken part in a dramatic, though unsuccessful, attempt at a death-bed conversion of the famous atheist and hero of the Revolution, Tom Paine.

These and other glimmerings of leadership led to Fenwick's appointment to the presidency of Georgetown University and his ultimate elevation to the Roman Catholic hierarchy. But on this first evening of his career as prelate, the newly-consecrated Bishop looked not so much to the past as to the future, and the future would have discouraged a lesser man. Boston, the site of his bishopric, had been a city for only two years though it boasted a population of over fifty thousand. Drunkenness and brawling were common among its heterogeneous masses of immigrants. There was bitter anti-Catholic prejudice among the Boston blue bloods and high caste descendants of the Colonists. The Gunpowder Plot, hatched among Catholics in England in revenge for stringent anti-Catholic laws, still rankled in their descendants. While *Guy Fawkes** Day* was being celebrated in England to commemorate the event, Americans, until recently, had their corresponding *No Pope Day* on which His Holiness was burned or hanged in effigy. Often rival factions sponsored rival

---

* One of the plotters for whom the day was named. Their aim was to blow up Parliament.

"Popes" and brawls broke out over which group would have the honor of hanging its effigy in the public square. Finally, there was a strong spirit of nationalism spreading over the United States, and the Roman Catholic Church was looked upon as a dangerous, subversive faction whose allegiance was given to a foreign power.

Aside from having to live with this prejudicial environment, there were many other problems already claiming Fenwick's attention. As yet no assistants had been appointed to help in the administration of his see. Seminaries for the training of priests were inadequate, and he would have to prepare young men for ordination himself. There were churches to be built, parishes to be founded, cemeteries to be acquired, and the difficult problem of providing educational facilities for Catholic children to be solved. But on that happy evening of personal triumph, the Bishop little knew just how stormy and difficult his reign was to be. As events were to prove, it probably would not have daunted Fenwick's Himalayan constitution and spirit in any case; but as he retired that night in 1825, he must have thought the evils of the day were more than sufficient thereof.

Four years later, in 1829, Fenwick had already accomplished much in the way of strengthening and improving his diocesan organization. A number of new churches had already been built or were under construction; novitiates were in training for the priesthood, and the Catholic faith was spreading, though slowly, in the face of bitter opposition.

One of the highlights of the Bishop's accomplishments was the erection of a new convent for young girls in Charlestown, Massachusetts. Fenwick was not the school's founder; it had been a going concern since 1820, five years before he was called to Boston. But Fenwick had decided at once that the original quarters in Boston were entirely unsuited to the purpose for which the academy had been established. At the time of Fenwick's appointment the sisters were living in an old residence, near the cathedral, which was neither large enough nor suitably located for a girls' school. Therefore, in 1826, Fenwick purchased twenty-seven acres near Bunker Hill in Charlestown on which to build a new convent. The property included an old farmhouse which the sisters occupied for a year and a half while their new home was under construction on the crest of the hill that sloped up from the old farmstead.

The new structure was worthy of the highest admiration. It stood three stories high overlooking vineyards, terraced walks and vegetable and flower gardens, including small individual plots for the students. A lodge for the Bishop had also been built a short distance from the convent. Fenwick, who was of a scholarly inclination, had acquired a fine library over the years which he installed in the lodge. The convent school was conducted by the Ursuline sisters who were noted in Europe for their efforts on behalf of the education of young females. Nor was this devotion lavished on Catholic girls alone; the good sisters attracted pupils from the best upper-class families of various religious persuasions. They were so highly regarded as educators, that when certain European governments ordered all convents in their principalities closed, the Ursulines were specifically exempt from the order and even encouraged in their work.

Much of this same attitude carried over to the Charlestown convent. It had been an immediate success and was drawing pupils from the best Protestant families in Boston and some from distant parts of the United States and Canada. The Mother Superior, otherwise known as Mary Edward St. George, ran the institution in a highly efficient, if somewhat totalitarian, manner. The future looked bright indeed.

There had been only one untoward incident to mar the brief history of the convent, and this occurred at the time the sisters occupied the little farmhouse before the completion of the main building. One of the Selectmen from Charlestown became so inflamed at the thought of a nunnery in his bailiwick, he threatened to gather a force of thirty or forty men to burn the house down. But the mild deportment of the nuns as they took their evening constitutionals on the hill soothed his ruffled feelings, and the ugly incident had long since been forgotten.

Yet, in spite of these accomplishments, the year 1829 heralded the appearance of the first storm clouds on the New England horizon that were to develop into a hurricane of anti-Catholic prejudice during the five years to follow. The spirit of nationalism was intensifying; thus there was correspondingly more anti-Catholic feeling directed against a church which was held to be essentially extra-national in its purposes and organization.

To make matters worse from the point of view of the Catholics, vicious anti-Catholic propaganda began streaming in from abroad. The very titles of these works—*Master Key to Popery, Jesuit Juggling, Forty Popish Frauds Detected and Disclosed, Female Convents,* with the sub-title: *Secrets of Nunneries Disclosed*—insured the widespread popularity of the books and at the same time fanned the fires of prejudice and hate. The book on *Female Convents* was typical of the lot. It was a kind of latter-day *Decameron* purportedly written by Scipio de Ricci, an ex-priest. Filled with allegations of

15

debauchery on the part of nuns and priests, it told of the discovery of infant bodies in hidden vaults under European convents and denounced Catholic educational institutions as Roman Jugend organizations in disguise.

By 1829, feelings in Charlestown were running so high that the Bishop's purchase of three acres on Bunker Hill for a Catholic cemetery produced such violent opposition Fenwick had to take the matter to the Supreme Court of Massachusetts. During the legal proceedings a stable on the convent grounds was burned by anti-Catholics; the houses of Irish Catholics in Boston were stoned for three nights in a row, and street brawls between Catholics and non-Catholics were frequent.

The next year saw the crystallization of anti-Catholic feeling to the extent that a semi-formal organization was founded along with an official weekly publication, *The Protestant*, to spread the gospel of hate. Other newspapers took up the cry, attacking Rome, the Pope, the Church, the priesthood and, of course, convents, or to use the preferred term of opprobrium, "nunneries." Events moved so quickly that in 1831, a formal New York Protestant Association was chartered. The organization proved popular and attacks on it by Catholics and their supporters only served to strengthen the bonds of prejudice which held it together.

During the next few years, the Protestant nativists gained ground rapidly. They had developed powerful leaders who were also first-rate orators and debaters. These merchants of prejudice used their pulpits to deliver violent tirades against the Catholic Church and attempted to engage priests in one-sided public debates. One of the mightiest of these harbingers of violence was the Rev. Dr. Lyman Beecher—more famous today as the father of Harriet Beecher Stowe, but in the early 1800's as a leader of anti-Catholics and a man who epitomized everything the extremists in the movement held dear. One of his favorite oratorical flourishes during a sermon was to repeat over and over the phrase, "the Devil and the Pope of Rome." It was against this background of prejudice and ugly rumor that violence erupted on the hills of "Bunker, Breed and Benedict" in 1834. It was a conflagration that spread through the entire nation and which took thirty years to extinguish and only then when it was swept into the greater holocaust of Civil War.

The fuse that detonated the explosion was the appearance in Charlestown of an "escaped nun" from the "accursed convent." The fugitive in question, Rebecca Reed, was neither a nun nor an escapee; but against the background of religious intolerance and in the face of rumors that were

16

beginning to circulate around Charlestown and Boston about the dark goings on in the convent, "escaped nun" she became—at least in the popular mind. The fact of the matter seems to have been that she was a rather stupid, lazy girl who was employed in no higher capacity than that of a menial in the institution's kitchen. Apparently, she had entertained aspirations about becoming a member of the Ursuline Order but showed neither the requisite talent nor necessary industry to fit into the life of the convent. The opinion among objective observers was that she was lazy and found the work too hard. In order to escape censure as a failure, she put her imagination to work instead of her muscles and thereby found a way to get out of her intolerable position with honor. She decided to flee the convent and spread the story that she was being forced to take orders against her will. Once out, she quickly got into the clutches of the Beecher group, and stories were soon circulated that told of "forced conversions," cruel and unusual penances imposed upon the nuns by the "monster" Fenwick, and hints of the presence of mysterious "vaults" under the convent whose dark purposes were left to the listener's imagination. The results of her experiences were later published in a book entitled *Six Months in a Convent*. There seems to be little doubt that she enjoyed considerable editorial help from her anti-Catholic mentors during its preparation.

Tales of the unholy activities going on in the "nunnery" became progressively more distorted and provocative. Threats, at first vague and under cover, then specific and in the open, began to circulate in Charlestown and Boston. Posters appeared in the streets whose wording was calculated to fan the flames of rising hysteria. The following example is taken from Billington's history of the era:

> Go Ahead! To Arms!! To Arms!! Ye brave and free the avenging Sword unshield!! Leave not one stone upon another of that curst Nunnery that prostitutes female virtue and liberty under garb of holy Religion. When Bonaparte opened the Nunneries in Europe he found cords of Infant skulls!!!!!

In spite of all that had happened thus far, it is possible that things might have quieted down if there had been no additional provocation. There were many who took Miss Reed and her wild tales with more than a grain of salt; but then a nun who had taken the veil did flee the convent, and from that time on passions reigned unchecked.

The fugitive's name was Elizabeth Harrison who, as Sister

17

Mary John, taught music in the academy and suffered a mental breakdown as a result of overwork at her assigned task. She had been preparing her pupils for an exhibition and had been giving fourteen music lessons a day of forty-five minutes duration each—enough to drive anyone of normal sensibilities to distraction. This formidable schedule gave rise to a "brain fever" just before school was dismissed for the summer; but under the ministrations of a physician and the sisters she had apparently recovered—in fact, seemed quite happy in spite of the music lessons until the psychotic episode of her flight shortly after school re-opened for the fall term.

After leaving the convent surreptitiously on July 28th, 1834, she took sanctuary at the nearby home of Edward Cutter, a gentleman whose daughters had been among her former pupils. According to one account, Miss Harrison burst in on the Cutters at suppertime clothed only in her nightgown and in a state of feverish distraction. Mr. Cutter, after Miss Harrison had been partially restored to her senses, took her at her own request to the home of an acquaintance living in West Cambridge. Cutter then notified Bishop Fenwick of the nun's defection and returned to his amazed family.

The convent at the time of these disrupting developments was flourishing. The original faculty of three sisters had been expanded to ten, two of whom were lay sisters acting as housekeepers. The student body consisted of approximately fifty girls, three-fourths of whom were upper-class Protestants whose families looked upon the academy as a kind of finishing school for their daughters. The pupils were charged $125 a year for tuition and board and were educated in eighteen subjects including the more delicate arts of Japanning, oil painting, music, needlework, and painting on velvet, satin and wood. There was also instruction in the more abstract subjects of chemistry, astronomy, botany "the use of globes," and rhetoric. No doubt the high tone of the establishment helped seal its fate, since half the townspeople were ignorant, unsophisticated laborers who were jealous of their betters and afraid of things they could not comprehend. There was, however, no substantiated evidence that the sisters were in any way proselytizing their charges to become members of the Catholic faith, though there were many rumors to this effect.

Once the news of Miss Harrison's escape got out, the rumors flew thick and fast. It was alleged that Bishop Fenwick had recaptured her and that she was held prisoner in a dungeon in the cellars of the convent. The following somewhat garbled account appeared in the *Boston Mercantile Journal* shortly after Miss Harrison's defection:

18

MYSTERIOUS—We understand that a great excitement at present exists in Charlestown, in consequence of the mysterious disappearance of a young lady at the Nunnery in that place. The circumstances as far as we can learn are as follows:—The young lady was sent to the place in question to complete her education, and became so pleased with the place and its inmates, that she was induced to seclude herself from the world and take the black veil. After some time spent in the Nunnery she became dissatisfied, and made her escape from the institution—but was afterwards persuaded to return, being told that if she would continue but three weeks longer, she would be dismissed with honor. At the end of that time, a few days since, her friends called for her, but she was not to be found, and much alarm is excited in consequence.

On the Saturday after Miss Harrison's disappearance, placards appeared on the streets of Charlestown bearing the following inflammatory exhortation:

To the Selectmen of Charlestown! Gentlemen—It is currently reported that a mysterious affair has recently happened at the Nunnery in Charlestown. It is your duty gentlemen to have this affair investigated immediately; if not, the truckmen of Boston will demolish the Nunnery Thursday night—August 14.

In the meantime, the object of this violent solicitude had come to her senses and had been conveyed back to the convent at her own request. She apologized to the Bishop and Mother St. George for having caused all the fuss, and her two superiors more or less considered the matter closed. They seemed to discount the threats and newspaper articles as no more than a further sporadic outcropping of the prejudice which had dogged the convent from its inception. But whether it was complacency or trust in the powers of righteousness, they failed to understand that the situation was fast approaching a climax. The smoldering prejudice had flamed into mass hysteria and was about to spell the convent's doom.

On Saturday, August 9th, passions were so inflamed that the Selectmen thought it advisable to follow the recommendations on the placards and conduct an investigation. Since the rumor that Miss Harrison was being held against her will seemed to be the chief cause of popular consternation, the Selectmen appointed a committee of five to demand an interview with her and at the same time to inspect the convent—no doubt to search for the "vaults."

The accounts of the inspection vary considerably depending upon the source consulted. Shea, in his *History of the Catholic Church,* reports a "number of evil-disposed men of the dregs of society" in company with some of the Selectmen appeared at the convent shouting, "Down with the Convent!" "Down with the Nuns!" They demanded to see Miss Harrison, and when the Mother Superior produced her and they were informed by the girl herself that she was not being held against her will, went away satisfied. Another historian (Catholic) claims that the Mother Superior invited the Selectmen on her own initiative and had Miss Harrison conduct them on a three-hour tour of the establishment.

However, the most engaging, if not entirely accurate, account was provided by Louisa Whitney, a pupil in the academy, who later published her reminiscences of the fateful events leading to the convent's destruction. She recounts that the committee of Selectmen was given a glacial reception by Mother St. George while the girls watched delightedly from hidden vantage points. When the Selectmen tried to assure the Superior of their good intentions she overwhelmed them with a torrent of invective, charged them with responsibility for the wild stories that were in circulation, and refused to allow them to search the cellar for the "dungeons and cells of iniquity." Miss Whitney goes on to report that Miss Harrison finally calmed the enraged Mother Superior and reassured the Selectmen of her own liberty. She then offered to conduct one of them through the cellars, but as he approached the gaping pitch-black entrance he lost courage and departed in company with his fellow Selectmen.

Whatever the exact nature of the inspection tour, there seems to be little doubt that in spite of their failure to reach the convent's underground passages the Selectmen were indeed satisfied Miss Harrison was not being detained against her will. In fact, they wrote a report vindicating the convent which was supposed to have been published in the local newspapers, but either through carelessness or deliberate malfeasance did not appear until after the convent was a smoldering mass of ruins.

For the next day, which was Sunday, we have only Miss Whitney's account of the state of affairs within the convent. According to her, things were relatively quiet. The girls attended Mass in a body as was customary although the majority who were Protestant spent the time reading from their own Bibles or prayer books. In the afternoon there was the usual influx of visitors, most of whom were parents and relatives of the girls. They brought gifts or conferred with the sisters on the scholastic progress of their daughters. If Miss Whitney's memory is to be trusted, several of the parents warned the Mother Superior of the dangerous temper of the townspeople and the increasingly pointed threats of the convent's impending destruction. However, Mother St. George appeared calm and reassured everyone that in the unlikely event of an attack there was a sufficient force of Irish laborers in Boston to come to their defense and repel the truckmen. So far as is known, none of the parents attempted to remove their children from the convent in spite of repeated urgings to do so on the part of more apprehensive or prescient friends. An almost unbelievable complacency seemed to have hypnotized not only the parents, but the Mother Superior, Bishop Fenwick and the civil authorities as well.

On Monday, the final day of the convent's existence, we must again depend upon Miss Whitney's diary for an account of the institution's internal state during the daylight hours. She recounts that the girls were awakened as usual (very early), by the voice of Sister Mary Austin as she walked slowly down the aisle of the dormitory reciting matins and pulling the bed clothes off the sleeping girls. They made their ablutions in the heavy bedside crockery which served for plumbing in those days, and were then paraded to a classroom for morning prayers. Next they marched to a breakfast which consisted of dry bread and a mug full of milk. For the rest of the morning the girls were occupied with classroom activities.

Apparently some of the hysteria that was rife in the town had at last penetrated the walls of the convent in spite of the Mother Superior's lofty air of assurance. There was a lack of discipline evident in the classroom that morning, and little learning had been accomplished by the dinner hour. Miss Whitney, like all students at all institutions in the world, dwells on the unpalatability and insufficiency of the establishment's cuisine. She did not recall the specific menu for that particular day, but dinners in general followed this pattern: Soup with vegetables, or soup-meat mixed with vegetables. On Fridays and fast days, salt fish or hasty pudding. For dessert, they were served a dish of dried figs or prunes, so tough the girls were convinced they must be chopped-up bits of the nuns' old shoes.

After this unsatisfactory meal, there was a period of relaxation followed by afternoon classes and then another recess before supper. During the afternoon, alarming rumors and reports kept filtering into the academy from outside. A Mrs. Barrymore, the dancing mistress and a townswoman, did much to increase the tension and restlessness among both faculty and students when she brought in the latest communiques from the Charlestown camp. Evidently Mrs. Barrymore was a better rumor-monger than a prophetess, since she expressed strong convictions that the convent would not be attacked.

Bishop Fenwick also called during the afternoon, and Miss Whitney caught a glimpse of his excellency and the Mother Superior taking snuff (an unecclesiastic habit to which both were addicted), and engaging in apparently lively and carefree conversation.

Eventually suppertime arrived, and this spartan meal consisted of bread, butter and water. Bedtime followed shortly after at 7:30 P.M. If Miss Whitney's account of the academy's comestibles is correct, it is something of a mystery that the girls did not attempt the destruction of the establishment themselves. No doubt her gastronomic memories were rendered somewhat bilious by homesickness and girlish rebellion.

When darkness had fallen, an interlude of quiet followed as the nuns performed their round of bed checks, said their evening prayers and made personal preparations for retiring. Down below the grounds of the academy, the scene was tranquil, even beautiful, for the fires from the kilns in the nearby brickyards cast a warm, cozy glow skyward. But this peaceful interlude proved all too short. At 8:30 a hideous yell pierced the night from the direction of a little bridge spanning a creek which cut across the road to the convent from Charlestown. The isolated yell quickly became the roar of a mob, and within a few minutes the building was surrounded by howling men and boys. There were shouts of "Down with the convent!", "Release your prisoners!" and demands to see the "secreted" nun.

Eventually the leaders, among whom was one of the Selectmen, pounded on the door and demanded to see Miss Harrison. This was undoubtedly the critical moment. Everything depended on how the Mother Superior dealt with a potentially explosive situation. She handled it in the same way she governed the convent—with a defiant, royal air which in this case was to serve her ill. Had she been more deferential the day might yet have been saved, but instead she hurled defiance at her tormentors and told Selectman Runey that he ought to be reading the riot act to the mob instead of demanding Miss Harrison. She then turned to the others and told them to go about their affairs instead of annoying the sisters and disturbing the children's rest. She added that she would receive a decently conducted delegation at some more suitable hour the following day. The leaders, seemingly pacified, started to retire, but not satisfied with her victory, she then shouted to the mob beyond. "Disperse immediately, for if you don't the Bishop has twenty thousand Irishmen at his command in Boston, and they will whip you all into the sea!" This unconciliatory remark brought a fusillade of stones from the exacerbated mob at which point the doughty Mother Superior herself retreated.

Some time passed while the rioters drew back in consultation, and then a pile of tar barrels was set afire in a neighboring field. Some reports attribute the mob's hesitancy to fear that the Bishop had secreted a force inside the convent to ambush the attackers. Whatever the reason, the light from the fire revealed about fifty ringleaders dressed in fantastic disguises including women's clothes; apparently the bonfire was some sort of prearranged signal for the main body of rioters to gather. Eventually, as estimated by the Boston *Post*, the total number grew to four thousand. While waiting for reinforcements, the ring leaders broached a hogshead of rum to liven things up and add fuel to their inner fires. Mr. Runey, the Selectman, after mildly remonstrating with the mob, washed his hands of the affair and "went home to rest his sore eyes."

Meanwhile both the students and sisters were in a state of abject terror. Most of the nuns fainted at one point or another during the proceedings, and some of the older girls found themselves suddenly thrust into the role of nurses to their erstwhile instructors. To add to the confusion, one of the nuns, a blood sister to the Mother Superior, lay dying of consumption, and Miss Harrison was again thrown into a deranged state by the events which her own actions had largely precipitated. Only the Mother Superior kept the inmates from fleeing in terror by exercising her iron will and defiant manner. To the very end she believed she was master of the situation.

The main assault began about midnight. The mob stormed the door, and this time there could be no doubting their nefarious intentions. Mother St. George tried a last desperate appeal, but she was answered by a musket shot and wisely retreated to the children's quarters. Here she marshalled her charges and led them out of the building through a back entrance and down to the edge of the garden which was the only place not occupied by members of the mob. Here the fugitives came up against a high picket fence and were forced to stop.

Inside, the mob had already begun the sack of the convent. They started with the cellars, seeking, no doubt, the dungeons and cells of iniquity. Next they ransacked the upper chambers.

Money was appropriated from the Superior's office—valuables belonging to the children, silverware, and other portables went into the ringleaders' pockets. As they went through the classrooms, they hurled musical instruments and books out of the windows to the courtyard below. When sufficient inflammable material had been collected, they made a bonfire of it in the reception room on the first floor. Bibles, prayer books and the crucifix from the chapel altar were thrown into the flames with curses and yells of delight. Others dashed from room to room setting fire to drapes and whatever else would burn. Within minutes the entire convent was a mass of flames. The Boston *Evening Transcript* gives a retroactive description of the revels in these words:

> What a scene must this midnight conflagration have exhibited—lighting up the inflamed countenances of an infuriated mob of demons, *attacking a convent of women, a seminary for the instruction of young females,* and turning them out of their beds, half naked in the hurry of their flight, and half dead with confusion and terror. And this drama, too, to be enacted on the very soil that afforded one of the earliest places of refuge to the Puritan fathers of New England . . .

Meanwhile, the terrified girls and sisters who had been listening to the last disonant notes of their musical instruments as they splintered on the pavement, were doubly terrified as the flames which lighted up the area for miles around revealed their sanctuary. They heard cries from the mob which made it plain that the Mother Superior was wanted in person and would no doubt be pursued to her place of hiding when she was not found in the convent. Fortunately, Mr. Cutter and some of his neighbors were also looking for the sisters and their charges and found them ahead of the mob. The rescuers tore pickets off the fence to provide an exit for the fugitives who were taken to the house of a Mr. Adams some distance from the convent. There they spent a sleepless night expecting to be discovered at any moment by the mob's patrols. Miss Whitney's last memory of the Mother Superior was a mental picture of the still-defiant woman sitting bolt upright on the Adams' sofa, clutching her silver snuff box.

Back at the convent grounds, the yelling, frenzied rioters who had done their worst at the main building now turned their incendiary attentions to the Bishop's lodge and proceeded to ransack it and make a bonfire of the contents. Mention was previously made of his grace's library which underwent a mock auction before being consigned to the flames. A young boy, Marvin Marcy, took up the volumes, read the titles or gave profane titles to them, knocked them off and cast them into the bonfire. Eventually the house itself was set aflame and a similar fate awaited the little farmhouse where the nuns first made their home while awaiting the construction of their convent.

While these riotous events were taking place at Mt. Benedict, fire bells were ringing all over Charlestown, Boston and Cambridge. Companies from each of these towns came in answer to the alarms, but either did nothing or were prevented from doing anything by the mob—the accounts differ. Some say the firemen came to watch the fun and that one engine came back bedecked with flowers, drapes and other loot from the convent. Others record that the firemen's hoses were cut by the mob and the firemen threatened with personal injury if they attempted to save the convent. It makes little difference except from an ethical point of view since the fire fighting apparatus of those days consisted of horse-drawn hand pumpers which would have been useless in fighting a fire set at many points simultaneously in a three story building.

The point has also been made that no civil authorities other than the sore-eyed and ineffective Mr. Runey appeared in defense of the convent. Again, the point while well taken is purely academic. There was no police force at that time fitted out as a riot squad. Instead, Charlestown and Boston employed "nightwatchmen" whose equipment was no more formidable than lanterns, pikestaffs and rattles for raising the alarm. The talents of this force were scarcely adequate to cope with isolated cases of breach of the peace much less a frenzied mob of several thousand determined men. The convent was doomed from the moment the attackers met the Mother Superior's withering counterfire.

To return to the scene: When the flames were dying, some of the rioters discovered the mausoleum where dead members of the community had been buried. They tore the silver name plates from the coffins and exposed the remains of the dead to profane view. Legend has it that another mocker of sacred things took some consecrated bread from the chapel and went to a "low den" in Boston where he displayed the wafers in derision. On the following Wednesday he is supposed to have cut his throat in a fit of depression in the same tavern.

All told, the riot went on until dawn. The mob returned from its night's work in triumph, cheering and singing, just

25

as the girls were being taken in carriages to temporary housing in Charlestown. The men's remarks, shouted to the young ladies as they rode by, indicated the rioters thought they had done the students a great service by liberating them from their "prison." Eventually all the girls were returned to their homes, and the sisters took temporary refuge in Boston. Sometime later they made one unsuccessful attempt to re-establish their convent, but public feeling was still so inflamed they gave up and eventually dispersed. Nothing is known of their subsequent history.

That night, twenty-four hours after the sacking and destruction of the convent, the mob returned and burned fences, trees and all other remaining inflammables they could lay their hands on. Before going to the ruins of the convent they paraded through the streets of Charlestown armed with pistols and knives and demonstrated in front of a Catholic Church in Franklin Street. The second night after the riot, a crowd of one thousand men and boys wandered through the streets of Boston alarmed by a rumor that Bishop Fenwick had at last called upon the Irish laborers so sorely needed by the Mother Superior the night of the fire. Presumably they were coming as an avenging army to extract justice from the truckmen. In actual fact, Fenwick had appealed to his flock not to attempt retaliation themselves but to trust to the law. He also dispatched six priests to surrounding communities to forestall any spontaneous Irishmen's march on Charlestown.

There was also a rumor circulating around Boston that Harvard College was going to be attacked by Irishmen who would serve the institution's library in the same manner that the rioters had dealt with Fenwick's. Forty or fifty graduates armed with muskets stood guard all night but no book-burning Irishmen put in an appearance. This ended the immediate violence and threats of violence.

The reaction in the press and among the better classes of townspeople was generally one of outraged indignation. Authorities in Charlestown and Boston called mass-meetings where resolutions were passed denouncing the mob's action and pledging that the perpetrators would be brought to justice. A committee was appointed to look into the truth of the rumors centering around Miss Harrison and Miss Reed, and to investigate the riot itself. It was also instructed to draw up recommendations for recompense. Even the powerful Rev. Beecher delivered three sermons in which he expressed the horror of all decent Protestants at the outrage. The authorities took measures to keep the peace, now that the damage had been done. Captain Howard of the revenue cutter *Hamilton* was stationed at Boston Harbor at the time. The Captain and his men were quartered in a hall in Boston for a week to suppress any further demonstrations; they were said to be well-armed with "cutlasses and blunderbusses."

In accordance with promises made by the civil authorities, the ringleaders of the mob were duly brought to trial. The first to face the bar of justice was John R. Buzzell, who was put up as a test case by the prosecution, since several witnesses were willing to swear they had seen him taking an active part in the riot. Sometime before the riot he had also distinguished himself by administering a ferocious beating to the convent's porter. However, the reaction of outrage had worn off, and many who were at the trial—some of them witnesses—would not have admitted it but nevertheless felt that a good deed had been done. Convictions in such an atmosphere were impossible and the case against Buzzell broke down when witnesses against him became vague. Anti-Catholics paraded through the streets carrying placards threatening the jury with reprisals if a verdict of guilty were brought in. Buzzell's counsel were cheered in the courtroom. The officers of the court were hanged in effigy and the Attorney General dubbed a "Catholic myrmidon." A paper, *The Daily Whig,* sprang into existence for the sole purpose of propagandizing the public in favor of the rioters. The old familiar theme of "vaults" was heard again even in the face of sworn testimony to the contrary by the mason who had laid the foundation for the building.

When Buzzell came out of court after his acquittal, a celebration was staged at Bunker Hill Tavern. He was carried through the streets like a hero, and a fifty-gun salute was fired in his honor. The crowd poured money in his hat to pay for his defense. He was so touched at this display of gratitude on the part of his fellow townsmen, he inserted a card of thanks in the local newspapers.

There were several subsequent trials of the lesser lights but each was a foregone conclusion. Then, as if feeling a little remorseful at the injustice they had been handing out, the jury brought in a verdict of guilty against young Marcy, the seventeen year-old self-appointed auctioneer of the Bishop's books. He was sentenced to prison, almost escaped by shipping aboard a New Bedford whaler, was retaken and served seven months of his sentence before being pardoned on a petition instigated by Bishop Fenwick and signed by the sisters and six thousand lay Catholics.

It turned out this was the only justice the Bishop and the Ursulines ever received at the hands of the State of Massachusetts. Time and again Fenwick appealed to the authorities for recompense against a loss that amounted to $50,000 —a veritable fortune in those days. Promises were made, bills introduced into the state legislature, but nothing ever came of these efforts at justice.

During the trials some curious sidelights and contradictory stories came out about the Mother Superior. It was reported in one of the records that her real name was Grace O'Boyle and that she was a low-class Irishwoman. Another historian identified her as Mary Ursula Moffatt, a learned French scholar from Canada. Still a third listed her as the daughter of Stephen Burroughs, a noted rogue, who was celebrated as a thief and counterfeiter. Finally, others gave her name as Burrill and said she had come from Burlington, Vermont. She was described by one witness as a "figure-head made of brass." Another testified that what she had shouted on the night of the burning was: "The Bishop has twenty thousand of the vilest Irishmen under his influence, who would tear down the houses of Cutter and others; and that the Selectmen might read the riot act till their throats were hoarse, and it would be of no use." Whatever her forebears or remarks on the fateful night, she evidently made a lasting impression on the historians of the affair.

The ruins of the convent were allowed to stand for fifty years as a symbol of protest against the outrage itself and the subsequent injustice meted out by the courts. Eventually, sentiment gave way to rising real estate values and the land passed into private ownership. Mt. Benedict was razed and the whole area became a residential development.

But the hate lived on. On the first anniversary of the fire, Bishop Fenwick was shot in effigy, and two years later St. Mary's Church at Burlington, Vermont was burned by "low shopkeepers and college students," and "Pope Day" was revived for a time. Maria Monk published her celebrated *Awful Disclosures* which, incidentally, became one of the all-time best sellers, and it was not until the 1860's that the violence and prejudice wore themselves out.

There could be no better final commentary on this strange incident in American history than the words of the committee appointed to investigate the outrage. They stand today as a warning to posterity and a valid testimony of the dangers of mass hysteria and mob rule:

> If for the purpose of destroying a person, or family, or institution, it be only necessary to excite a public prejudice, by the dissemination of falsehood and criminal accusations, and under its sanction array a mob; and there be neither an efficient magistracy nor a sense of

public duty or justice sufficient for its prevention, and if property may thus be sacrificed without the possibility of redress, who among us is safe?

The cry may be of bigotry to-day, and heresy to-morrow; of public usurpation at one time, and private oppression at another; or any other of those methods by which the ignorant, the factious and desperate may be excited, and the victim may be sacrificed without protestation or relief.

2: The End of the World

OF THE MANY DELUSIONS which have plagued the human race, one of the most extraordinary and persistent is a recurrent belief that the end of the world is imminent. In every generation from Biblical times down to our own day a prophet of doom has appeared, and each of these seers has succeeded in attracting a considerable following—often with tragic results. To begin with, the ancient Jews tormented themselves with forebodings of doomsday. The Old Testament is liberally sprinkled with prophecies concerning the world's destruction and the day of judgment. Then, there are the well-known passages in the book of Revelation and in Matthew 24: 29-31. Most of the subsequent prophets based their predictions on such Biblical sources.

Since the Apocalypse gives the term of the world's duration as a thousand years, the most remarkable of the perennial epidemics of fear of doomsday was that which spread over Christendom in the middle of the tenth century. Throughout the period a number of fanatics appeared in France, Germany and Italy prophesying that time was running out and urging the populace to wind up their earthly affairs. The site of the last judgment was expected to be Jerusalem, and in the year 999 a vast army of pilgrims moved eastward to the Holy City, there to await the coming of the Lord. Most had sold their homes and chattels before leaving Europe, and were using the proceeds to finance the strange pilgrimage. Many famous buildings in Europe, including churches, were allowed to fall into ruin since there seemed to be no point in trying to maintain them in the face of the fiery whirlwind that was soon to come. All classes of people fell under the spell of the delusion—noble knights, serfs, citizens, women and children—and all travelled eastward in large bands leaving their castles, homes and business establishments to fall into decay. On the safari to Jerusalem, the deluded masses intoned psalms and gazed skyward from time to time expecting the heavens to open at any moment to let the Son of God descend in clouds of glory.

During the thousandth year the number of pilgrims increased markedly. Most of them were ridden with terror, and every time a thunder storm rolled up, or a celestial phenomenon such as a meteor appeared in the heavens, the entire population of the Holy City rushed into the streets

30

weeping and gibbering with fear. Fanatic preachers kept fanning the flames of terror, and every shooting star became the occasion for a homily on the impending judgment.

In subsequent centuries, similar waves of terror swept over Europe, especially during times of calamity such as occurred when the great plague ravaged the continent between 1345 and 1350. Another occasion for such mass hysteria was the appearance of a comet, a shower of shooting stars, earthquakes or floods. Any of these fearsome events was sure to lift up a prophet of doom to announce that the end of all things was at hand. And so on right down to World War I when the global nature of the conflict caused many to believe that the fulfillment of the Biblical prophecy to the effect that a general war would precede the earth's destruction was at hand.

However, in modern times there has never been such widespread hysteria as a result of cataclysmic auguries as that which spread over New England in the early part of the nineteenth century. Between 1800 and 1834 a whole host of prophets rose up to announce that the judgment was near. One of the oddest of the lot was Harriet Livermore, the daughter of a congressman from Massachusetts, who, for several years, preached the second coming of Christ in various parts of the country. She believed the advent would take place in Jerusalem where the Lord would begin His thousand year reign over the Twelve Tribes of Israel. Included in her itinerary were four lectures in the House of Representatives at Washington. She had conceived the curious notion that the American Indians were descendants of the Tribes and had come to the capital to urge Congress to transport them to Jerusalem in order that their savage spirits might be prepared for the Millennium.

Another female eccentric who preached the *Dies Irae* about the same time was Lady Hester Stanhope, a niece of William Pitt, who installed herself in a house on Mount Lebanon to be ready for the dread day. She kept two huge Arab stallions to provide transportation for herself and the Savior on His glorious re-entry into Jerusalem. Among her other peculiarities was an addiction to oriental pipes and the wearing of turbans.

There were a number of others, but the real giant among the prophets of destruction was William Miller. He began prophesying the end of the world in 1831 and did not desist until 1834, the year this fearsome event was to take place. He was the instrument of widespread excitement and alarm that ranged from Canada to Pennsylvania and from Boston westward to Ohio. It is estimated he had 50,000 close adherents at the height of his career and an equal number of fellow-travellers who were half convinced of the truth of his awesome message but unwilling to commit themselves openly. It is with Miller's strange prophecies and the resulting wave of hysteria that the rest of this study is concerned.

Prophet Miller was born in Pittsfield, Massachusetts, February 15, 1782. He was the oldest of sixteen children of humble rural parentage. Like other boys of his day he attended a rural district school and in the summer worked on his father's farm. But unlike the typical farm boy, Miller was given to wide and indiscriminate reading. He bought, borrowed and begged every book he could get his hands on, touching every subject under the sun. As a result, he became something of a village prodigy, respected above and beyond his years and station in life.

When he reached his twenty-first year, Miller married Lucy Smith of Poultney, Vermont, and the young couple started what ordinarily would have been a typical rural married life on a small farm. However, Poultney boasted a fair sized library for so small a community, and this discovery delighted Miller. In fact, he occasioned a certain amount of ribald gossip by spending most of his honeymoon poring over its books instead of with his bride. It soon became apparent to his village friends, most of whom were God-fearing men, that Miller's voracious appetite for literature was leading him along devious and ungodly paths. Among others, he was studying the works of Voltaire, Hume, Paine and worst of all, he delighted in Ethan Allen's atheistic treatises. The end result of Miller's unholy studies was the loss of his faith. Worse, he became a scoffer at all things sacred. In conversations with young men of the village, he treated the Bible and theological works with sarcasm and profane levity. He mocked the devotions of his friends and family by imitating their prayers in a ludicrous voice and by caricaturing their devotional gestures. He took up with a circle of irreverent young men who seemed to accept Miller as a natural leader of their renegade group. Miller's apostasy prostrated his wife and mother; and the rest of his family, among whom were ministers of the Gospel, thought of him as already doomed to everlasting hell fire.

Miller's unhallowed mode of life might have gone on indefinitely if the War of 1812 had not intervened and taken him away from his profane books and unholy companions. Miller, in company with many of the Green Mountain Boys, heeded the call to arms by enlisting in the Army. He won a commission as a lieutenant, and because it was believed that most of the action would take place along the Canadian border, he was ordered to take his company to Burlington, Vermont on Lake Champlain. During the whole of his military career the young officer was plagued by disasters and strange experiences which those skilled in neuropathology may find significant in the light of subsequent developments. On the journey northward, he was thrown out of a wagon and suffered a severe brain concussion. Then, after he arrived at the encampment at Burlington, a raging fever broke out among the soldiers. Miller caught the disease and was left with a large ulcer of the arm as an aftermath. Something of the man's character may be gleaned from the fact that when the medical students, who were attached to the army as Surgeon's mates, began to eye Miller as a possible subject for the dissecting rooms, or at least as promising material for experiments in surgery, he reminded them that there was nothing wrong with his sword arm. He thereupon brandished his weapon and promptly routed the would-be surgeons who showed mortal fear of sharp instruments not of their own choosing. He managed to keep the diseased limb which eventually recovered; but his unfortunate military experiences permanently weakened his constitution, and he was plagued with recurrent attacks of fever and ulcerations of his limbs for the remainder of his life.

It was during the great battle at Plattsburg, New York, that the most significant event of Miller's life took place. Late one night he found an enlisted man's tent lighted up, and thinking that the men were gambling Miller crept up to catch them in *flagrante delicto*. Much to his amazement he discovered that they were praying. He withdrew quietly, and the next day, hoping to indulge his profane sense of humor, he called up the man whose tent was the scene of the previous night's prayer meeting on the charge of gambling. He intended to mock and embarrass the lad when he owned up to the prayer meeting. However, the earnest, candid answers given by the young soldier and his devout attitude took Miller completely by surprise. He found himself abashed and unable to carry through with the projected joke. He noticed, too, that many of his men addressed themselves to their Maker before going into action. For days Miller brooded on the sincerity of the mens' devotion in the midst of the ribald life of the camp.

A little later, one of his close friends became seriously ill, and Miller sat up all night with the dying man. As he kept the death watch, he was put into a profound depression by the thought that life was so short and death so final. He found himself unable to bear the hard prospect of death as signalling the end of all existence and discovered that his diestic views were not able to sustain him in his hour of need. In spite of these melancholy thoughts he nevertheless managed to acquit himself honorably in battles against the British.

When Miller returned from the war he entered a prolonged period of depression during which he continued to brood over the mysteries of life and death. He even took the unprecedented step of attending religious services and stealing into churches at odd hours to sit and wrestle with his thoughts. On one such occasion, while meditating in a little Baptist church, he suddenly experienced conversion and decided he would embrace the Scriptures with their heaven and hell in place of his former views.

The immediate effect of his being saved was to plunge Miller into another bout of reading, but this time his library consisted of a single volume—the Bible. For a total of fifteen years he pored over its books, especially the prophecies where he found support for his desperate need to believe in a life after death. Most appealing to his keen mind were the prophecies of Daniel and the book of Revelation. He became obsessed with the problems of interpreting the dream of Nebuchadnezzar found in Daniel 4:1-37, and discovering the significance of such symbols as the Beast with seven heads and ten horns mentioned in the thirteenth chapter of Revelations. He tortured himself with endless calculations based on the prophecies in Daniel as to when such events would come to pass as the destruction of nations, the end of Papal rule, the baptism of the world by fire and the beginning of the thousand years' reign of Christ. By five different and independent formulas Miller finally concluded the world would end in A.D. 1834, and at the same time Christ would enter upon His thousand years' reign. There would be a glorious resurrection of the righteous dead who, with the living faithful, would be ascended into heaven. The living wicked would be destroyed, and Satan would be rendered powerless for the duration of the Millennium by being bound and cast into a bottomless pit. At the end of the thousand years, the wicked dead would undergo a resurrection and once more the Foul Fiend would be loosed. But he and his legions of the damned would be defeated by the power of God and cast into hell while the righteous would live in eternal bliss.

It must be emphasized that Miller took these matters in their most literal sense. He believed implicitly that the beginning of the Millennium would take place in 1833, and that graves would open so that all the chosen ones could be translated at one and the same time. Moreover, like all the prophets before him, Miller was certain these dread events would be preceded by signs and portents, chiefly astronomical, which would give warning of the impending cataclysm.

At first Miller kept his curious theories to himself, pondering over them endlessly and rechecking his calculations in every conceivable way. But one Saturday morning in the autumn of 1831, as he sat down for still another bout with the Scriptures, a voice seemed to say, "Go, tell it to the world!" The implications of this ghostly message were so overwhelming Miller was dazed and frightened, and he cried aloud, "I can't go, Lord." But the Lord seemed to answer, "Why not?"

In the next few minutes Miller underwent a profound inward struggle. He was fifty years old and not in the best of health. He was only a farmer with no education or oratorical powers. He had no pulpit from which to speak; in fact, he was not even licensed to preach. But his rationalizations for refusing the call only seemed to deepen his despair, and he finally made a compact with the Lord that if he were ever given the opportunity to preach he would tell his listeners of the propinquity of the Lord's second coming. In doing this, he later confessed, he was not altogether sincere, since he saw no possibility of such an opportunity being tendered to a mere farmer.

Thus, he experienced great momentary relief. However, by one of those curious strokes of fate that make the naive believe in miracles and predestination, a young man appeared at the farm just half an hour later explaining that there was no preacher to fill the pulpit at Dresden the following day. Because Miller was noted as a deep student of the Bible, he had been sent to invite him to fill the vacancy. Miller was shocked by the news. He immediately regretted his agreement with the Lord, but compact it was and he would have to go through with it. Perhaps, he told himself, it had all been foreordained.

When he mounted the pulpit of the little Baptist church that Sunday morning he was frightened and feared that he would appear ridiculous, but as he warmed to his subject it seemed as if a miracle had taken place. He found the words flowing out, and his arguments supporting the nearness of the second coming were holding the audience spellbound. The little congregation sat half terrified and half anxious at the prospect Miller depicted so vehemently and which he bolstered by so many calculations and with such powerful logic. It was as if the resurrection of the dead and their glorious translation were about to take place then and there in the little village chapel.

The spark Miller cast to the winds in Dresden that Sunday morning started a conflagration. His first audience spread the news of the prophet and his apocalyptic message, and country folk from miles around came to hear his strange views. Some were curious; some profane; some were half persuaded before they arrived, and Miller's curious powers of oratory soon convinced all but the most skeptical that a seer of great prowess had been raised among them. Officials of the Baptist Church were sufficiently impressed to grant Miller a license to preach, and a growing circle of Baptist, Methodist and Congregationalist churches were thrown open to the new prophet who was employed as a kind of itinerant revivalist. Hundreds of skeptics and derelicts were converted to Christianity as a result of Miller's preaching, and he made many converts to his particular views of the Second Advent among both the long-standing and newly won believers.

It is doubtful, however, that Miller's unaided efforts would have resulted in the hysteria and panic to come if it had not been destined that he was to meet one Joshua V. Himes, pastor of a Baptist chapel in Boston. Himes was a natural-born forerunner of modern press agents, hucksters, and publicity men, and he saw a golden opportunity to exercise his talents in support of the rude farmer from Vermont. It happened that Himes had heard of Miller's strange doctrines and growing influence in the rural districts. He decided, therefore, to invite the prophet to give a series of lectures in the Boston chapel, and Miller accepted the invitation for the 8th of December, 1840. He remained for the next eight days speaking for the first time to relatively large and sophisticated audiences.

Himes was immediately taken with Miller's evangelistic, emotional approach, though he was by no means convinced of the truth of the prophet's curious beliefs. But this made little difference. Himes could see the effect Miller was having in his congregation—every night people had to be turned away—and so was convinced that Miller could be the instrument of a great religious revival whether the world came to an end or not.

In his *Life of William Miller*, James White records the following conversation between Himes and the prophet which heralded the beginning of the long and remarkable ministry of the two men.

ELDER HIMES: "Do you really believe this doctrine?"
MILLER: "Certainly I do or I would not preach it."
HIMES: "What are you doing to spread or diffuse it through the World?"

MILLER: "I have done, and am still doing all I can."
HIMES: "Well, the whole thing is kept in a corner yet. There is but little knowledge on the subject after all you have done. If Christ is to come in a few years, as you believe, no time should be lost in giving the church and the world warning in thunder-tones, to arouse them to prepare."

Miller replied that he was willing enough to give testimony of the coming Millennium, but after all what more could he do. He was an old farmer without a church or the means to spread the word except through the kindness of clergymen who were willing to extend him invitations as a visiting preacher. Himes made light of the prophet's reservations and promised to go ahead of Miller and use his influence to open churches in cities to the prophet so that large numbers could be converted at once.

True to his word, Himes persuaded ministers in various metropolitan areas throughout New England to lend their facilities to the prophet. As a result, Miller was soon launched on a lecture tour whose success was immediately apparent. Word of his strange doctrines went ahead of him; their subject-matter alone was enough to ensure crowds. But Himes was not satisfied with a one-sided campaign. He conceived the idea of publishing adventist literature which would explain Miller's doctrines and which could be broadcast wholesale in the form of flyers. The initial result of his campaign was a paper, "The Signs of the Times" which carried full particulars about Miller's apocalyptic doctrines and the supporting calculations. Eventually, these journalistic efforts were greatly expanded, and millions of pages of literature were circulated throughout the United States. The prophet's lecture audiences became larger, and he began to win converts even among the clergy who up to that time had been either opposed to Miller and his works or at best were lukewarm to the seer's teachings. Some of the converted ministers became inflamed with millennialism and elected to go out on their own to preach the second coming. Because of these unexpected clerical conversions, Miller's one-man enterprise began to take on the characteristics of a sect or church.

But Miller and his disciples were not always received with open arms. When he arrived for a lecture in Newburyport, Massachusetts, a great crowd gathered to hear him speak. But just as he started to deliver the sermon, an ancient egg was flung at the lectern. Miller stood his ground and went on with the sermon, but towards the end a mob who had meanwhile gathered in the street began to hurl stones through the windows. In the quaint language of biographer White they also "indulged in some characteristic hootings and kindred noises." The barrage of stones and flying glass routed the congregation, and as a consequence of the unfortunate disturbance, the meeting was held in a safer place the following evening.

Miller did a great deal of travelling in the course of spreading his doctrines; consequently he rubbed elbows with many strange people. One day while on a ferry boat he was introduced to a phrenologist. The latter, however, was unaware that this was *the* Miller of doomsday fame. The bumpreader was quite taken with the adventist's head and requested permission to give a reading. Miller acquiesced, and the phrenologist reported that the "organs of calculation" were very large—an interesting coincidence, to say the least, in view of Miller's penchant for the book of Daniel. However, the pseudo-psychologist misfired badly on the "organs of marvelousness" which he deemed underdeveloped. Still unaware that his subject was the prophet, the phrenologist added that in view of the lack of imaginative development the subject in question would never make a convert to "Mr. Miller's harebrained theories." Finally, the skull specialist expressed a desire to examine prophet Miller's head which he said, "he would like to give a good squeezing," and added, "he doubted not it would be the reverse in every particular to the head under examination."

It will be remembered that one of Miller's canons involved the predicted appearance of signs and portents in the heavens announcing the imminence of the end. This aspect of his views was based on Matthew 24: 29-30 which, in part reads: "Immediately after the tribulation of those days shall the sun be darkened, and the moon shall not give her light, and the stars shall fall from heaven, and the powers of the heavens shall be shaken. . ." By another of those singular coincidences that dogged Miller's footsteps, "signs and portents" actually did begin to appear in the heavens during his ministry of gloom. One of these had already appeared before Miller began to preach publicly, but because of the awesomeness of the spectacle it was still fresh in the minds of his hearers. The phenomenon in question was the great meteoric shower of November 13, 1833. An old edition of *The American Encyclopedia* describes the showers as ". . . brilliant, and probably no spectacle so terribly grand and sublime was ever before beheld by man . . ." According to the *Handbook of the Heavens*, this was a shower associated with the Leonids, a typically extensive display, but which in this case produced so many "falling stars" that 250,000 were counted at one station between midnight and dawn.

Meanwhile, Miller had set the end of the world for April of 1843, and in the spring of that year a magnificent comet appeared in the skies. So outstanding was the celestial visitor it has since become known as the "Great Comet of 1843." The *Handbook* cited above gives the length of its tail as 200,000,000 miles. The entire comet was so bright that it could be seen even at high noon. Naturally the Millerites, as they had come to be called, gazed at it in fear mingled with hopeful anticipation believing it to be a sure sign of the impending Millennium forecast by the Scriptures. In addition to the comet, other curious celestial phenomena began to make an appearance. Strange rings appeared around the sun, crosses were seen in the sky and sundogs or mock suns occurred from time to time. The entire community was profoundly stirred by these awesome apparitions, and many who had considered Miller a crackpot now believed him to be a prophet in a class with the mighty Isaiah.

That spring, Miller and Himes started a series of camp meetings. A huge Tabernacle tent was pitched in a field, and a great crowd of praying and singing Millerites and hangers-on would come to hear the prophet preach the impending doom. He spoke from a crude pulpit in front of which a large canvas was suspended, depicting the seer's calculations and bearing illustrations of the Papal Beast, the Pagan Dragon, the Beast of the Revelations with seven heads and ten horns, the Scarlet Woman and other such symbols from Daniel and the book of Revelation. Naturally, as April approached, the excitement at these meetings reached fever pitch, and there seemed to be an odor of fire and brimstone in the spring breezes.

But April passed into May and the old world appeared to be as sound as ever. Miller's followers were not only disappointed but also shaken in their faith at the failure of the prophecies. However, their leaders kept pointing out the difficulties of being precise in such metaphysical matters and assured them that the Advent would surely take place *sometime* during the year 1843-1844. Confidence was quickly restored, and the Millerites' attention was taken up with the building of a Tabernacle in Boston. This became the focal point of their activities and it also developed into a center of public curiosity for Bostonians. Rumors began to circulate that the building was insured for a period of seven years. Scoffers and antagonistic newspaper editors questioned the Millerites on the point, dwelling on the inconsistency of announcing the Millennium within a year but taking out insurance on their Tabernacle for seven. The Millerite leader-ship denounced the report as a cruel rumor circulated by their enemies and calculated to undermine belief in the prophecies. A statement to the effect that the building was insured for only one year was finally published by Himes. To add to their troubles, members of the sect were continually pestered by scoffers who asked when the faithful were to be taken up. Some of the more credulous among the unbelievers loitered near the Tabernacle when services were in progress expecting to see the Millerites rise up through the roof on their way to glory.

Meanwhile, the indefatigable Miller continued his lectures and conducted camp meetings still testifying to the imminent coming of the Lord. The prophet, of course, looked forward to being translated in the glorious resurrection and this gave him an air of serenity and confidence which stilled doubts among the faithful and won him many converts. He claimed that his prophecy could come true any time during the Jewish year which, according to his calculations, would carry over to March 21, 1844. As the date drew near, Miller waited calmly for the end at his home. He had worn himself out travelling and lecturing. Now he rested in hope and confidence, reading his Bible and listening for the blast of Gabriel's horn.

But Elder Himes and the rank and file of the Millerites were anything but calm. Himes was busy getting out the "Midnight Cry," the official Millerite publication, and exhort-ing the other leaders in the movement to even greater efforts on behalf of those who were yet unsaved. He also used the columns of the paper to answer scoffers, of whom there were many.

With the approach of March 21st, the hysteria reached its height among Miller's followers. They began to make ascen-sion robes and devoted themselves entirely to ghostly matters. Crops were left untended; some even sold their farms and homes. Shopkeepers closed up in honor of the King of Kings. While such extreme reactions were largely confined to rural New England, the delusion also gripped segments of the urban population. Clara Sears, quoting from a *History of Philadel-phia*, reports that in the City of Brotherly Love a group of wild young fellows went to a Millerite meeting and sur-rounded the auditorium. At a signal, torches were lighted and fireworks set off; the "saints" inside "went wild with terror, for they thought the fiery whirlwind was come."

Sears also collected a number of personal reminiscences from old people in various sections of New England who still remembered family stories of the hysterical reactions of the

Millerites on the eve of the Millennium. Some of the more extreme cases are summarized here.

In Salem, a large band of the faithful marched in their ascension robes to Gallows Hill, where the witches had been hanged, and watched for the second coming from that melancholy site. Others went to graveyards to be with departed loved ones when they rose up to be translated into eternal life. Among these was a particularly benighted man who stood by his first wife's grave waiting for her resurrection. His second wife who was so incensed at his behavior that she refused to live with him after the predicted resurrection failed to occur.

Some climbed into trees or went out on roofs of barns or houses. Among the latter were those who had constructed wings and on the stroke of midnight of the 21st, tried to fly upward into the arms of their God. One of these aeronautical adventists ended up with a broken leg and a badly bruised caboose.

But by all odds the most amusing incident from Sear's collection had to do with a crowd of believers in Westford, Massachusetts. They had gathered in a large house in their ascension garments and were ready to be transfigured. Living nearby was "Crazy Amos," the village half-wit, who was also distinguished as a victim of drink. He was fond of blowing on a large brass trumpet; and when he heard the tumlt in the neighborhood, he rushed outdoors to join the fun. He loosed a terrific blast on his horn, and the Millerites thought that Gabriel was heralding the day of judgment. They rushed into the street shouting Hallelujahs and jostled each other for advantageous positions to be taken up. When calm had been restored, they realized that the great Day had not arrived and that they had been badly taken in. Crazy Amos added insult to injury by telling them to go home and dig potatoes since Gabriel was unlikely to do it for them.

When midnight passed, the Millerites realized they were doomed to a second disappointment. Not only did they have this to live with, but they also faced the jests of mockers and infidels. In this they were not disappointed. The following passage is quoted from White:

> And some are tauntingly inquiring, "Have you not gone up?" Even little children in the streets are shouting continually to passers-by, "Have you a ticket to go up?" The public prints, of the most fashionable and popular kind, in the great Sodoms of our country are caricaturing in the most shameful manner the "white robes of the saints," the "going up," and the great day of "burning."

Even the pulpits are desecrated by the repetition of scandalous and false reports concerning the "ascension robes," and priests are using their powers and pens to fill the catalogue of scoffing in the most scandalous periodicals of the day. England and France with their sinks of pollution, London and Paris, cannot, will not, and dare not, compete with our own Boston, New York, or Philadelphia in scoffing. If these will not open the eyes of our good men in these cities, then I shall believe there is none there. At any rate, the world must and will be burned up, and few men left. . . .

Father Miller was prostrated with disappointment and bitterness. To add to his misery, doctrinal controversies and personal quarrels broke out among the leaders of the sect when they realized their glorious hopes were broken on the rocks of reality. The result was a breakdown in the organization of the sect and a splitting up of the followers into factions. Ludlum, in his *Social Ferment in Vermont,* cites instances of extremist behavior among groups of Adventists who were unable to adjust themselves to a mundane existence after their imaginary flight into celestial realms. Near Brattleboro, Vermont, there were many such fanatic meetings and on one occasion a young man selected as a scapegoat for the sins of the whole company was beaten into unconsciousness by way of reparation. Sexual aberrations were reported among the faithful in several localities, and the story got around that at one camp meeting a spinster appeared before her brethren in God stripped to the pelt.

As reports of these untoward developments got back to Miller, he sank into a deeper and deeper despondency and never again took an active part in the management of his sect which, after the hysteria and fanaticism died down, eventually became the Seventh Day Adventists. Elder Himes was of stronger stuff and stuck to his guns for the next thirty years; he continued to publish pamphlets and tracts exhorting the faithful to watch and wait. Then he, too, renounced millennialism and took orders as an Episcopal clergyman. Still, he asked to be buried on a hill so that he would be in a convenient spot for the resurrection. Evidently he kept some remnants of his earlier faith.

Little needs to be added to the foregoing account by way of explanation of the Millerite mania. It has already been pointed out that this is a more or less perennial delusion associated with social upheavals and celestial phenomena. As indicated in the introductory paragraphs, there was no dearth of the latter during the decade of Miller's prominence. But what of the social background? Strictly speaking, there was nothing approaching the disruptive force of a plague of war, but Vermont appears to have been fertile ground for religious cranks and radicals who flourished at the time. Perhaps the long cold winters and bleak landscape of those latitudes had something to do with it; perhaps the otherwise canny Vermonter is singularly credulous in religious matters. Whatever the reason, Swedenborgianism found a home there, and Joseph Smith and Brigham Young, the founders of Mormonism, were both Vermonters. In addition, there was a great deal of philosophical and political agitation in the Green Mountain State during the first half of the century. For a full account of these movements in Vermont the reader is referred to Ludlum's book.

However, in fairness to the Vermont character, it should be pointed out that Miller's chief influence was among the Methodists and Baptists, and many of his followers and evangelists were drawn from the ranks and clergy of these denominations. (One of the clergymen who went over to Miller's camp had the provocative name of Chilian Wines.) The more conservative groups denounced Miller and his followers as crackpots. Thus, to summarize, the delusion spread among the more evangelistic sects, finding a receptive hearing because of the general religious and social unrest.

Finally, it must not be forgotten that according to all contemporary accounts Miller was a man of great persuasive power. Thus, his singular personality was probably the most important single factor responsible for the furor. With his deep study of the Bible and complex mathematical calculations, he must have made the conventional preachers of his day seem like second raters. On the average he had probably spent three or four times the amount of effort preparing for his ministry of doom as compared to the time spent in more conventional study by the rural preachers of the day. In many ways he must have been an early variety of Billy Sunday or Billy Graham, the great difference being the curious nature of his doctrines. Undoubtedly if one of these latter-day evangelists preached the Millennium, he too could attract a considerable following even in our time.

It is appropriate that this study end on a hopeful theme for the deluded prophet. He remained faithful to the end. Deserted by all but a few of the believers, he died in the hopes of a glorious resurrection crying at the end, "Victory! Shouting in death!"

3: The Great Airship of 1897

WHEN THE AVERAGE AMERICAN hears the expression "The Gay Nineties," it brings to mind Gibson Girls, bicycles built for two, the Clarence Day stories and an era of musical comedy life which forecast the froth and furor of the Mad Twenties. Yet, running through the decade was a series of social, political and economic upheavals that impelled historian Herbert Lyons to entitle an article about the period, "The Not-So-Gay Nineties." The last ten years of the dying century witnessed a rash of economic reversals which gave rise to vicious labor-management clashes, such as the Pullman strike of 1892, and ultimately culminated in one of the most serious depressions in American history. Between 1893-1897, unemployment rose to two million, and public confidence in the monetary system was badly shaken. At the height of the panic an event took place which foreshadowed one of the blackest episodes of the great depression of the Thirties. This occurred in 1894 when a band of down-at-the-heel workers known as "Coxey's Army" marched on Washington to protest the widespread unemployment and were arrested for deploying in tents on the Capitol lawns. It was also during the Nineties that the Republic engaged in some of the most irrational international maneuvers in its history. These were the diplomatic blunders leading up to the fiasco of the Spanish-American War which, historians agree, was an unwarranted and senseless conflict. From the American male's point of view, one unfortunate trend which began in the Nineties was the domination of social life by the female. American women began to experiment with "mixed drinks," went unescorted to matinees and took over the folkways and mores of courtship. Only in the sanctuary of his business chambers was the male safe from feminine interference, and even here his days of independence were numbered.

Despite the fact that only a few generations have passed, the newspapers of the latter part of the Nineties read like a preface to antiquity. The fashion plates in the clothing advertisement depict the well-dressed women of those days in such baroque costumes that they appear to be fugitives from some ultra-antique period of history and somehow much more dated-looking than their trimmer colonial grandames. On turning to the sports page, one is likely to be carried away by the impression he is reading accounts of the very birth of boxing and football as national institutions. In the prize ring, Jim Corbett and Bob Fitzsimmons were the heroes of the hour. On the college gridiron, football was coming into its own but not without a struggle. It was under heavy criticism from gentler folk, among whom was a contingent of Mexican bull fighters that had witnessed an American college game. The matadors expressed themselves to the effect that "the game was too rough." Finally, from the vantage point of the automobile age, it seems equally incredible that the greatest menace in downtown New York during the Nineties was the bicycle. Daily arrests of "scorchers" were reported—men and boys who sped through the streets of Manhattan endangering the lives and limbs of long-suffering pedestrians.

Primarily, however, the antiquarian mood is induced in the modern reader by the format of the front pages of the daily journals of those days. They were bedecked with dozens of advertisements announcing the merits of a bewildering variety of nostrums, philtres, pills, liniments, gargles, salves and quack medical appliances. The appearance of nearly any one of these ads in a modern daily would put medical practitioners in a state of near apoplexy and send them to the nearest telephone to notify Federal drug enforcement officers of a serious menace to public health. A few of these panaceas are worth describing in a book devoted to human credulity even though somewhat aside from the main purpose of this study.

Carter's Liver Pills, one of the few products familiar to the modern reader, were highly recommended for "sick headaches." There was no mention of the great benefits accruing to the liver with its divers weaknesses and miles of tubing. Johnson's Anodyne Liniment, dropped on sugar, attacked a multitude of not always logically related but at least alliterative ailments:—colds, coughs, croup, catarrh, cramps, cholera, chills, colic, cracks, chaps and cuts. Some medicants, as though foreshadowing today's wonder drugs, specialized, and directed their curative powers at diseases of one or two organs. In this category was Prof. Dr. Dixi Crosby's "Puritana"— "a prize formula of Dartmouth"—said to be capable of warding off "Weak Lungs and Fagged Brains." In contrast to these all too human pharmaceuticals was "Merchant's Gargling Oil," used, apparently, not as a gargle but as a liniment so powerful that it benefited both man and beast. The cut accompanying the advertisement testified to the drug's versatility by depicting its application to the withers of a huge draft horse.

Some purveyors of medications based their appeal, in part, on the use of esoteric names. There was, for example, "Salvacea" which cured the most stubborn cases of catarrh, burning, itching and painful skin diseases, chaffings, piles chilblains, toothache, burns, earache, wounds, boils and bites. This formidable concoction had rivals in S. C. Knight's "Ammoniated Opodelodoc" and Ayer's "Cherry Pectoral."

Some of the personal messages accompanying the advertisements were downright touching since they reproduced testimonials from desperate, pain-racked people who had swallowed gallons of elixirs and pills without relief until, of course, they discovered the powers of the product in question. Lydia Pinkham, for example, ran a kind of letters-to-the-health-lorn column from which the following pathetic appeal was gleaned:

> Lucy E. W. writes: "I am desperate. Am 19 years of age, tall and weighed 138 pounds a year ago. I am now a mere skeleton. From your little book I think my trouble is profuse menstruation. My symptoms are . . . etc.*
>
> Our doctor tells father I am in consumption and wants to take me to Florida. Please help me! Tell me what to do, and tell me quickly. I am engaged to be married in September. Shall I live to see the day?

Lydia recommended large draughts of her vegetable compound, reassured her correspondent, and then took a backhanded swipe at the medical profession of her day: "Women want the truth, and if they cannot get it from their doctor, will seek it elsewhere."

Lydia's compound also revealed unsuspected versatility when an experimental-minded wife discovered that huge doses of it cured her husband's "kidney trouble."

Finally, there were the mystifying medicines whose names or descriptions failed to make their purpose clear—such as a "magnetic blood pumper," "H-O," "Indian Elixirs," "Athlo-pho-nos," and most curious of all was this terse announcement from the pre-Freudian era:

"NEUROTIC PILE OINTMENT CURES PILES."

It may be that overdoses of these powerful medicants had something to do with the appearance of the airship. Perhaps the strange vessel would have appeared in any event in an era credulous enough to make millionaires out of the manufacturers of the pills and potions described in the preceding paragraphs. Whatever the case, it was against the background described in these pages that the "airship" was first sighted.

---

* The ellipsis of modesty is Lydia's, not the present writer's.

46

The vessel made its initial appearance in California in the fall of 1896. However, the first sightings were scattered and confined to the coast, and, when cold weather set in, the airship was seen no more until the spring of 1897. Perhaps the craft was not suitably equipped for winter flights, or it may have been that inclement weather kept people indoors at night when the ship was usually aloft. Whatever the reason, most of the vessel's activities were reported during the following spring, and, as a result, it has since come to be known as the "Airship of 1897."

The first detailed reports of the mysterious craft's celestial visits appeared in the April papers for that year. The New York *Herald* led off the accounts with an article summarizing the ship's sporadic activities up to that time. It seemed there had been numerous sightings between California and Chicago for several weeks previously as if the craft were bound for the Midwest or the East. By April 9, the vessel had arrived in Chicago and was observed by thousands of people who stood about the streets until 2:00 A.M. to watch its maneuverings in the early morning sky. There was general agreement among viewers that the apparition was either an airship or some kind of floating object hovering miles above the earth. Some—"men of unquestioned veracity"—declared it was definitely an airship. They described its shape as "cigar-like" and alluded to its "great wings."

There was also striking agreement among Chicagoans in their descriptions of the vessel's lights. The headlight was reported to be white and "wonderfully" resembled a searchlight in its penetrating powers and side to side excursions across the evening skies. The ship also boasted a green light at its midsection and a red tail light at the stern.

The apparition was so awesome that the populace was apprehensive about the nature of the ship's mission. As is natural in such cases, astronomers were consulted about the strange phenomenon that was appearing in their provinces. A professor of astronomy at Northwestern University obligingly turned his powerful telescope on the celestial visitor and concluded that it was Alpha Orionis. The professor argued that the red and green lights reported by Chicagoans must have been due to the star's light changing color as it penetrated atmospheric disturbances on its earthward journey. A second professor agreed with his colleague's diagnosis and went on to suggest that the apparent motion of the lights could be an illusion of movement caused by misty clouds speeding in front of the star and making it appear to move just as the moon sometimes seems to race across the sky when large fluffy clouds are blown across the lunar visage.

A less hypothetical explanation was offered by the secretary of the Chicago Aeronautical Society who asserted he *knew* that the nocturnal visitor was an airship. Moreover, he reported the machine was capable of carrying three men aloft. At the same time he brushed off a rumor that the ship was fabricated of steel. Instead, the gas bag was the usual type of paper reservoir. However, the most significant statement attributed to the secretary was to the effect that the three aeronauts in charge of the vessel had discovered the long-sought secret of controlled propulsion. He added, finally, that the vessel was on its way to Washington, D.C. where it would make its first public descent. This seemingly knowledgeable description of the elusive dirigible only whetted reporter's appetites, and the secretary was questioned closely for further details. However, he refused to divulge any additional information other than to remark that he and certain wealthy men had supplied the necessary funds for the vessel's construction. To give out more data, he believed, would be unfair to the inventor and might "take the edge off public interest."

The next day, the New York *Herald* reported that two photographs of the airship had been taken while the craft was in motion. This fortunate occurrence pleased the editor since, as he pointed out, if the photographs were genuine such concrete evidence would disprove all theories that had accounted for the apparition as a mere optical illusion. The plates, the *Herald* added, had been "tested with acid" and were, indeed, found to be authentic. Moreover, there were two witnesses who had been present when the vessel was being photographed and both were willing to testify as to the reality of the airship and the authenticity of the photographs. However forthright these statements might be, the Chicago *Daily News* was unable to agree with the conclusions expressed by the *Herald*. The midwestern paper's photographic expert denounced the pictures as fakes. After sarcastically describing the image on the plates as "an eliptical gas-bag, with a fish tail, and a basket the shape of a Vienna loaf," the *News* added that the pictures demonstrated nothing more than the enormous strides recently made in the art of photography.

While this clash of experts was taking place, men-in-the-street witnesses were in general agreement that the airship was a cigar-shaped gas bag fitted around a metal framework and carrying a basket or gondola suspended underneath. Some keen-eyed sighters were able to discern a man in the basket whose actions suggested that he was steering the craft.

In Omaha, Nebraska, the secretary of the Trans-Mississippi Exposition announced that he had received a telegram from the inventor of the vessel. The inventor included a promise that he would land the ship in Omaha if the Exposition would provide him with 87,000 square feet of landing space. Moreover, the secretary was able to add two hitherto unknown details to the general fund of knowledge about the ship's performance characteristics. It could carry twenty passengers and was capable of ascending to altitudes of ten to twenty thousand feet. But just as was true in the case of the photographs, there were those who disagreed with the Exposition's secretary. A lawyer in San Francisco asserted that the dirigible belonged to one of his clients. According to the attorney, the latter had spent five years and $100,000 on the vessel's development. He went on to describe the ship as having been fabricated of metal, measuring one hundred and fifty feet in length and capable of taking aloft fifteen passengers. The vessel, he added, was equipped with two canvas wings eighteen feet in width. The attorney further claimed to have seen his client-inventor take off with the wings flapping gently as the craft rose slowly and majestically into the sky. To add to the confusion, an electrician in San Jose revealed that he had made a round trip to Honolulu on the airship but could only describe the craft's much-debated motive power as propeller-driven "neither by steam or electricity."

On April 12th, there was no news of further sightings. However, an amateur inventor, Oscar D. Booth of Peoria, Illinois added still another inside story to the accounts of the airship's origin. He claimed to have positive knowledge that the vessel had been constructed by Charles Clinton of Dodge City, Kansas. The airship, Booth added, "has wings or large propellers placed at both ends of the cigar-shaped car." This statement, at least, had the merit of leaving considerable latitude as to the ship's method of propulsion.

On the 13th, the news of the elusive craft was on the front page, and the news was bad. The airship, it seemed, had exploded, the New York *Herald* headlined the unfortunate development in detail and with considerable emotion:

AIRSHIP BLOWS UP!

The Strange Wanderer of the
Western Sky Passes Away
with a Dull Thud

ITS SAD INGLORIOUS END

Was Sailing Through the Atmosphere
Sunday Night, When "Bang"
and All Was Over

NEWS IS FROM KALAMAZOO

Shower of Propeller Blades, Electric Wires and Steel Splinters, so Says Cruel Rumor

The body of the report gave credit for the eyewitness account of the vessel's doom to two "old soldiers," George W. Somers and William Chadburn, who, it appeared, had been up late Sunday night in attendance upon a "sick horse." On their way home from this melancholy mission, they saw the cigar-shaped balloon speeding through the sky; but as they watched, to their amazement and dismay, there was a dull report like the discharge of distant cannon, and the apparition disappeared before their eyes. Much grieved at the ship's "inglorious end" they spent a sleepless night. A recently married couple was found in the vicinity who were also "up late" and had heard the "explosion" but at the time attributed it to nothing more out of the ordinary than thunder.

The following morning a search was undertaken at the site of the catastrophe which turned up scattered bits of the exploded vessel. A large coil of heavy copper wire and a partially fused propeller blade constructed of light metallic material were discovered in the area. In a nearby township, steel splinters were found embedded in a barn by men engaged in re-shingling the structure. These poor relics proved to be the only remaining traces of the airship.

However, the reports of the ship's untimely end proved to be premature, since it was sighted the very next day in various localities. In Carlinville, Illinois, there was a daylight sighting at a farm, which for the first time also involved a witnessing of the vessel's landing ability. Two men saw the dirigible alight in a field where it remained for a quarter of an hour before continuing north. At six that same evening, the dirigible was again discovered on the ground—this time near an Illinois mining camp. A large crowd of miners gathered and began to approach the craft, but when they had come within half a mile of it, the ship rose up and sailed away. One of the sighters saw a man working about the vessel as if he were fixing machinery. This latter report lent credence to a theory that the ship was in mechanical difficulties since it had been forced to alight twice within a single day. The only inside story of the vessel's purpose in cruising about the Midwest came from far away Boston where two men announced they had reason to believe the ship was in reality a giant searchlight sent aloft near Troy, New York by the celebrated inventor, Thomas Edison.

On April 14th, the hysteria reached its height. The reports of sightings vied with each other in exaggerations and contradictions concerning both the ship's construction and performance characteristics. In Chicago, the papers complained of a dearth of reliable information about the vessel despite the plethora of reports that were coming in. Many of the sightings turned out to be mere rumors or reports that proved to be the doings of pranksters. It appeared that some of the latter breed were sending aloft homemade dirigibles with lights attached which resulted in many various airship sightings. As if in answer to the Chicago papers' lament, Appleton, Wisconsin reported the discovery of a message from the elusive craft itself. An iron rod had been found sticking in the ground with a letter attached. The epistle, as quoted in the New York *Herald,* read as follows:

Aboard the Airship "Pegasus" April 9, 1897. The problem of aerial navigation has been solved. The writers have demonstrated to their entire satisfaction that the ship is a thorough success. We h; .ve been able to attain a speed of 150 miles an hour anu have risen to a height of 2,500 feet above sea level.

The "Pegasus" was erected at a secluded point ten miles from Lafayette, Tenn., and the various parts of the machine were carried overland from Glasgow, Ky., to that point, being shipped from Chicago, Pittsburg and St. Louis. We have made regular trips of three days each from Lafayette to Yorktown, and no harm has come to the "Pegasus" thus far.

Within a month our application for the patents for a parallel plane airship will be filed simultaneously at Washington and the European Capitols. It is propelled by steam and is lighted by electricity, and has a carrying power of 1,000 pounds.

The difficulty seemed to be that the flying horse was everywhere at once. In Indiana, Prof. Keeley, watching her from his astronomical observatory, described the craft as sixty feet long, cigar-shaped and with a gondola suspended under the balloon. He was able to make out that two men rode in the gondola. One man was fifty years old with a beard, the other young and clean shaven. The older aeronaut wore a stiff hat, the younger a Cuban crush hat. The ship was making a speed of ten miles an hour at the time of these sartorial observations but in departing attained the great speed of one hundred and fifty miles an hour. Back in Chicago, a patrolman *captured* the vessel late that same night and excitedly brought his booty to the 13th street station just before daybreak. Unfortunately, the patrolman's find proved to be a hoaxter's flimsy creation of sticks and tissue paper instead of the elusive *Pegasus*.

The next day reports from the Midwest revealed that great crowds of watchers were gathering in the streets, on roofs, and at the outskirts of cities in order to avoid artificial lights and thus insure better viewing conditions for observing the ubiquitous airship. In Iowa, five men observed the aircraft cruising through the sky and apparently making landing preparations. The curious Iowans jumped into a wagon, followed the ship until it had descended on a farm four miles from town, and then attempted to approach the vessel in order to make a closer inspection. Unfortunately, when they had come to within 700 yards of the ship, it discharged two bags of ballast and took off. The ballast, at least, was available to put on exhibition at the local drug store.

Appleton, Wisconsin making a testy reference to the letter purporting to have come from the airship, made it clear that no *reputable* citizens in that city had seen the apparition. The report added, "This is a university town and we are too sober for such things." Grand Rapids, Michigan was not to be outdone in civic virtue by her sister city. She let it be known that her citizens were also "sober, law abiding and truthful. The airship has not been seen here."

The reports were, in fact, making such heavy demands on the speed and versatility of the airship that the Chicago *Daily News* published a large front page cartoon on April 17th showing a hypothetical day in the life of the vessel. The successive drawings depicted the dirigible cruising over Kalamazoo at breakfast, hovering near Cleveland for fishing in the afternoon, then being sighted in Valparaiso, Indiana in the evening. By the dinner hour it had been identified as Alpha Orionis in Evanston and at the same time discovered *sui generis* at a dinner stop in Paris, Illinois.

The *Daily News* went on to speculate that the airship might, in fact, be a gigantic cigar advertisement sent aloft by some entrepreneur who subsequently intended to put an *airship cigar* on the market and promote it thereafter in a more conventional manner. The cynical editor ended the article with some rather pointed remarks about the relative number of sightings in prohibition versus non-prohibition districts in Chicago.

The following day most of the sightings took place outside Chicago. The *Daily News* comments of the previous day evidently dampened the imaginations of Chicagoans. However, no such effect was felt in other midwestern cities. In Cleveland, a remarkable report came in from one S. H.

52

Davis who happened upon the airship while he was on a fishing expedition. At first sighting the aircraft appeared to be a "queer looking boat" floating in the water. Aboard were a man dressed in a bathing suit, a beautiful woman and a boy of ten. But as the fisherman drew near, the *boat* sprouted a gaily-decorated balloon which rose above the occupants. When the balloon was fully distended, the entire apparatus became airborne. It circled for awhile like a hawk, discharged an enormous swordfish, and then sailed away. The swordfish joined the ballast bags as exhibits jettisoned by the airship.

In Birmingham, Iowa, the aeronauts (this time two men) appeared to be of a more friendly disposition. Two sighters approached the ship which they had chanced upon in a field. As they closed in, it rose according to custom, but this time the balloonists at least waved friendly adieux as they sailed away. The ship's crew were even more convivial in Bloomington, Indiana. Mr. Haney Savidge of that city declared the vessel had landed in his fields whereupon six persons disembarked. After conversing with him for a few minutes, the aeronauts re-embarked, and the craft sailed away. Apparently, no record was available of what must have been an extremely interesting conversation.

On this same date in Waterloo, Iowa, a reliable report that the airship had at last really landed brought thousands to the scene. There they saw a forty-foot cigar-shaped balloon which in its other dimensions was twenty feet in width and ten feet high. The ballon had been constructed of light lumber and covered with a canvas skin. However, the *airship* turned out to be an unusually elaborate practical joke perpetrated by a man known to have a "waggish disposition."

While these sightings and alightings were keeping newsmen busy chasing the airship all over the Midwest, rumors and reports began to circulate about a mysterious inventor who was said to be involved in lighter-than-air areronautical research. The inventor in question was Frank Brinton, and it was believed significant that he had been missing from his customary haunts for ten days prior to the rash of sightings. Rumors as to his whereabouts continued to appear in the news columns throughout the middle part of April until a friend in Iowa asserted that he *knew* the inventor was in Washington seeking patents. The report added, darkly, that Mr. Brinton knew more than he was willing to tell. Whatever the basis of these rumors, the missing inventor was never found, and it mattered very little since the odyssey of the airship was just about over. There were a few scattered sightings until the latter part of April, but these added nothing to previous descriptions of the vessel's appointments. Then the airship burst like the proverbial bubble when it was denounced as a fraud by no less an expert on mechanical devices than the wizard of Menlo Park, Mr. Thomas Edison. The denouncement came about this way.

An individual named Bert Swearingin of Astoria, Illinois found a length of reed in a pasture. The stick was three feet long with a red, white and blue streamer attached to its top. An egg-shaped stone weighing three pounds was fastened to the bottom as if to carry the unique contrivance downward from great altitudes. Halfway up the reed, a packet had been attached which contained the following letter as quoted by the New York *Herald*:

From Air Ship—Notice to finder—Please mail letter inside. Passed over here about half-past two P.M. April 16, 1897 about 2,300 ft. high, going east and north. Excuse dirt, as just got done oiling.

The communication was signed *Harris*, and addressed to Thomas Edison, New York City.

The next day the inventor was shown the letter as published in the *Herald*, and denounced it as a fake. He asserted that it would be impossible to construct such a ship and keep the process a secret. The remainder of his analysis proves Edison was not always one hundred per cent right as a prophet despite his genius with mechanical apparatus. He stated that when practical aircraft were constructed they would not be airships but would take the form of mechanical devices and would be raised into the atmosphere by means of light but powerful motors. He denied that he was attempting to invent such a ship, and said to the *Herald* reporter, "I prefer to devote my time to objects which have some commercial value. At best airships would be only toys."

Edison's great prestige was evidently sufficient to kill the illusion, and it was not until half a century had passed that mysterious objects were again appearing in the western skies.

In attempting to account for the "airship" three-quarters of a century after its appearance, it seems reasonable to assume the immediate cause for the hysteria was some kind of astronomical phenomenon. If anything at all was sighted, only a celestial object such as a star would have been sufficiently distant to be observable at such widely scattered points. It may have been Alpha Orionis, a Nova, or any one of a hundred other similar phenomena that have given rise to periodic waves of excitement and hysteria down through history. There is also the distinct possibility that once some such astronomical freak was reported as an "airship," pranksters sent aloft balloons with lights attached thereby triggering a wave of sightings. Seen from a great distance, such contrivances would have appeared much larger than they actually were. The immediate cause, however, is not so significant or interesting as compared to the reasons why the hysteria spread so rapidly once it got underway. The main explanation would seem to lie in the widespread interest in aeronautics characteristic of the Nineties. Inventors were on the threshold of solving both the problem of controlling airships in flight and of devising heavier-than-air flying machines. Experiments seeking the solution to both of these aeronautical puzzles were going on all over the world in the 1890's.

The problems of heavier-than-air flight were conquered by the Wright brothers just six years after the events described here, even though as late as 1901 an aeronautics "expert" announced that the final solution of the difficulty of providing powerful but sufficiently light engines "was beyond the limits of the vaguest possibility." Controlled balloon flights, as a matter of fact, had been made as early as 1852 when Henri Giffard succeeded in constructing an *air-steamship* which was propelled by a 350-pound steam engine of three horse-power capacity. The engine turned an eleven foot propeller at the rate of 110 r.p.m The trouble with Giffard's ship, and others like it that were constructed in the latter half of the nineteenth century, was that they could not attain sufficient speed to be controllable in winds. Ships which had been flown successfully could make only ten to twelve miles per hour and as a consequence were at the mercy of anything stronger than a light breeze.

Many of the devices employed by inventors in their attempts to overcome propulsion problems are even more fantastic than some of the details in the airship reports of 1897. Two French balloonists constructed a huge melon-shaped bag which was to be propelled by six sailors who were to "row" the atmosphere with windmill-like oars covered by silk. Similarly, Musnier designed a ship to be propelled by eighty aeronauts cranking a shaft which extended through the gondola and on the other end of which a propeller was to be attached. Airships with large sails erected on the top of the gas bag proved equally impractical. The canvases were designed to propel the craft and at the same time serve as a means of controlling the vessel's direction and speed of flight. Although these experimental devices were impractical, they led to the development of successful Zeppelins in the early 1900's. There can be little doubt that the interest generated by these pioneer experiments provided an aura of credibility to the reports of an airship cruising over the Midwest.

Finally it should be pointed out that many of the details in the reported sightings read like pure fabrications. We shall never know whether the individual who *saw* a swordfish discharged from the ship, or those who composed the mythical letters, were actuated by the spirit of fun or belonged to the ever-present lunatic fringe. It really doesn't matter. It was a good story while it lasted.

4: Bombs, Bolsheviks and Babbitts

I

SOMETIME BETWEEN THE HOURS OF 6:00 AND 8:00 P.M. on the evening of April 25, 1919, two men drove up to a mailbox on 28th Street near 6th Avenue in New York City. The man on the passenger side of the car got out quickly, and, after a glance or two up and down the street, deposited a number of small packages in the box. He hurried back to the car and the two drove across to Broadway, where more of the little brown-paper wrapped cartons were dropped into a box on 29th and Broadway, and again on 32nd and Broadway. After carrying out this seemingly innocent mission, the two men disappeared into the city's millions, never to be identified.

Four days later, and hundreds of miles to the south in Atlanta, Georgia, the United States Postal Service carried out its traditional mission of getting the mails through in spite of such elemental difficulties as rain, sleet, dark of night and the more mundane problems created by the Service's patrons. Despite the fact that one of the packages mailed in New York had been incorrectly addressed to Sandersville, Georgia, it was duly delivered to the home of the addressee, Senator Thomas Hardwick (Dem. Ga.), former chairman of a committee advocating restrictions on immigration. A little later, the Hardwick maid collected the package along with the rest of the morning's mail and took the lot to Mrs. Hardwick. The Senator's wife glanced at the small package and noted that it was addressed to her then absent husband. But since the return address was Gimbel Brothers, the celebrated New York department store, and because the pencil-box size package bore the inscription "Sample," Mrs. Hardwick assumed that it contained a free gift of pencils for promotional purposes and gave it to the maid to open while she looked through the rest of the mail. When the girl untied the knot and started to remove the cord, there was a terrific explosion accompanied by a blinding flash of flame and a barrage of deadly shrapnel. Both of the maid's hands were blown off, Mrs. Hardwick was severely burned about the upper part of her body, and both victims were deeply lacerated by small fragments of metal which had been packed around the explosive. Later, experts from the

57

Department of Justice expressed surprise that the two women were not killed instantly, for such was the force of the explosion that furniture in the room was badly damaged.

For all its diminutive size, the infernal machine, as it came to be called, was one of the most diabolical and deadly devices ever contrived for mail-order bombing. As subsequent events proved, it consisted of a six by three inch stick of hollowed out wood about one inch in thickness. Inside the core was a stick of dynamite that had been soaked in nitroglycerin. Three fulminate of mercury percussion caps were attached to the cord in such a way as to detonate the device when the package was untied.

Apparently the Atlanta bombing was no isolated incident. Twenty-four hours earlier, a similar device had been discovered in the mail of Mayor Ole Hanson of Seattle, Washington, who had been stumping the Pacific Northwest denouncing radicals. It was described as powerful enough to "blow out the entire side of the County-City Building." Fortunately the Mayor's aides became suspicious of the unordered package and turned it over to the local bomb squad.

On the following day, April 30th, Charles Caplan, a New York City postal clerk, purchased a newpaper at a kiosk on his way home from work. After boarding his train, he folded it for subway reading in the curious manner of New Yorkers, and was soon absorbed in the lead story of the Atlanta and Seattle outrages. Since the package addressed to Mayor Hanson had not been destroyed, the news story carried a detailed description of its wrappings and return address. There was something oddly familiar to Caplan about the description. He racked his memory for a hint as to where he had previously seen a number of similar packages. Suddenly he remembered that he had set aside sixteen identical parcels in the sorting room of the Post Office because they had insufficient postage and would have to be returned to Gimbels.

Caplan hurried back to the Post Office and found the little packages neatly stacked on a shelf where he had set them aside several days previously. They were destined for some of the country's most prominent citizens, including Attorney General A. Mitchell Palmer, Postmaster-General Burleson, Chief Justice Oliver Wendell Holmes, Kenesaw Mountain Landis (then a jurist, later baseball commissioner), and the famous capitalists J. P. Morgan and John D. Rockefeller. The remainder were addressed to other government officials and high magnates of the business world who were prominent at that time.

The following morning a nation-wide alert went out to all

post offices in the United States ordering postmasters to intercept any additional packages similar to those found in New York. At the same time a massive investigation was launched to discover the perpetrators of the bomb plot. It appeared obvious from a study of the intended recipients of the infernal devices that those responsible must be anarchists. Attention was at first directed toward Gimbels personnel, since all of the packages discovered thus far had identical return labels bearing the store's address. However, Isaac Gimbel, the store's owner, while promising an investigation, announced that his hundreds of employees had been carefully screened by "experts" at the time of their employment. Consequently, there was virtually no possibility that the famous store harbored a nest of bomb-manufacturing nihilists. He accounted for the labels on the packages by suggesting that they had been secured by persons making legitimate purchases who subsequently removed them for their own nefarious purposes.

In point of fact the anarchists were never found. Every clue, such as the source of the packaging material, the origin of the dynamite and caps, and the identity of fingerprint-like smudges found inside the packages, led to dead ends. At the close of the investigation only one thing was clear. Thirty-six bombs had been destined to wipe out thirty-six governmental officials and business moguls who by word or deed had taken a stand against radicals, socialists, Bolsheviks, members of the I.W.W. and aliens. The bombing had been calculate to initiate a reign of terror and confusion among those unsympathetic to left-wing causes. The frustration of the plot saved its intended targets (the maid and Mrs. Hardwick were its only victims), but to the subsequent discomfort of the plotters it served as the stimulus that brought to a head the incipient antiradical hysteria of the period. The Red Scare of the Twenties was on.

II

In order to understand the dynamics of the Red menace of 1919-1920 that was responsible for this fantastic plot, we must first turn to certain domestic and foreign developments which had grown out of World War I; for the roots of the postwar hysteria were deeply imbedded in the emotionalism of the war years and were well-nourished by the superpatriotism created by the barrage of propaganda put out by the Wilson administration. A study of this scope cannot, of course, attempt to provide a complete history of this phase of the war. Rather, its purpose will be to survey the highlights of those consequences of the conflict which provided a receptive environment for what was to come.

To begin with, various official and semiofficial patriotic organizations mushroomed into existence during the 1914-1918 era. Their purpose was to whip up a white heat of anti-German prejudice and at the same time to encourage super-Americanism. Such was the aim of the National Security League, a group of virulent patriots whose great contribution to the war effort was to invade motion picture houses and harangue their captive audiences with four-minute speechs designed to arouse anti-German passions and sell Liberty Bonds. The American Protective League, working under the Department of Justice, made its mission the ferreting of "spies" and "German agents." Virtually everyone with a name that smacked of Teutonic antecedents was investigated and sometimes harassed to the verge of suicide. One of their suspected traitors was H. L. Mencken, who was denounced as a cohort of the "German monster, Nitzsky." Through a subterfuge, Mencken himself wrote the report which was sent to the League's headquarters in Washington. Needless to say he was completely exonerated of subversive activities.

To insure "right thinking," a Committee on Public Information was set up by the Wilson administration. Among its functions were those of censoring the mails, getting the German language thrown out of college and university curricula, and proving (with the help of hired historians) that American and British propaganda ought to be taken as literally as the Gospel of St. John the Evangelist. Finally, there were the Vigilantes, who made a specialty out of smearing yellow paint on the houses of those suspected of less than two hundred percent patriotism or of anyone of military age who failed to rush off to France fast enough to suit members of the organization. Occasionaly these patriots engaged in bodily assault to bring home their message to reluctant citizens. The temper of the times was such that even women were under suspicion if they failed to knit socks and sweaters for the boys at the front.

In addition to the stimulus provided by such Ku Kluxer organizations, good Americanism was also encouraged by various laws enacted by the Congress between 1917-1920. These statutes not only favored the tactics just enumerated, but also resulted in the first real break in the American tradition of freedom of speech. In effect, the legislation meant that for the first time opinions per se were labeled objectionable. The severest penalties were provided for minor crimes—sometimes for nothing more than the advocacy of such crimes. A censorship of the press and mails was established, and the time-honored privileges of the soapbox orator were suspended. In short, the Bill of Rights was put in grave jeopardy by oppressive legislation under the guise of dealing with wartime emergencies.

While such extreme, totalitarian measures were being taken in the United States, Nikolai Lenin brought off his Bolshevik coup d'état in Russia in November of 1917, and centuries of Czarist rule ended in a bath of blood. Naturally, Americans were revolted by the whole Russian mess, and, in the United States, the Russian name "Bolshevik" (meaning originally the "larger" or "majority" party), came to stand for all the pentup hate, prejudice and frustration generated by the organizations described above and by the war itself. After the war, "Bolshevik" became the symbol of everything sinister, un-American and revolutionary. The overwrought emotionalism of the war years had no opportunity to dissipate itself, since the United States was an active participant for a relatively short time and even this contribution was more disillusioning than cathartic. The transition from anti-German to anti-Bolshevik was, therefore, an easy one. Moreover, the American brand of Bolsheviks, Reds, Radicals, or Socialists —the name really made no difference—became scapegoats for the disillusionment, economic upsets, labor troubles, and other domestic upheavals that follow in the wake of any war. Eventually things became so bad that the most innocent departure from conventionalism was suspect, and anyone advocating the slightest change from oppressive legislation or intolerable labor conditions was looked upon as an anarchist with a bomb in one hand and a dagger in the other. The Republic, in short, was hagridden by the specter of Bolshevik anarchism.

When the bomb plot described in the opening paragraphs came to light, the antiradical element found a Führer in the person of Attorney General A. Mitchell Palmer, one of the intended targets of the would-be assassins. The bomb outrage set Palmer off like a jolt of lightning. He became the knight-errant of the forces of righteousness and the avowed enemy of anyone who was not a native-born, one hundred percent Babbitt. He turned his legal talents and high intelligence to formulating programs of hate and propaganda which rivaled anything Goebbels was able to conjure up two decades later.

Palmer was a Pennsylvania Puritan driven by overwhelming ambition; he had designs on the presidency and had made an unsuccessful bid for nomination on the Democratic ticket in 1920. He was undoubtedly a brilliant man (he had been graduated from Swarthmore in 1891 with the highest honors ever received), but his emotions and ambitions ran away with his intellect. He was, of course, aided and abetted by all sorts of hangers-on who sensed a golden opportunity to cash in on the hysteria for their own personal advantage by following his lead.

Palmer launched a twofold attack: as Attorney General he had the unquestioned right to recommend legislation for coping with any domestic dangers not covered by existing federal laws. He chose to ignore the fact that there were already adequate codes in existence to deal with criminals who sent dynamite through the mails or who were disloyal to the United States and suggested instead the most sweeping legislative enactments which, if put into effect, would have abridged the Constitution. He became terrified—not only of bombings—but also of soapbox orators, propagandists, professors of economics, strikers and, above all else, aliens. He thought he detected dangerous loopholes in the federal laws, since there was no provision for the punishment of single persons who hired a hall and made a speech against the government. Such individuals could not be prosecuted for the simple reason that conspiracy was not involved. Moreover, there was no way to stop the insidious perils of pamphleteering. Again, unless conspiracy could be proved, radicals could not be arrested for handing out inflammatory literature on the streets. Palmer, in fact, wanted legislation broad enough to allow him to deal with long-haired men and short-haired women—anything from avowed anarchists to parlor Reds. As a result of the Palmer agitation, Congress had no less than seventy bills under consideration in 1919-1920 which dealt with unlawful naturalized citizens, and a proposal by one enterprising Senator from Tennessee that an American Devil's Island be established on Guam for the transportation of radicals.

But Palmer was not content with restricting his efforts to legislative proposals. He hired spies and agents provocateurs whose orders were to secretly join labor unions and the Socialist and Communist* parties. Once entrenched, their mission was to become leaders in the movements so that Palmer would be privy to the organizations' secrets and revolutionary plans. He was careful to warn his henchmen never to *incite* to violence, but only to *appear* to encourage the Reds to the point where they would either be lulled or provoked into doing something illegal. As Judge Anderson of Boston noted later, the United States was put into the

---

* At that time the Communist Party was legal.

doubly curious position of encouraging its own downfall and actually owning part of the Communist Party which was striving to bring about that unwelcome event.

Making good use of his spies, Palmer rounded up radical leaders in a series of raids largely directed at the alien population. Those caught in his dragnets were deported to Russia by way of Finland on a ship originally commissioned the *Buford*, but which came to be known during Palmer's reign as the "Soviet Ark." None of those deported had committed any known crime. Palmer also obtained illegal injunctions against strikers, and loosed devastating propaganda blasts against radicals of every description. He told a women's political league in New York that the people of that city would be treated to the edifying spectacle of the "second, third and fourth Soviet Arks sailing down their beautiful harbor."

Nor was the Attorney General without support. Public opinion, that last court of appeal in all matters political, supported and applauded him. To quote Palmer: "I was shouted at from every editorial sanctum in America from sea to sea; I was preached upon from every pulpit; I was urged —I could feel it dinned into my ears—throughout the country to do something and do it now, do it quick, and do it in a way that would bring results to stop this sort of thing in the United States."

That summer Mr. Palmer's house was bombed, and after this counterattack on the part of the radicals the Attorney General's hysteria knew no bounds.

The bombing took place in June 1919, just a month after the mail bomb plot described earlier. Palmer was home at the time*, and it was evident that the attack was an attempted personal reprisal for the Attorney General's war on radicals. Palmer had just left his library on the first floor and was getting ready to retire in his upstairs bedroom when he felt the house shake as if it had been hit by a truckload of bricks. He rushed downstairs, to find the front of the house blown in. Had he lingered in the library for a few moments longer, he would have been killed or seriously injured. Windows were shattered for blocks around by the force of the blast.

In the street, police found the blown-to-bits remains of the would-be assassin. Evidently the bomb went off prematurely,

---

* Palmer had attended a social affair earlier in the evening in the company of Franklin D. Roosevelt, then Assistant Secretary of the Navy. Roosevelt drove Palmer home but did not join Palmer for a nightcap. If he had, the course of history might have been changed, since both men would have probably been in the library at the time of the explosion.

killing the anarchist before he could leave the danger area. In the dead man's clothing was a copy of *Plain Words*, a radical publication, hence there was no doubt the deed had been perpetrated by Bolsheviks. Palmer vowed it would be a war to the death from that time forward until they were all eradicated.

He began by terrifying Americans with threats and sinister innuendoes. He saw Bolsheviks lurking everywhere ready to steal Liberty Bonds from private homes, blow up capitalist factories and foment strikes. The very government of the United States was in grave danger from all quarters—even from within. The National Security League issued a chart in which three hundred members of Congress were charged with disloyalty. The lawmakers were greatly incensed at this sweeping allegation, and an investigation followed forthwith which, of course, exonerated the legislators.

On the educational front, teachers were required to sign loyalty oaths, and college professors were denounced by their students if they appeared to be anywhere left of center in their pedagogy. Radcliffe, the female version of Harvard College, was subjected to heavy censure for allowing the girls to debate the affirmative of such an obviously un-American question as the right of labor unions to organize. In New York, the Board of Education drew up a creed for school children the essence of which was to make them swear a terrible oath to defend the flag, respect the President, put patriotism above all other loyalties, and to oppose Bolshevism, anarchism and the I.W.W. One New York paper suggested that if such a manifesto were adopted, graduation from New York educational institutions might come to depend more on patriotism than scholastic ability, and at the same time, relatively harmless potential radicals would become confirmed Bolsheviks, since they were left with virtually no alternative. But the real hotbed of radicalism in those days was Yale. It came under fire for harboring liberal professors who openly spoke out against Palmerism; and, as a consequence, Yale enjoyed about the same position in the Twenties as Harvard was to find itself in during the 1950's when the late Senator McCarthy charged that the institution was a sanctuary for Fifth Amendment Communists.

On the labor front, one hundred and fifty alleged members of the I.W.W. in West Virginia were forced to kiss the flag and were then deported. The laboring class, in fact, was the sorest spot in the country from Palmer's point of view. Prices were high, hours of work unreasonably long—in some cases twelve hours a day for seven days a week—and working conditions left much to be desired. As a result of such conditions strikes were frequent, and every labor dispute was seen by Palmer (and many employers) as a potential revolutionary uprising fomented by Bolsheviks. For much the same reason, every time organized labor unions or socialistic organizations were allowed to march in a parade in a major city there was sure to be trouble. Serious disorders broke out in Cleveland when a May Day parade precipitated a riot which spread through the entire city resulting in one death and scores of injuries. In Centralia, Washington, four were killed outright in an Armistice Day parade in November, and one man was lynched in disorders that followed the riot. As a consequence of these developments every workingman everywhere was suspect. The war cry of the times was S.O.S.—"Ship or Shoot."

If the Attorney General's calculations had been correct, one out of every four adult Americans at that time would have been an avowed Bolshevik—a member of a hidden army ready to revolt and overthrow the government at the first opportune moment. More reasonable estimates put the figure at one-tenth of one percent of the total population—this was the "Bolshevik Army" which had the entire nation knocking its knees in terror.

While the laboring man was considered the prime tool of the Bolsheviks, other social groups came in for their share of attention. Anti-Negro and anti-Jewish prejudice, anti-intellectualism and anti-Catholicism ran rampant through the United States and led to a resurgence of the Ku Klux Klan of the Reconstruction period following the Civil War. During the next few years, the knights of the white sheet enjoyed a tremendous success terrifying Negroes, down-and-out aliens, hobos and others who were unable or unwilling to fight back. Intellectuals came under heavy fire for discussing the merits of the Bolshevik plan of free love, for reading the *Nation* and the *New Republic,* and, in general, for refusing to take Palmer and his Gestapo seriously.

As summer moved into fall and winter, the wave of fear and intolerance reached the proportions of an abject panic which, according to Zechariah Chaffee in his *Free Speech in the United States,* brought about the following state of affairs:

> One by one, the rights of freedom of speech, the right of assembly, the right to petition, the right to protection against unreasonable searches and seizures, the right against arbitrary arrest, the right to a fair trial, the hatred of spies, the principle that guilt is personal, the

principle that punishment should bear some proportion to the offense, had been sacrificed and ignored.

However, the worst was still to come at the end of the year. Palmer's spies and agents had been devoting full time to their jobs and all was ready to cleanse the Republic of Bolsheviks by New Year's Day of 1920. Massive raids were unleashed all over the United States that day, and over six thousand persons were arrested—some on illegal warrants* issued by the Attorney General—some on no warrants at all. In many cases officers received the warrants after arrests had already been made. A few sample descriptions of incidents typical of the raids and their aftermath are given from reports in newspapers and magazines of that year.

Frederick M. Davenport, in the *Outlook* for August 1920, gave the following picture of the raids in Utica, New York. Eleven "anarchists" were arrested on the charge that they were guilty of inciting "to riot, disorder, breach of the peace, destruction of property, and general revolutionary activities among the people of the state; and that it is their intention by such means to offend the public decency and to annoy and endanger the life, repose, health and safety of a considerable number of persons, and to render such persons insecure in their life and the use of property—that it was their intention to incite the breaking of contracts of service or hire, with the intention of endangering human life, causing grievous bodily injury, exposing valuable property to destruction."

The net result of the raid initiated on these formidable charges was exactly nothing. The eleven "anarchists" were hustled out of their beds at midnight, and the total haul from their rooms turned out to be some Red literature and a sinister-looking "ripper" knife. The eleven were mostly ignorant young Polish immigrants who were eventually released and subsequently became good citizens.

In Boston, six hundred persons were arrested. The raids consisted of Palmer's storm troopers bursting into meeting halls, ordering everyone present to line up against the wall, and then searching and questioning the victims without the benefit of warrants or provision for defense counsel.

In Lynn, Massachusetts, thirty-nine people holding an innocent meeting for the purpose of discussing the formation of a co-op were jailed. All but one had to be released the following day for lack of evidence of any wrongdoing.

---

* Since the raids were on aliens who were under the jurisdiction of the Department of Labor, Palmer's warrants were illegal.

In Chelsea, Massachusetts, the mother of three children was arrested during the night and taken with her thirteen-year-old daughter to the police station. A short time later the child was sent home alone to a remote part of the city. The mother was lodged in jail overnight and taken to a wharf the next morning where she and another "Bolshevik" were held in a dirty toilet for six hours. They were finally conveyed to Deer Island and imprisoned for an additional thirty-three days.

In Nashua, New Hampshire, a raid brought in thirteen women, five of whom were held incommunicado for over twenty-four hours in a cell without so much as a mattress to sleep on.

In Washington, Edward J. Irvine, a member of the Workers' Party of America, was arrested at a meeting. Detectives rushed to his home looking for radical literature. They informed his mother that he was making a speech in which he expressed the desire to see the streets running with blood. When he was subsequently brought to trial and asked how he had become a radical, he replied through reading the Harvard Classics, the life of Jesus and the writings of Thomas Jefferson.

In Detroit, one hundred men were imprisoned for a week in a bull pen whose dimensions were twenty-four by thirty feet and which was maintained under such filthy conditions that even the mayor of the city was moved to protest.

Nor were those suspected of Bolshevism the only victims of Palmer's ferocity. In Boston, Minnie Federman, a witness, was asleep in her bedroom at 6:00 a.m. when several of Palmer's minions entered her chambers. They showed no warrant or subpoena, but peremptorily commanded her to dress and accompany them to the station. When the men refused to leave the bedroom, she had to dress in a closet. While she was getting ready her room was searched for "literature."

The persons arrested in these raids were, in most cases, harmless working people. They were ignorant aliens recently of the European peasant class who had no idea of their rights and were therefore afraid to protest at being handcuffed, chained and thrown into dirty jails, there to be held incommunicado with no charges leveled against them. Altogether this "Army of Bolsheviks," presumably armed to the teeth with bombs, daggers and other such un-American weapons, were found to have a total of three pistols in their possession. Some were jailed, some deported—including a few American citizens who eventually got reinstated when they proved their citizenship—but most were eventually released for lack of evidence of criminal intent or activity.

During the new year, the hysteria went on apace. The

"Fighting Quaker" promised to keep up "an unflinching war" against Bolshevism no matter how it was "disguised or dissembled." In January, he got out a long letter to mass-circulation magazines warning editors of the dangers of radicalism and, in effect, urging them to propagandize their readers against every shade of Red. It seemed Palmer was trying to edit the nation's magazines from Washington. With this form of suppression the Attorney General had come full circle, since he was now subscribing to every method employed by the very Russians he anathemized: censorship, raids and seizures without warrants, persecution for opinions, and deportation. Something of the temper of the nation in that first month of 1920 can be gauged by a quotation from a speech delivered in a church by Secretary of State Langtry of Massachusetts. He said: "If I had my way I would take them [radicals] out in the yard every morning and shoot them, and the next day would have a trial to see whether they were guilty."

In addition to Palmer's fulminations and pogroms, two events which turned out to be highly significant had their origin during the year. One of these occurred on the educational front; the other was largely political in nature. By an ironic twist of fate it was the political development which spelled the doom of the Red hysteria.

The first case involved a New York educational institution known as the Rand School. The latter was a college established in 1906 by the American Socialist Society. By 1920, it boasted approximately 5,000 students. None of its activities had ever been held to be illegal; however, a state legislative committee, known as the Lusk Committee, set up a fearful agitation in 1920-1921 charging that the institution had too many radicals on its staff. The committee's agents seized letters from the institution's administrative files and offered in evidence incendiary passages from these communications to prove that the school was a veritable training ground for Bolsheviks. Some of the letters, incidentally, had been written *to* the school by extremists and in no sense reflected the institution's purposes or teachings. The investigation almost resulted in legislation which would have put all New York educational institutions at the mercy of licensing boards such as those certifying plumbers, barbers, beer wholesalers and gas-fitters. Fortunately, when Al Smith became governor he vetoed the bill, and the whole thing collapsed. In the Thirties, when the school was about to close for lack of funds, such outstanding Americans as Helen Keller, Elmer Davis, Charles Beard, Stuart Chase, and John Dewey supported a drive for donations to keep it in operation.

The political incident involved five duly elected members of the New York State Legislature who were denied their seats by more or less Star Chamber proceedings. They were members of the Socialist Party, which was neither an illegal nor subversive group. Nevertheless, it was asserted that the elected representatives could not be Socialists and still remain loyal to the Constitution. While the Socialists remained unseated, the unprecedented result was that a segment of the American people was being deprived of legal representation in the state legislature. They were, in effect, disenfranchised. During the battle that followed, it became apparent the witch hunt had gone too far. Even conservative elements began to decry the excesses to which postwar hysteria had carried the Republic. The distinguished Charles Evan Hughes, among others, took up the cudgels for the New York Socialists. Public opinion began to move slowly at first, then in an avalanche of revulsion against Palmerism. The wholesale cancellation of deportation warrants followed, and once more the voice of the liberal could be heard throughout the land.

But the end was not quite yet. The Red menace was destined to end much as it had begun—with an explosion of gunpowder, not words. The time was 12:05 p.m., September 16, 1920—the place Wall Street, the financial heart of the United States. The sidewalks that noon were filled with clerks, stenographers, and messenger boys hurrying to lunch in the time-honored manner of New Yorkers. Inside the House of Morgan, a conference taking place in the back parlors kept the financial leaders of that mighty institution working past the lunch hour. It was a conference that probably saved their lives, however it may have affected their purses. A few minutes earlier, just ahead of the noontime exodus, a somewhat incongruous and seemingly trivial incident took place across the street from the Morgan establishment. An unshaven, dirty-looking workman had leisurely driven up the street in a delivery wagon and reined his horse along the curb by the Sub-Treasury Building. But in the hurry of the midday rush-hour scarcely anyone cast a glance in the direction of the patient animal whose now absent driver had left him tethered to a hitching post.

Suddenly, and without warning, there was a blinding flash of blue-white light which illuminated the whole of Wall Street. An instant later a deafening roar accompanied by a shock wave spread through lower Manhattan and across the river into Brooklyn. For the next split-second there was silence—then the tinkling rain of thousands of splintered windows falling to the streets. A great mushroom cloud* of yellowish-black smoke rose one hundred feet into the air; this was followed by a spreading pall of dust from broken plaster and chipped building facings.

When the reverberations of the explosion died away, the screams of the injured and dying cut through the clouds of dust and smoke—strangely thin sounds after the deafening roar of the explosion. The lifting haze revealed a scene of incredible destruction and horror. A half-naked woman whose flesh was seared tried to rise, then fell back dead. A dying messenger begged for someone to guard the pouch of securities he had been carrying when he fell. Some of the injured were afire—screaming with the pain of burning flesh. Their blood ran in the gutters.

All told, twenty-nine people were killed outright, and six died later in hospitals. Plate glass was shattered for blocks around, and in the immediate vicinity of the explosion the facades of buildings were chipped and scarred by bomb fragments. Over one million dollars worth of damage had been done in an instant. The interior of the House of Morgan, the presumed target of the attack, looked like a no man's land: glass was strewn all over the floor, and much of the beautiful imported marble work had been wrecked. A clerk lay dead amid the splintered furniture. Outside, the front of the building was pock-marked by chunks of iron that had been used to reinforce the bomb.

Across the street there was no sign of a wagon—only a shallow crater left by the bomb—and the horse, who had been the unwitting bearer of the infernal machine, was reduced to unrecognizable bits.

Soon ambulances arrived to gather up the dead and injured. A huge, hysterical crowd of people, some from as far away as Broadway, were drawn to the scene by the noise of the explosion and the wail of ambulances. An alarmed Assistant Secretary of the Treasury requisitioned one hundred regulars from the 22nd Infantry Battalion stationed on Governor's Island to protect the Sub-Treasury from looting. In the soldiers' wake, the Red Cross and a small army of city officials and workmen arrived to carry out their several tasks of mercy, investigation and reconstruction. Thirty detectives were hurriedly dispatched to guard the Morgan residence, and eight separate investigations were launched to ascertain responsibility for the outrage. One of these manhunts was under the direction of the famous detective William Burns.

---

* The psychological effect of such an explosion in the atomic age can readily be imagined.

70

But in spite of thousands of man hours spent in tracking down leads, the perpetrators of the crime were never found. This much seemed clear: the explosion was caused by a huge time bomb made of TNT and reinforced with slugs of cast iron cut from old-fashioned window weights. In confirmation of this analysis, pieces of the homemade shrapnel were dug out of the bodies of the victims. There was no doubt the infernal machine had been brought to the site by the man who left the horse and wagon; however, the only concrete clue to his identity was the horse's shoes. Theoretically, at least, they should have been traceable; and the blacksmith who had forged them was eventually found, but here the only promising lead petered out.

The consensus among the investigators was that anarchists were responsible for the crime. One supporting fact in favor of this hypothesis was the discovery of crudely printed threats in nearby mailboxes. Frank Francisco, of the Department of Justice, also thought it significant that the explosion took place soon after the Department's "Red Square" had been abandoned. The bombing, it seemed, was the last horrible gasp of the dying Red menace which had been threatening the security of the United States ever since the closing days of the first World War. But the nation had recovered its equilibrium to such an extent that everyone recognized so senseless an outrage could have been perpetrated only by a small group of men with twisted mentalities and in no way reflected the wishes of any significant number of Americans. The hysteria was over.

III

In accounting for the Red hysteria of the Twenties, the influence of World War I legislative and patriotic factors has already been discussed. It has been demonstrated that the epidemic was primarily a domestic disease rather than the result of an international conflict with Russia. Aside from these etiological factors, several additional points are worthy of brief mention as a kind of concluding commentary for this study.

To begin with, this episode of mass hysteria illustrates the ever-present danger in a democracy such as ours of what psychologists call "displaced aggression." In social upheavals this form of aggression manifests itself as scapegoating. Americans, in common with people all over the world, suffer from a high level of personal frustration, anxiety and conflict. In a civilized community there is little outlet for the tensions generated by such psychological forces. Paradoxically, war

71

provides a safety valve at the same time that it intensifies the very forces for which it is serving as a cathartic. Perhaps this is why wars of the pre-atomic variety were not as unpopular as they might have been. Perhaps this is why the incidence of neuroses and psychoses markedly declines during periods of international conflicts.

But during World War I, the fires of emotion forged a curious mixture of idealism, hatred of things foreign, and superpatriotism which never found a satisfying outlet in the conflict itself. "Bolsheviks" therefore became the scapegoats, and in the name of fighting them every tradition Americans held sacred for over a century was thrown overboard. Minority groups suffered the most, as they always have and always will, since the worst sort of people invariably get in the driver's seat in times like these. And the worst sort inevitably attacks at odds of ten to one.

Another contributory factor was the lack of leadership in the White House while the furor was going on. Since the end of the war, Wilson had been preoccupied with the famous Fourteen Points for peace and the establishment of the League of Nations. When Congress renounced his programs, the President took the stump in a direct appeal to the people. After an extensive tour, he collapsed from fatigue and strain in Pueblo, Colorado, in September of 1919. Shortly afterwards he suffered a paralytic stroke which rendered him unable to carry out the duties of his office. Therefore, as the hysteria was gaining ground, there was no national leadership to dampen it. When the madness reached its height, Warren Gamaliel Harding had been elected—a popular leader but hollow as a jug. It was a ripe opportunity for a totalitarian like Palmer, of whom Wilson once said, "He would make a good President." Wilson, as well as the majority of the American people, had succumbed to the human weakness of looking up to authoritarian leadership in a time of crisis irrespective of whether this leadership was good or evil. The dangers of this sort of thing were made all too clear by the events in Germany and Italy not too many years afterwards. The moral would seem to be that democracy needs strong leadership, just as is true of any other form of government. It cannot run itself or be allowed to drift with the whims and passions of the moment.

In conclusion, a careful and much more detailed study of the events outlined here also makes it clear that loyalty cannot be legislated by a welter of hastily passed laws and the activities of high-pressure patriotic groups. The Constitution provides us with broad, liberal principles which give the greatest possble latitude to the loyal opposition. Nothing in

American history has ever demonstrated that allowing these principles their broadest interpretation both in theory and practice results in serious danger to the Republic. The world's greatest philosophers, musicians, artists and statesmen—including our own founding fathers—have always been in opposition to their times and their governments. The price of progress has always been opposition expressed in free debate. That the minority point of view is sometimes shouted from soapboxes in inflammatory language need not cause a panic. Neither should isolated cases of criminal behavior inspired by radicalism, such as the bombings of 1919-1920. It is precisely on the hysteria generated by unwise retaliation for such outrages that members of the lunatic fringe thrive.

We might well follow the example set by Britain while the Red scare was going on in the United States. A British radical introduced into Parliament a bill advocating sweeping reforms. He was invited to talk the matter over at dinner with the King and Queen. In the United States in those days he would have had his dinner in jail and probably added dozens of fringe cases to the ranks of confirmed radicals by arousing sympathy for his cause. Political mass hysteria is the most dangerous of all types of hysteria. The events of 1919-1920 show all too clearly that it should be kept at the dinner table instead of in the cellar.

5: The Last Days of Rudolph Valentino

ON AUGUST 24TH, 1926, one of the worst riots in the history of New York City erupted on Broadway near 66th Street. Between sixty and eighty thousand persons were involved, hundreds of whom were injured. An emergency hospital had to be set up at the scene of the disturbances to care for those trampled under foot or lacerated by fragments from broken windows. A task force of nearly two hundred policemen was eventually mobilized to bring the mob under control and then only after mounties repeatedly charged the rioters, most of whom were women. The cause of these unruly legions in the heart of New York City was the dead body of Rudolph Valentino, the greatest movie hero of the day, and possibly of all time. The milling throngs had come to pay their last respects to the dead actor as he lay in state in a Broadway funeral parlor.

The times were ripe for such an outbreak of hysteria. It was an era celebrated for excesses and exhibitionism in every facet of human behavior. The gin of the F. Scott Fitzgeralds set the pace along bibulous lines. Extraordinary public demonstrations of physical prowess were common, and nearly every woman who boasted a good set of muscles and any swimming ability whatever took to the nearest body of water in an attempt to emulate Trudy Ederle's feat of feminine endurance in the English Channel. Those with lesser talents, but an irrepressible urge for the limelight, put on hair-raising deeds of derring-do for no better reason than putting on deeds of derring-do. In cities of any appreciable size, men and women were hauled aloft while dangling from the landing gear of barnstorming airplanes. Others performed tight rope stunts on the edges of roofs on the highest buildings in town. Meanwhile their more dexterous brethren exercised their curious talents by escaping from strait-jackets while suspended head downward eight or ten stories above the streets. There seemed to be no limit to human ingenuity in contriving masterpieces of sheer foolishness. If, however, one preferred more sinister, if vicarious, forms of excitement, he could find much to admire in the Hall-Mills murder case with its romantic motive and a *Pig Woman* as a witness to the fatal deed. The reports of the trial headlined every newspaper for weeks, not excluding the staid New York *Times*.

74

But however much one might admire marathon parties, macabre murders or super-stuntsters, the real idol of the hour at the mid-point of the Twenties was Rudolph Valentino. His movie love-making gave his female fans high voltage emotional jolts. In person, he was a handsome Latin reported to be worth millions. He could dance with the grace of a ballerina and fence like a musketeer. He won and took to wife an heiress and two glamorous movie actresses in his three unsuccessful experiments with matrimony. Wherever he went he was besieged by adoring flappers, and his mail was full of mash notes. Men, too, came under his spell, and many copied his oiled back hair-do, gaucho-style sideburns and broad-bottomed trousers. In short, he made *sheiks* out of young American males, and in the process entrenched the word in the language. The only segment of the population that took a jaundiced view of Valentino and all his works were middle-aged men, and this, of course, could be put down to jealousy.

In the closing days of the summer of 1926, Valentino was at the height of his career. His three unhappy marriages were mere memories, and he was reputed to be in love again—this time with Pola Negri, the most devastating female on the Hollywood lots. With his great hits, *The Four Horsemen*, *Blood and Sand*, and *The Sheik*, bidding fair to become celluloid immortals, Valentino had arrived in New York for the grand opening of his latest tour de force, *The Son of the Sheik*. He was thirty-one years old, apparently in good health, and with every indication of a long and eventful life ahead of him. There had been only one untoward incident to mar his happiness that summer. The unpleasantness had occurred on his trip east when the actor ran head on into a gang of Chicago reporters who had been deputized by their editors to find out what Valentino thought of a waspish editorial in the Chicago *Tribune* protesting the effeminization of the American male. It seemed that a reporter had discovered a machine for dispensing pink talcum powder in the men's room of an elite Chicago hotel, and the unkind editor had linked this alleged symptom of masculine degeneracy with Valentino's ultra-fashionable dress, wearing of slave bracelets and performances in the sheik movies. Instead of laughing the whole thing off as a joke, Valentino got his Latin blood up and challenged the editor to a duel. The weapons were to be swords. Receiving no reply, the enraged actor next suggested the more typically American method of resolving affairs of honor—a fist fight. Still there was no answer, and Valentino took the editor's silence for a tacit apology. But by the time the great lover had arrived in New York, the tabloids were full of the Chicago affair, and Valentino continued to brood over the fancied insult to his manhood. Within two weeks the newspapers were full of Valentino again, but this time the giggles had changed to tears.

On Sunday afternoon, the 15th of August, Valentino was in his hotel room in the company of his valet. Suddenly the actor gasped, clutched at his abdomen and collapsed with pain. The time was shortly past the noon hour. The frightened valet telephoned a stockbroker friend of the actor's who, upon arrival, decided the situation demanded the talents of a physician rather than those of a financier, and promptly called a doctor. There was some difficulty in diagnosing the cause of the illness, and the stricken man was not taken to the hospital until four o'clock. He was immediately operated on for a perforated gastric ulcer and inflamed appendix. Since these were the days before the antibiotics, postoperative peritonitis was virtually certain, liquids and particles of food having spilled out of the stomach into the actor's abdominal cavity. All Dr. Meeker, the surgeon, could do was sew up the perforation, remove the appendix, clean out his patient as thoroughly as possible and rely on nature to complete the cure. However, the following day the star's condition gave rise for guarded optimism. The peritonitis had developed as expected, but appeared to be localized. The great lover was said to be in sufficient strength to pat a nurse on the cheek. The nurse, incidentally, was reported to be as beautiful as any of the current batch of leading ladies in the film capital.

Besides Dr. Meeker, the actor's postoperative condition was watched closely by two physicians with the oddly assorted names of A. A. Jaller and Golden Rhind Battey. In addition, the local newspapers felt it worth noting that Rudy was in the *lucky room*—the most luxurious suite of the Polyclinic Hospital—where America's Sweetheart, Mary Pickford, had recently weathered a serious illness. The only sour note was struck by the New York *Evening Post* which pointed out that the sheik had been forgotten by his admirers. The article alleged that, hospital hints to the contrary, Valentino had received but one telegram and a single visitor. A *Post* reporter, who played detective about the hospital grounds, saw no messenger boys delivering "thousands of telegrams" and no trucks with "loads of flowers." This same journal added a postoperative note to the effect that the first thing Rudy said to Dr. Meeker upon coming out of the anesthetic was, "Doctor am I a pink puff?" Finally, from Hollywood, there was a report describing Pola Negri as "stunned and shocked" upon being informed of the actor's collapse.

On Tuesday, the 17th, there could be no further doubt that the missing messages and floral offering had materialized. In fact, the hospital was forced to establish a special information bureau to handle the flood of inquiries coming in by telephone and telegraph. Flowers appeared in such embarrassing quantities there were enough to stock several florist shops. Besides sending tokens of good will, some of the well-wishers appeared in person. Among these was a girl accompanied by her pet monkey who came to the hospital to "amuse Rudy." Another young woman identified as Maire Markiewicz arrived and asked leave to read the actor a poem which she had written and entitled *A Dreamer's Thought*. When Marie was denied admission to her dream lover, she became "unmanageable" and had to be treated for a "nervous condition." A little later, a distracted male admirer found wandering about the hospital corridors, offered to pray at the sick man's side.

In view of these unwelcome attempts on the star's person, S. George Ullman, the actor's manager, engaged a detective who was stationed in the hall near the sick man's suite with orders to intercept all unauthorized visitors.

Bulletins on the target of all this veneration were terse. They simply indicated that his recovery was probable and his condition sufficiently improved to allow him to take a meal of broth, French vichy and peptomized milk. In spite of the monastic hospital fare, the actor was sufficiently alert to sit up in bed and order boxes of chocolates dispatched to the hard-pressed telephone girls.

There were no further reports from Hollywood on Miss Negri's nervous condition. However, she expressed hope to reporters that she would be able to arrange a trip to New York upon completing her current picture.

The next day, the 18th, Valentino was reported out of danger, and his physicians announced that as a consequence of the marked improvement there would be no further medical bulletins on his condition. Nevertheless, inquiries continued to flood the hospital, including one from Miss Negri, who called before breakfast from her Hollywood home.

On the 19th, a cruel rumor was spread through the city that Valentino had died. Calls immediately began to pour into the hospital to reach a peak rate of two thousand an hour for over four hours. Two extra operators were required to handle the load. In some sections of the city, premature mourning began. Saleswomen in department stores lowered their heads to their counters and sobbed, unmindful of their bewildered customers. But aside from these unwarranted developments, there was little else for the papers to publish on the case save a report that among the gifts arriving at the

77

hospital were a number of Bibles and a sandalwood box contaning *sacred oils* guaranteed by the donor to bring about the actor's speedy recovery. According to Dr. Jaller, neither the holy ointments nor a supply of metephen (a mercurial antiseptic) sent by a Philadelphia admirer were used in the actor's treatment.

And so it went for the next three days. The news on the star's condition was so undramatic it had been dropped from the front page, and the only matters of any significance to appear in the news columns were a statement by Pola Negri that she was definitely arranging for a three-day trip to New York and a denial by Dr. Jaller that the actor's illness was a mere publicity stunt. Dr. Jaller denounced the rumor as an ill-disguised attempt to cast aspersions on the integrity of the hospital and its staff.

On the 22nd, the actor was back in the headlines and the news was all bad. He had suffered an unexpected relapse and was fighting for his life. Septic poisoning had set in, and pleurisy was developing in his left lung. The nursing staff was immediately doubled, and four doctors were in constant attendance on the sick man. Public reaction to these discouraging developments was rapid. Major Edward Bowes, who in those days ran a popular amateur hour on a national radio network, asked the nation over station WEAF to "hold an encouraging thought" in support of the idol's recovery. And, once again the amateur doctors rallied to the star's side. Some offered advice and others more tangible evidence of their concern. Among the latter was one Elias P. Turbin who engaged a pilot with the earthbound name of Casey Jones to fly a special "antiseptic medicine" to New York. The medicine, according to the actor's doctors would not be used.

Twenty-four hours later the "greatest lover of them all" was dead at the age of thirty-one. He died at noon after being given the last rites of the Catholic Church. There was no one who loved him for his own sake at his side—only hirelings. Even S. George Ullman, Valentino's manager, was unable to bear the end, and when it appeared imminent, he stepped out into the corridor.

When the news leaked out, throngs estimated in the thousands gathered in the streets around the hospital; many were weeping. Nurses and telephone operators inside the hospital broke down in grief.

The evening edition of the papers were full of sympathetic statements and eulogies from high moguls of the screen world and others in all walks of life. Most of the statements praised Valentino's acting in fulsome terms and deplored his untimely end. Not at all typical was boxer Jim Jeffrie's terse encomium: "That's too bad. He made good." In Hollywood, Pola Negri was reported to be prostrated and unable to talk when requested to make a statement. Two doctors were said to be struggling to control her hysterical condition.

The body meanwhile, had been placed in a wicker basket, covered with a gold cloth, and removed to the Campbell funeral parlors on Broadway and 66th Street. Even before the undertakers had agreed to a period of lying in state, the mass hysteria which had been festering since the beginning of the actor's illness came to a head. Strangers began to call at the funeral parlor attempting to gain admission by means of stratagems and ruses. There were many who claimed to have known the actor before he became famous. One shabbily dressed woman asserted that she knew him in Italy, so well indeed, that she was the first girl that he had ever kissed. Others brought funeral offerings hoping to be allowed to place them near the body. Typical of these was a "foreign-appearing" woman who arrived with a fourteen inch crucifix inlaid with a mosaic of forget-me-nots. Her uncle, she maintained, had been one of the actor's dearest friends, and in recognition of the relationship, she wished to lay the crucifix on the deceased's chest. Her offering was received by the management without comment as to its disposition. But these premature visits were only a portent of what was to come. When Valentino's manager agreed to let the body lie in state beginning at four o'clock the following afternoon, the stage was set for a greater drama than Valentino had ever starred in during his celebrated movie career.

By the time the funeral parlor opened at four, twelve thousand people had gathered in the streets in a soaking rain in anticipation of viewing the remains. The funeral directors, in view of the "heterogeneous character" of the mourners, hastily changed their arrangements. All bric-a-brac and statuary were removed from the anterooms, and while the original plan had been to expose the entire body in a high catafalque, it was placed instead in a bronze coffin under unbreakable glass in the Gold Room—so called from the gold cloth draperies adorning the walls. Aside from the ornate textiles, the only appointments in the Gold Room were four candles and a statue of a woman at the head of the bier, her head shrouded with a black veil and bowed in an attitude of grief.

When the doors were opened, the mourners entered in force. There were stylish flappers, shabbily dressed women with shawls over their heads, well-dressed matrons in furs, men and boys—all classes, colors and races. They shuffled past the dead lover for a two-second look at his emaciated face. Outside, the crowd swelled to an estimated sixty thousand. The mourners formed a line, in some places four abreast, which extended for eleven blocks. The melancholy queue started at Sixty-sixth and Broadway, extended east to Columbus Avenue, north two blocks to Sixty-eighth Street and West to Broadway. There the police thinned it to a single line which stretched an additional two blocks to end at the entrance to the funeral parlor. Time after time the crowd got out of hand, and mounted police were forced to charge in order to restore order. Despite this display of municipal prowess, the crowd spilled into the street and traffic was interrupted for hours along Broadway. Women, who made up most of the crowd, shrieked in terror of the pounding horses' hoofs. Clothes were torn from their owner's bodies, and twenty-eight ownerless odd shoes were collected by the police during the afternoon. Two women had to be arrested for disorderly conduct in the course of the disturbances. At the height of the crush, the windows in the funeral parlor gave way, and ten persons were lacerated—some of them severely—by fragments of plate glass. A room in the funeral parlor was pressed into service as an emergency hospital to care for the victims. By evening, however, the crowd had been brought under control; and at midnight, when the establishment closed, a long but orderly line waited patiently for admittance.

While Valentino was drawing the largest crowd of his career, other manifestations of the hysteria were going on elsewhere. Inside the funeral chambers, telephone calls from all points in the nation arrived at the rate of twenty a minute. Downtown, rumors were circulating that the body would be interred in a solid bronze coffin weighing a ton and a half. However, this improbable estimate was subsequently denied by S. George Ullman. More sinister rumors charging that Valentino's death had resulted from poisoning gained sufficient credence that an assistant district attorney let it be known he was unable to take action on such unsubstantial charges. An equally irresponsible story was circulated to the effect that the squadron of doctors who had attended the actor were ill as a result of their prolonged vigil. Finally, that same day, a bulletin arrived over the wire services from the other side of the nation with the latest intelligence on the condition of Miss Negri. She was being attended by two physicians and two nurses, having suffered a complete nervous collapse when informed of her reputed fiancee's death.

In light of the first day's disconcerting events, the police, at least, took a realistic view of matters, and the following day assigned one hundred and eighty-three officers to the task of keeping order at the scene of the previous day's disturbances. This formidable detachment was made up of a captain, two lieutenants, ten sergeants, one hundred and fifty patrolmen and twenty mounties. Those officers not on active duty on the Broadway front were kept on reserve in the 104th Field Artillery Armory. The gentlemen of the undertaking parlor also strengthened their defenses for an anticipated invasion. They ordered heavy planking mounted across the front of the building, and moved the corpse from the Gold Room on the third floor to the Rose Room on the first. In this way, by avoiding the delay involved in taking the mourners to the third floor by elevator, the undertakers anticipated that one hundred viewers could be handled every minute. Subsequent sample counts made by an experimental-minded reporter proved that the directors' judgment was faulty. Only thirty-eight mourners a minute filed past the actor's bier in the course of the afternoon.

When the doors were opened, some persons had been waiting in line for hours, their ardor to view the remains undampened by a steady rain. Again, the same heterogeneous collection filed past the bier. Among those paying their last respects to the movie idol was the widow of a notorious Baltimore bandit who had recently been hanged for murder. There were the 1926 version of bobby-soxers such as Dolly Toth, a nineteen year-old girl from New Jersey, who, upon viewing the body fainted, was revived and fainted again. But not all who came that afternoon were girls and women. Fashionably dressed men, sheiks, and Bowery bums shared the grief and curiosity of the weaker sex.

Those not overcome by the sight of the dead actor were surprised to see two black-shirted and ribbon-bedecked Fascisti in full regalia standing at attention at either end of the coffin. These martial minions had appeared sometime during the previous night, and when understandably curious reporters inquired as to their status, the Fascisti's only reply was to the effect that they were there because they wanted to be there. This unsatisfactory explanation was subsequently challenged by anti-Fascists who arrived later in the day and demanded that the Fascists withdraw forthwith, on the grounds that Valentino had been anti-Fascist with the result that his pictures had been banned in Italy to his considerable economic detriment. The Fascisti then amplified their previous statement, claiming that Benito Mussolini had ordered them to their melancholy posts. No understanding between the two factions was reached, and the black-shirts remained at the coffin.

While these developments were taking place near the remains, plans for the obsequies (to be held upon the arrival of the actor's brother) were under discussion in the offices of the funeral directors. Mr. Campbell favored a funeral procession of a hundred cars with an airplane hovering overhead and periodically dropping red roses on the procession. He hinted that some civic organizations might be invited to march, but qualified this with the most remarkable statement made by anyone during the entire affair. He said, "It is desirable to have the arrangements as simple as possible."

Meanwhile the funeral directors planned a ceremonious changing of the guard that same evening at the bier. Twelve of the Fascisti were to be present, and both American and Italian flags were to be placed in standards as all present executed the Fascist salute. Elsewhere, in Tin Pan Alley, a new song had been composed in honor of the dead actor. The tune was entitled, *There's a New Star in Heaven Tonight,* and the music was said to be so simple that anyone could render it on a piano by using only two fingers. Finally, out in Hollywood, a communique had been released by Pola Negri's managers to the effect that the actress would be present at the funeral services. It had been reported previously that she would resume work on her picture thus losing herself in her art in the face of inconsolable grief.

That night when the funeral parlor closed, between sixty and eighty thousand mourners had passed the remains. All night long crowds milled about the street, and four policemen were on duty to prevent untoward demonstrations. Inside, the Fascists found themselves faced with unexpected competition in the form of a rival honor guard sponsored by the Italian Artists Association. Meanwhile, a consultation was being held among the principals, and the decision was reluctantly reached not to reopen the parlors on the morrow. Moreover, there would be no state funeral. Mr. Ullman, who was responsible for these decisions, was not satisfied that the mourners had come in reverence, since he had personally observed flappers painting their faces just before entering the parlor, girls reentering the line for a second look, and the not-to-be-forgotten injuries and unseemly street scenes of the previous day. Mr. Campbell, on the other hand, subscribed to the view that the rain had caused the riots, and accounted for the remarkable turnout as an expression of true regard for the deceased rather than idle curiosity or irreverence. However, he agreed to cooperate fully with Mr. Ullman, and the cancellation of the elaborate cortege and the closing of the parlors were ultimately announced to a disappointed public.

On the 27th and 28th, there was some apprehension that

a riot might be precipitated by the closing of the funeral home. However, such fears proved to be groundless A score of persons milled about the entrance demanding to be let in, but only those who presented tickets issued by the actor's manager were permitted to view the body. The only unfortunate incident occurred when an eight-foot wreath from United Artists was being delivered. The crowd attempted to take advantage of the situation and storm the entrance. But the assault was beaten back, and from that point on the spell was broken; thereafter the mass hysteria confined itself mainly to those who had been professionally or romantically associated with the actor before his death. The masses had found greener pastures in the homecoming of Gertrude Ederle, and a near riot had to be broken up by the police when she returned to her home in New York City.

Meanwhile, with the special permission of the Department of Health, the actor remained unburied. Final arrangements awaited the arrival of his still absent brother, Alberto, who had sailed from Italy immediately upon being notified of the star's death. All was now quiet at the funeral parlor. The Fascists had been dismissed to prevent a possible clash with anti-Fascists and the crowd outside had thinned out to a few diehards.

During the lull, scattered reports from various corners of the world kept the mass-wake in the news. Among these were the following: Jascha Heifetz had been operated on under the pseudonym of *John Smith* in order to prevent any possibility of disturbances such as those associated with Valentino's illness and death. An unnamed hospital attendant with a shrewd appreciation of human nature expressed doubt that such precautions were necessary. He felt there was no comparison between the public's love for music and its adoration of movie idols. In London, a twenty-seven-year-old actress, Peggy Scott, took poison and left this message to posterity anent her feelings for Valentino. "With his death my last bit of courage has flown." Also on the international front, *Osservatore Romano* described the scenes at Valentino's bier and then added this philosophic commentary on the times: "It would make us laugh if it did not cause the most profound pity. It is a collective madness, incarnating the tragic comedy of a new fetichism, the last logical consequence of a materialist civilization which has given man dominion over everything but himself." Finally, back in Hollywood, the actor's horse took part in a memorial service held at a breakfast club. The animal was paraded in military fashion with his master's boots reversed in the stirrups.

On August 29th, six days after the screen idol's death,

Miss Negri arrived in New York after a three thousand mile journey which had been "expedited" by railroad officials and minutely reported by the newspapers. When the news filtered out that the actress was in town, hysteria broke out anew. Crowds began to gather at the funeral parlor, and when she arrived at the scene, a way had to be forced through the mob by police. The casket was opened by special permission of the Health Department. Miss Negri was overcome by the sight of her reported lover and collapsed. A nurse and Mrs. Ullman worked for thirty minutes to revive the stricken *tigress* of the screen. When she was able to leave the funeral parlor and had entered her limousine, a patrolman had to dismount forceably several persons who had broken police lines and leaped on her car as it began to move away. Safely back at her hotel, having been aroused by reporters' questions to reply to allegations that she and Rudy were not really engaged, Miss Negri issued the following statement: "My love for Valentino was the greatest love of my life; I shall never forget him." Then she added apparently by way of clarification, "I loved him not as one artist loves another, but as a woman loves a man."

On the 31st, the long week was over. The actor's brother had at last arrived from Italy and was met at the pier by Miss Negri, an Italian delegation with crepe be-ribboned flags and such a vast number of onlookers that customs inspections at the Port of New York broke down for several hours. Pola kissed Alberto three times and later remarked to reporters that he had told her of losing twenty pounds as a result of his brother's untimely death.

The next day the funeral took place on schedule with solid walls of humanity lining the route of the cortege. At intervals knots of people broached police lines and halted the march. In the procession were the Hollywood greats whose every sob was reported by an army of newsmen. The sob-sisters also noted that the casket was covered with a blanket of red roses from Miss Negri; these, significantly enough, replaced earlier yellows from Norma Talmadge.

At the solemn High Requiem Mass, Miss Negri appeared to be on the verge of collapse on several different occasions during the ceremony, but managed to control herself until the services were over. Miss Acker, a former wife of the dead man, was overcome and had to be revived in an emergency first-aid station that had been set up at the rear of the church to care for such a contingency. When the services were over and the procession was on its way out, a little man rose in his pew and shouted "Goodbye Rudolph! Goodbye my friend. I will never see you again." He was forcibly conveyed from the church by detectives. As the cortege started back to Campbell's, Miss Negri finally collapsed. "He was so dear to me," she is reported to have said afterwards by way of explanation.

The police re-routed the procession to the funeral parlor to prevent possible riots. By this time there were six thousand persons along the projected route which was closely guarded by two hundred policemen. When the remains were once again under the protection of Campbell's there to await shipment to Hollywood for final interment, the principals departed on their several ways. Before leaving on a fishing trip, Dr. Meeker, through the kind offices of Mary Pickford, delivered a note to Miss Negri which had reportedly been written by the actor just before his death. Upon reading the note Miss Negri again suffered a collapse.

The dead idol remained in New York three more days while arrangements were in progress for shipping his remains to Hollywood. During this interim, reports that Miss Negri had not actually been engaged to Valentino became so persistent that the actress was stung into making public the letter from Dr. Meeker which was responsible for her collapse after the funeral. The letter read:

I am asking Miss Pickford, an old friend and patient of mine, to deliver this message to you, as I am going to Maine. About 4 o'clock Monday morning, he stretched out his hands and said, "I'm afraid we won't go fishing together. Perhaps we will meet again. Who knows?" His mind was very clear and this was the first time he seemed to realize that he would not get well. Then he said: "Pola—if she does not come in time, tell her I think of her!"
I feel under obligation to get his message to you immediately.

Precisely how the letter established her engagement to the screen idol was never made clear by Miss Negri.

For several days after the funeral, the rumors hinting at the possibility of poisoning having been the true cause of Valentino's death, continued to crop up, and Mr. Ullman publicly denied reports of an autopsy in the hope of quieting public misgivings. For the same reason, Dr. Meeker released a lengthy technical report defending his care of the actor after submitting it to a board of three medical experts. The Church, too, came in for its share of criticism and felt compelled to defend the actor's Catholic funeral on the grounds that Valentino's spiritual state at the moment of death was known only to the priest who had administered the last rites to the dying man. The Church authorities added, however, that the actor must have renounced all past divorces and any current engagements to qualify for sanctified burial. Miss Negri made no public comment on this last statement.

On the 3rd of September, the actor at long last entrained for Hollywood on his own round trip return ticket which he had been unable to use in life. The expected crowds of morbid sightseers and admirers gathered in railroad stations and terminals at all points west. In Chicago, six persons were injured when a multitude gathered on the concourse, on roofs and in the streets to view the casket as it changed trains. The body, however, was switched to the westbound line while still in the freight yards and the gathering was all in vain.

As the train moved westward, Miss Negri, who accompanied the remains, finally admitted to reporters that there had been no formal engagement, but an equally valid *informal* betrothal existed as a result of a verbal understanding between herself and the actor.

When the train reached Los Angeles on September 6th, the casket was removed at a suburban station "to prevent disorderly scenes." Miss Negri was described as "in an extremely nervous condition" when she debarked. A motorcycle escort led the procession to a funeral parlor where several hundred women had gathered, one of whom was found secreted in the establishment and had to be evicted. The next day a quiet funeral was held and Rudolph had at last found peace.

By any reasonable standards this would have been the end of the affair, but the standards were not reasonable, and the hysteria went on for years. On the anniversary of the actor's death in 1927, women erected shrines to him in their boudoirs. Others were growing flowers beneath his photograph. One member of the ghoulish cult kept an old shirt of the dead actor's in an embroidered casket. So numerous were his British mourners, they decided to share their mutual grief and organized a club whose motto was *Toujours Fidele.*

In 1928, the first *lady in black* appeared to kneel at Valentino's marble mausoleum in Hollywood. In his book on hoaxes, Curtis MacDougal presents two views of this curious event which was destined to become more or less traditional. One theory held that Russell Birdwell hired the girl for the purpose while a one-reel short, *The Other Side of Hollywood,* was being filmed. Hedda Hopper gave a different version claiming it was a florist's hoax perpetrated in order to encourage the purchase of wreaths for laying at tombs. Whatever the truth of the matter, unexplained *women in black* appeared at the actor's resting place in many succeeding years.

By way of a closing analysis for this study in mass-hysteria, it may be argued that several casual factors combined to result in the unprecedented demonstrations over a dead movie star. First, as was pointed out at the beginning of the chapter, it was, in part, a manifestation of the *Zeitgeist*. The American people were bored with prosperity. Coolidge was in the White House—a President who, according to H. L. Mencken, the scathing critic of the times, spent most of his administration "snoozing" with the result that the Capitol was a "peaceful dormitory." Isolationism was the order of the day in international relations. As a joint consequence of this domestic and foreign tranquility, disturbing ideas were neither emanating from Washington nor emigrating from across the seas to use up Americans' surplus mental energy. In their desperation for a taste of excitement almost anything would draw a mob. Heroes came and went by the dozen, each causing a near riot wherever he appeared. In Ohio, even the poor relics of a mastodon drew thousands for a brief view of the remains at twenty-five cents a head. Then there were the dare-devil and exhibitionistic stunts mentioned at the beginning of the chapter; they never failed to draw crowds. Thus it was a time for superficialities, excitement, and restlessness—not a time for soul-searching. The coming depression would bring that.

Secondly, as Frederick Lewis Allen points out in *Only Yesterday*, there had been a revolution in manners and morals. Women had been emancipated from ethical and social restraints and were flexing their moral muscles. They could smoke, drink, drive fast and live fast without exciting adverse comment. There were serious discussions of Freud, sex and companionate marriage—all carried out without raised eyebrows. One manifestation of this new freedom was the great quest for romance characteristic of women of the times. Obviously, the lives of most women are a round of cooking, having babies, washing diapers, and enduring tired husbands. At that time there were no soap operas, television serials or happiness pills to make life bearable for the Hausfraus, so that the focal point for all their dammed-up emotion became the "greatest lover of them all." He symbolized everything their husbands and boy friends were not—his name spelled Romance. Something of this same psychology seems to have become a national folkway as a consequence of the Valentino affair as has been demonstrated by the perennial crooner-crazes that have been with us ever since.

Finally, the whole business was to a large degree phony from the very beginning. Had the lying in state been conducted with decorum, it would never have attracted such crowds. However, the actor's manager engineered the affair

87

with almost ghoulish skill. The undertaker's press agent provided the newspapers with photographs of the chambers where the dead man would lie; and, in addition, gave them posed pictures of the funeral cortege, one of which accidentally got out before the funeral took place. Similarly, the exaggerated newspaper reports of wild grief suffered by the principals and others at the bier, and the long delay between the actor's death and departure for Hollywood added fuel to the fires of madness.

So it was in New York in the summer of 1926. *Requiescat in pace.*

6: The Martians Invade New Jersey

NINETEEN HUNDRED AND THIRTY-EIGHT has been described as one of the darkest years in the history of the world. Just a year previously the Berlin-Rome-Tokyo Axis had been cemented, and the principals were now engaged in their rapine of Europe and Asia. Hitler launched his *Anschluss* in Austria in March, 1938, and by September had brought the whole of Europe to its knees at Munich. Japan was boring deep into China's vitals and announced her intention of pursuing a "sacred war" in the Pacific for the creation of a new East Asia once the Chinese "incident" could be brought to a successful conclusion. Mussolini, characteristically, hovered vulture-like waiting for a chance to scavenge on the victims felled by his more powerful brother-in-arms, the Führer.

In the United States, which was still reeling from the economic devastation of the depression, the events in Europe cast a pall of gloom that lay over the land from coast to coast. And on the domestic front, too, there was little cause for optimism in the closing days of the summer. President Roosevelt was struggling to block a general railroad strike, and the problems of widespread unemployment still plagued his administration.

However, for the benefit of those who sought escape from the depressing problems overshadowing the world, Hollywood was in its heyday and producing some of its best movies. Rosalind Russell, Janet Gaynor, Deanna Durbin and Dougles Fairbanks, Jr. were the leading lights on the marquees. The Dr. Kildare movies starring Lew Ayres were proving to be one of the most popular series ever filmed. For those who preferred their entertainment in the medium of fiction, *Rebecca* and *All This and Heaven Too* were highly recommended best-sellers.

But the focus of attention was in Europe, and Americans were becoming more and more radio-conscious as the networks took on an international scope in covering the rapidly deteriorating political situation in the Old World. With electronic speed and precision the statesman-like voices of radio announcers girded the earth in fifteen minutes taking the listener to all the major capitals of the world without his having to stir from his own living room.

On the lighter side of the airwaves, Charlie McCarthy, Edgar Bergen's celebrated wooden stooge, and Orson Welles, the boy genius, were competing with each other on Sunday nights. In October of 1938 Welles was not happy though his state of mind had nothing to do with McCarthy's high audience rating. Rather, he had been planning something special for Halloween—something harrowing in the spirit of the season—and he was having trouble with the proposed selection. An old tale of H. G. Wells, *The War of the Worlds* had been chosen for dramatization. But after the preliminary rehearsals, the producers felt the story was too fantastic; it simply could not be made credible for an audience of twentieth century Americans. The consensus of opinion among the show's participants was that it should have been shelved in the musty limbo of such classics of science fiction as Jules Verne's *Twenty Thousand Leagues Under the Sea* and *Off on a Comet*. Then the twenty-three year-old prodigy took over. Welles had virtually nothing to do with the writing of the script and had shown only superficial interest in the preliminary rehearsals, but with a few touches of his peculiar genius applied during the first full rehearsal, the play seemed much improved. At any rate it would have to do. The Mercury Theater was committed to put it on over the CBS network on Sunday, October, 30th.

Sunday evening radio fans in those days were of three types. Some were in the Welles camp, some were died-in-the-wool McCarthyites and some, much to the annoyance and confusion of audience surveyors, statisticians, and advertising agencies, listened to McCarthy first (who was on at the beginning of Bergen's hour-long program), and then switched networks to Welles.

That fateful Sunday evening, the Welles devotees heard the usual "Bulova Watch Time" announcement followed immediately by another to the effect that Orson Welles and the Mercury Theater were about to present a dramatization of *The War of the Worlds* over CBS and its affiliated stations. Then Welles himself came on with a long prologue the gist of which was that other intellects had been spying on the earth for a number of years. He went on to give the state of the nation at a hypothetical period in the future and included such realistic details as a weather report and a sample of dance music by Ramon Raquello from the *Meridian Room* at the Park Plaza Hotel in New York City. All this preliminary material was to show how Americans would be disporting themselves when the events to be unfolded in the rest of the drama took place.

The dance music was suddenly interrupted by a bulletin from "Intercontinental Radio News" announcing that a "Professor Farrel" of "Mount Jennings Observatory" in

Chicago had observed several explosions of incandescent gas on the planet Mars. A "Professor Pierson" of Princeton had been contacted by the news service, and he not only confirmed his colleague's observations, but had already identified the gas as hydrogen by means of a spectroscopic analysis.

Back to Ramon Raquello—then another interruption: a huge flaming object, perhaps a meteorite, had fallen on a farm near "Govers Mill" in New Jersey. A CBS official announced that the network was dispatching one of its mobile units to the scene immediately and promised further details on the celestial visitor as soon as the unit arrived—then more music.

The next interruption was the last. The "meteor" proved to be a huge cylinder, and "Carl Phillips" of CBS was breathlessly describing the terrifying events near Govers Mill. The interplanetary missile was emitting a curious humming sound; its end was being unscrewed—monsters were coming out with bodies like grizzly bears, faces like wet leather and eyes like a serpent's. Meanwhile, the New Jersey State Police had been called to the scene to deal with the spacemen—then all hell broke loose.

A monstrous humped shape like a huge mechanical man rose out of the crater left by the explosion. It struck the advancing troopers with jets of flame—there were explosions—the announcer screamed that the ghastly device was coming his way—there was a crash as of a falling microphone—then utter silence.

When CBS had re-established contact, New Jersey was in grave danger of annihilation at the hands of the Martians. It seemed that seven thousand guardsmen had been drawn up in battle array and had been over-whelmingly defeated. Highways were clogged by fleeing civilians—more cylinders were landing—gas released by the Martians was spreading toward Newark.

The news bulletins were interrupted long enough for the Secretary of the Interior of the United States to make a nation-wide appeal for "calm and resouceful action." But by the time the half-hour station break came, the entire United States had already fallen to the Martians.

Long before this unfortunate state of affairs had been reached in the radio drama, millions of Americans who had been listening to the program, along with many who had been victimized by rumors, were already in the grip of mass hysteria. The result was a nation-wide panic unprecedented in both violence and extent. The most profound effects were, of course, felt in the New Jersey and New York areas, since these were in imminent danger from the "Martians." However, no section of the country was entirely free from the terror inspired by the extraterrestrial invasion. A rapid survey of the nation from east to west on that fateful evening would have revealed the following conditions: In New York City there were thousands of calls to police precincts, radio stations, and newspapers. The police, in fact, received so many calls their switchboards became jammed, and they were forced to dispatch a cruiser to the radio station to find out what was going on. Mostly the callers wanted advice on how to get out of the city before the Martians arrived. Newspapers, too, came in for their share of terror-inspired inquiries. The New York *Times* alone reported eight hundred and seventy-five calls, one from as far away as Dayton, Ohio, requesting information as to what time the world would end.

From Mt. Vernon, a man called in to find out "where the forty policemen had been killed." Another said his brother had been ill and confined to his bed while listening to the broadcast and had become so frightened that he rose from his sick bed, took the family car, and fled the city. The caller begged police assistance in locating the terrified and ailing man.

Over thirty Harlemites rushed to police stations in person, and one especially imaginative denizen of the district swore to the officers that he "heard" the President of the United States announce that all citizens were to flee the cities. However, among the Negro population in Harlem there was far less panic that Sunday evening than might have been expected on the basis of the popular stereotype of the Negro as overly emotional and terrified by extraterrestrial creatures of every variety. Many colored people in that district make a practice of holding Sunday evening services in what are called "parlor churches," that is, the living room of private homes. Consequently, they were not isolated from news of the dramatic events in New Jersey. When enquiring reporters asked how the Sunday orisons had been affected by the radio drama, they were informed that services went on as usual but that in some cases the evening supplications were hastily changed to "end of the world" prayers when news of the invasion filtered into the little congregations.

There were some in New York who "saw" or "heard" the battle of the Martians and Earthmen that was being waged in their neighboring state. A man equipped with binoculars could "see" the flames of the holocaust from his vantage point on top of a tall office building. One "heard" the bombs from aircraft fall in New Jersey and was convinced they were heading for Times Square. Another "heard" the swish of the Martian machines as they plummeted through the atmosphere to earth. In Brooklyn, a man called the police demanding that he be issued a gas mask; he had "heard" the distant sounds of the battle going on over in Jersey and believed a gas attack imminent. When informed it was just a play, he shouted, "We can hear firing all the way here, and I want a gas mask. I'm a taxpayer." Half a dozen women—some with children—showed up at the West 47th Street station to ask where they might find sanctuary. Some intrepid New Yorkers, however, ran to street corners in anticipation of witnessing hand-to-hand street battles between the Martians and terrestrial forces.

On the Jersey sector of the front, conditions were much worse. At various points in Newark persons had to be given sedatives and treated for shock and hysteria. In one section of the city, twenty families living in a multiple-dwelling unit were under the impression that a gas attack had, in fact, started. They summoned the police, giving such a lurid description of their critical circumstances that an ambulance, three radio cars and an emergency squad of eight men equipped with inhalators were dispatched en masse to the stricken area. This formidable squadron found the residents in the street holding wet towels to their faces and gasping for breath. Some of the least afflicted were trying to load clothes and furniture into their cars before fleeing the danger zone. It took officials an hour to restore quiet to the neighborhood.

In Orange, New Jersey, an excited motorist who had heard the announcement of the Jersey landing over his car radio rushed into a theater and shouted that the state was being invaded. The customers all fled in panic.

In Jersey City, scores of excited persons had to be urged off the streets by policemen. Parents rushed to hospitals requesting that their children be released immediately so that the stricken youngsters might be conveyed to a safer part of the country. A Negro housewife tried to collect her family so that all might die together when the troops entered the city. She was under the impression that Hitler was invading the United States in retaliation for a stinging telegram Roosevelt had dispatched to the Führer earlier in the month. National guard headquarters were swamped with calls from members of that organization wanting to know where to report for duty. The guardsmen had heard that all units were being mobilized to fight the extraterrestrial invasion forces.

In Caldwell, New Jersey, a parishioner rushed into the First Baptist Church and announced the impending destruction of the world by invading spacemen. The congregation began to pray for Divine deliverance from the catastrophe.

Meanwhile, in a nearby rural area, an embattled farmer took matters into his own hands. He got down his shotgun and began to erect a fort of sandbags with which he intended to hold off the enemy singlehandedly.

In Trenton, New Jersey, public communications systems were completely tied up by panic-stricken callers who sought information on the progress of the invasion or on conditions on the highways leading out of the besieged state. The following day, City Manager Paul Morton demanded an investigation of the communications breakdown pointing out the dangers of such a state of affairs in the event of a real emergency.

In Groveville, New Jersey, hundreds of automobiles appeared, loaded with persons whose curiosity to see the scene of the catastrophe had overcome their fear of the spacemen. Undoubtedly a confusion in names had arisen between "Govers Mill," the presumed locus of the holocaust, and "Groveville," (a small town near Princeton) which was innocent of any part in the interplanetary dramatics.

In Princeton, a professor of geology at the University got out his hammer, joined forces with a mineralogist, and took off for a field study of the Martian meteorite. Parents of dozens of Princetonians called the university demanding that their sons be sent home at once in view of the conditions in New Jersey. One such hysterical mother shouted over the telephone, "Hell has broken out! It's hot even where I am!"

Eventually things got so bad in New Jersey that the State Police put out reassuring messages over their teletype network, and radio station and newspapers telephone operators just plugged in every time there was a call and said, "It's a radio show."

While the panic was spreading through the immediate area of the invasion, other sections of the country were feeling the effects of the broadcast in their own way. In the South, in Birmingham, Alabama, and Richmond, Virginia, people gathered in the streets to pray. In North Carolina, persons with relatives living in New Jersey called in tears at newspapers offices seeking information about casualties. Similarly, in Atlanta, Georgia, a rumor got into circulation that a planet "bearing monsters" had struck New Jersey killing from forty to seven thousand citizens. In Wilmington, North Carolina, one housewife became so upset by the dreadful news from New Jersey that she had to be given bromides to quiet her nervous condition by her do-it-yourself doctor-husband. In Asheville, North Carolina, five boys at Brevard College were so overcome by hysteria they lost consciousness, and even among their more stalwart fellow student pandemonium

94

reigned. In some parts of the South distress was caused by stories of great destruction in New Jersey resulting from "meteors" or "planetoids" that had run afoul of the earth. For example, in Martinsville, Virginia, the saddened guests of a newspaper publisher left a social gathering prematurely when informed that a "meteor" had struck New Jersey "killing hundreds." And in Louisville, Kentucky, a panic-stricken family pulled up to a filling station for a fast refill. They informed the bewildered attendant that they were headed West to "get away from the destruction by meteors as quickly as possible." In the more Fundamentalist sections of the South there was widespread fear that the end of the world was at hand. The anxiety, in turn, led to widespread prayer, and one woman remarked of the drama, "Well, if it didn't do anything else it made a lot of people pray."

In the conservative latitudes of New England there was little actual panic, although many people were undoubtedly frightened by the drama. However, one woman who had been driving along the highways of Connecticut and listening to the play on her car radio called Hartford for "more information." When informed of the truth she expressed considerable indignation and added that such programs were scarcely conducive to highway safety. Rhode Islanders, too, failed to take the drama with typical New England aplomb. In Providence a number of terrified citizens called the municipal power company urging that the city's lights be blacked out to prevent the Martians from spotting the city as they flew earthward in their space vehicles.

The Midwest, in company with the East, was having its share of flooded telephone switchboards. In Kansas City, the Associated Press Bureau received inquiries from points as far away as Los Angeles, Salt Lake City, and Beaumont, Texas. In Indianapolis, a hysterical woman ran into her church screaming the dreadful news from the East, and suggested that her fellow worshipers be allowed to go home to die in the bosoms of their families—the minister obliged by dismissing services. In Detroit a Pennsylvania motorist asked the police if it were true that New York and New Jersey were "conquered" and that "hordes" were marching on Pennsylvania.

In the far West, in Concrete, Washington, the city power system failed at that critical point in the radio drama when the monsters were leaving their space ships in New Jersey. For a time Concrete was on the verge of panic, cut off as it was from communication with the rest of the United States. Women fainted and men made preparation to flee with their families to nearby mountains. Southward, in San Francisco, an excited gentleman called International News Service and told of details which were not in the broadcast. In his state of mental terror he had "heard" reports of the disaster on radio stations which were not carrying the Mercury Theater broadcast. An equally confused San Franciscan, obviously female and elderly from her voice, called a local newspaper for confirmation of the New Jersey disaster, and when informed of its fictitious nature, replied, "Oh, that's fine, but what are they going to do with those poor people from Mars?" Shortly afterward one of her more belligerent, if less excited, fellow Californians called police headquarters in Oakland offering to do battle with the invasion forces. "My God!" he shouted, "Where can I volunteer my services? We've got to stop this awful thing!" In Los Angeles, women not only fainted but some terrified citizens actually did flee to nearby mountains, and, as reported in the *Examiner,* there was "wild excitement" and a flood of telephone inquiries.

However, not all citizens were affected by the broadcast in such a way that they took positive action. A survey conducted by Hadley Cantril of Princeton sometime after the event, whose purpose was to determine what factors had been responsible for the widespread panic, turned up many curious and unexpected reactions. A few of these are summarized here.

One listener reported that he did nothing, since everyone had to die anyway, and being killed by Martians was as good a way to go as any. Then there was the gentleman whose only regret was that he had no bourbon on hand with which to facilitate his exit at the hands of the celestial monsters.

Some were more than merely indifferent or philosophical. One housewife told Cantril's pollsters that she was actually happy upon hearing of the impending catastrophe because she would not have to pay the butcher under the circumstances. Another woman tried to get her husband to dress up so that he would not meet his Maker in dirty working clothes. He answered her to the effect that we are placed on earth for the glory of God and it was up to Him to decide which garments we should wear to greet Him on that dread day.

An especially pessimistic man actually looked forward to the destruction of the human race, since he felt that there was no point in living in light of the fact that the Nazis were destroying civilization. A like-minded woman was discovered by her husband in the act of poisoning herself. She explained that she preferred dying by her own hand to death by the Martian's gases.

Finally, Cantril cites the amusing report concerning a young couple caught on the street who, when informed of the invasion, asked a grocer if they might take refuge in his basement. The tradesman misunderstood their intention and angrily inquired if they were trying to ruin his business with their unseemly conduct.

While millions of Americans were in the throes of this super-Halloween scare, all was not well back at the studio. Even before the program had ended, unpleasant reactions had begun to come in. CBS was repeatedly requested to interrupt the show with announcements designed to quiet the panic it had unwittingly started. John Houseman, founding partner of the Mercury Theater, gives this graphic description of the scene at the studio as the program was nearing its close:

> I remember during the playing of the final theme, the phone starting to ring in the control room and a shrill voice through the receiver announcing itself as belonging to the mayor of some Midwestern city, one of the big ones. He is screaming for Welles. Choking with fury, he reports mobs in the streets of his city, women and children huddled in the churches, violence and looting. If, as he now learns, the whole thing is nothing but a crummy joke—then he, personally, is coming up to New York to punch the author of it in the nose!"

The morning after brought additional reactions that in some respects were just as hysterical as those of the night before. Orson Welles, "sleepless and unshaven," faced an infuriated nation. He told representatives of the press he was "stunned" and regretted the Frankenstein's monster he had created, but said that he was unable to understand why his dramatization had caused such a panic. He felt its futuristic setting, the fact that the H. G. Wells story was well known, and the additional point that three announcements had been made during the play bearing on its fictional nature, should have prevented the panic. As to the highly dramatic nature of the broadcast, the *Herald Tribune* quoted Welles, in part, as follows: "There was an explosion, but it was only a small one, much like the sound of thunder. We don't believe in putting too much emphasis on sound effect."

In spite of these not too convincing explanations, both CBS and Welles were under fire from various quarters. Senator Clyde Herring of Iowa announced that he was going to introduce a bill into the next Congress "to prevent just such abuses." He went on to denounce radio bedtime stories, as well as the Halloween broadcast, asserting that "Radio has no more right to present programs like that than someone has in knocking on your door and screaming." In the same speech the Senator denied he was in effect urging censorship of public communications. The enraged Senator had plenty of public support, for there were many parents, ministers, and educators who agreed with the legislator that the play's effect on children had been deleterious. The Federal Communications Commission promised to look into the matter, but nothing was ever done. It might be noted that the present writer found no reports indicating that children were frightened by the broadcast; it was their parents who were terrified.

In the United States, three-quarters of a million dollars in damage suits were instituted against CBS by persons who claimed grievous bodily or mental injury caused by the broadcast and ensuing panic. None of these claims was ever substantiated or legally proved. In Britain, agents for H. G. Wells threatened the harassed producers and CBS with court actions on the grounds they had greatly overstepped their legal rights in modifying the original novel to the extent which they had. The British author was quoted by International News Service as follows: "I consider the liberties taken with my story an outrage, and am seriously perturbed by the interpretation that the broadcast has been caused to be put on my work throughout America."

As if this conflict between Welles and Wells were not enough, a report got out, and had to be denied, that the whole thing was a publicity stunt put on for the purpose of promoting a new play by H. G. Wells that was being published by Scribners. There was also talk that Welles perpetrated the panic to promote his own Mercury Theater. Whatever the truth of the latter rumor, the Theater was signed up by Campbell's Soup at a lavish figure shortly afterwards. But within a week the rumors, charges and countercharges had died down to scattered rumblings, and the affair quickly faded into nothing but an unhappy memory for all concerned.

Aside from the reactions from those directly involved in the terrifying broadcast, there were editorial comments and "expert" opinions aplenty by the "Monday morning quarterbacks." Most of these either denounced the highly realistic nature of the broadcast or took a depressed view of the mental processes of the American people. In the latter vein was the opinion of psychologist Rudolph A. Archer of Indiana State Teachers College, who compared the hysteria to the then popular dance craze of jitterbugging. The professor attributed both phenomena to a mass case of jitters caused by the World War and aggravated by "persistent economic chaos."

The Chicago *Daily News* angrily editoralized on the subject of "Morons at the Mike," and, after deploring the drama's overly realistic staging, offered the opinion that none but "trained, responsible hands" should be allowed to use the "awful powers" of radio. In a more humorous vein, the same paper reported in a news-item on a study of the Martian "vegetable" crop for 1938. It was said to be excellent; but the paper's astronomer-informer, who had been studying the red planet for some days prior to the broadcast, had seen no evidence of the mobilization of Martian armed forces.

Among the professional columnists, reactions were generally sarcastic. Dorothy Thompson suggested that Orson Welles be given a congressional medal for having "cast a brilliant and cruel light upon the failure of popular education . . ." Walter Winchell pointed out how the highly popular Buck Rogers space dramas had not frightened anyone. This, he felt, was attributable to the fact that the space hero's audience was composed of children, whereas it was largely adults who were victims of the Mercury Theater presentation.

Heywood Broun, while taking a beneficient attitude toward the technical brilliance of the broadcast, expressed concern that its aftermath might lead to radio censorship. Finally, the scintillating Walter Lippman took a most depressed view of those who had reacted hysterically to the radio drama. He felt the panic demonstrated the sad state of American values—indeed, he felt the hysteria was a phenomenon of the "spiritual proletariat."

So much for the symptoms. The problem remains of explaining the disease. Why should a panic of such incredible proportions have occurred in the first place as a result of an admittedly fictional radio presentation? Three factors, one of the background variety and two which were inherent in the dramatization itself can be adduced to account for the hysteria.

The background factor was the gathering war clouds in Europe. The drama came within thirty-five days of Munich. All during the spring and summer, conditions on the European Continent had deteriorated rapidly, and it was apparent to all but the most naive that war was inevitable. As a result of the growing war anxiety, Americans had come to accept radio as the source of emergency news and on-the-spot reports. The days of newspaper extras had been superseded forever. Therefore, it seemed perfectly natural that an invasion from any source whatever would be announced in the form of an interruption of a regularly scheduled program followed by on-the-spot reports from the battleground itself.

However, in and of itself this anxiety-ridden atmosphere would not have been sufficient to cause the panic, in view of the fact that the program was clearly identified as fictional. But what no one associated with the play's production until it was too late was the fact that many listeners pay little attention to preliminary announcements made at the beginning of a program, since these are almost certain to be followed by advertisements. In addition, in the case of the Mercury Theater, many listeners first tuned in to Charlie McCarthy, as has been indicated earlier in this study. A CBS post-mortem survey designed to cast illumination on the reasons for the panic revealed that the number of such delayed tuners-in was forty-two percent of those who heard the Welles program at all. Whatever the reason for their tardiness, it was late listeners who became panicky when they heard a "regularly scheduled" program of dance music being interrupted by a "special bulletin," or, if they tuned in still later, a description of the awe-inspiring events in New Jersey.

Finally, to lend credibility to the drama, there were the brilliant technical details added by Welles himself. Since it started by building a realistic frame of reference, the dramatization captured the credulity of its audience before it moved into its more fantastic phases. By that time it was too late; the power of suggestion provided by the initial softening-up phase of the broadcast made the subsequent events believable. Besides this introductory material, the use of "mobile units," the announcer moving up to the front lines and becoming a victim himself, the introduction of a "professor of astronomy," and the like, all added to the credibility of the dramatization. That it was well done is attested by the fact that the Mercury Theater received nearly fifteen hundred letters in the days following the show, ninety-one percent of which were congratulatory.

It was a Halloween to remember.*

---

* A year later, the same play was broadcast in Ecuador. A similar panic resulted. When the South Americans realized they had been badly taken in, they got their Latin blood up and burned down the radio station killing six of the show's participants.

7: The Mad Gasser of Mattoon

IN THE EARLY DAYS OF SEPTEMBER, 1944, newspaper editors had little difficulty making up eye-catching headlines from bulletins pouring in over the wire services. The momentous events of World War II were nearing their climax—the overthrow of Hitler's Reich—and the Allies were speeding toward that goal with incredible swiftness after the long years of build-up and delay. American troops poised on the frontiers of Belgium were ready to strike at the heart of the Rhineland. "Old Blood-and-Guts" Patton was dashing all over the French countryside with his Third Army Tank Corps leaving decimated German regiments to be mopped up by plodding infantry units. The long Battle of Britain had at last been won, and the lights would be on again in London before the end of the month. In Italy, the decisive campaigns were shaping up for control of that front. Indeed, in Europe things were going so well for the Allies that hero-of-the-hour Eisenhower was openly spoken of as the man to run the war in the Pacific once his "Crusade in Europe" had been brought to a successful conclusion.

On the domestic front, equally ferocious battles of an entirely different variety dominated the headlines. The chieftains of the G.O.P. were waging their unsuccessful quadrennial war against Roosevelt. Governor Dewey, the Republican candidate, in the opening barrage of his campaign condemned what he called "super government," Roosevelt's failure to prepare the United States for war, and the Democratic ghostwriters, whom, he alleged, were the real formulators of Roosevelt's policies. A little later, the President's dog Fala was dragged into the campaign along with other members of the Roosevelt kennels. The Republican high command charged that the animals had been transported about the country in airborne luxury at taxpayers' expense. Finally, in Congress, a fierce debate over the debacle at Pearl Harbor filled the legislative chambers with sound and fury.

On the lighter side of the news, a public opinion poll of women provided convincing statistical proof that their greatest needs, at least along material lines, were for nylon stockings and girdles. And for those jaded with news of battles both foreign and domestic, there were daily communiques on the condition of the Duchess of Windsor's appendix. The inflamed organ ultimately surrendered unconditionally to surgeons much to her admirers' relief.

In the Midwest, in Mattoon, Illinois (a community of 18,000), a different and far stranger kind of conflict was being waged—a war which ultimately reached such proportions that the latest bulletins from the beleaguered city rated headlines in many newspapers second only to those marking the latest advances of Eisenhower's armies. It was a weird kind of war—perhaps the strangest fought since the days when the fathers of Salem Village tilted with the Foul Fiend Himself. The people of Mattoon were locked in deadly combat with a phantom who struck in the night spraying poisonous gas into his victims' bedrooms and then vanished into the darkness leaving them paralyzed, nauseated and suffering from swollen, bleeding lips. So elusive was the ghostly anesthetist that would-be pursuers caught only glimpses of a "tall, thin man wearing a black skull cap" disappearing into the night. During a two-week reign of terror, the phantom claimed over thirty victims while the local police augmented by citizen volunteers and six squads of state troopers armed with riot guns stood by helplessly.

The phantom launched his initial attack on the first day of September at the home of Mr. and Mrs. John Corbin.* Mr. Corbin, a taxi driver, was at work, and Mrs. Corbin had just retired about 11 P.M. after a long and rather difficulty day. To begin with, there was the daily routine of policing her two little girls—Helen, four, and Diane, two—a task sufficiently demanding to tire any woman. But besides these members of her immediate family, the household was augmented by the presence of a sister, Mrs. George Palmer and her two-year-old boy, who were living with the Corbins while Mr. Palmer was in the Navy. Finally, in addition to the routine chores, the two sisters had company that day. As a result both women were over-tired and perhaps a little excited by bedtime. When the welcome hour arrived, Mrs. Corbin took Diane to bed with her, while Mrs. Palmer retired to the living room. The two youngest children were bedded down in another part of the house.

As Mrs. Corbin was reading herself to sleep, a sickening-sweet odor swiftly permeated the bedroom. At first she thought it might be perfume from flowers being wafted in on a breeze through the open window. This was a reasonable explanation since a large bed of flowers had been planted on that side

---

* The names of all victims have been changed to prevent embarrassment to persons still living.

of the house. But this reassuring line of thought was short lived. The odor grew increasingly more powerful, and as she started to get up, her legs and trunk became paralyzed. In her terror she screamed for her sister who immediately rushed in to find out what had happened. Mrs. Corbin inquired whether Mrs. Palmer could smell the sickening odor. Indeed, Mrs. Palmer noticed the odor at once. It was a heavy, unpleasant smell "like cheap perfume." Following a hasty consultation, the ladies were convinced the attack was the work of a prowler; and, after quickly ministering to her stricken sister, Mrs. Palmer summoned a next door neighbor, Mrs. Harding, to their aid. Mrs. Harding called the police while her husband hurried over to the Corbin home and searched the yard, but he could discover no trace of the supposed prowler. When the police arrived they, too, combed the area, but without success.

While the manhunt was in progress, Mr. Corbin had been summoned from his taxi stand to his wife's bedside. Upon arriving, he found that she had already begun to recover the use of her legs and was ministering to their daughter, Diane, who had also been overcome by the fumes. By now the police had departed since the incident seemed to be closed. However, as Mr. Corbin had pulled up to his beleaguered home, he thought he saw a man at the side window of the house and forthwith gave chase, but the man escaped. This demonstrated that the prowler possessed physical agility as well as ingenuity in administering anesthetics, since the Corbin home was surrounded by a four-foot picket fence. From the brief glimpse he had obtained, Corbin was able to describe the prowler as a tall man dressed in dark clothing with a tight-fitting cap on his head.

In view of Mr. Corbin's experience, the police were recalled to the scene, and this time they carried out a more thorough search of the neighborhood, but again to no effect. As a result of her husband's discovery, Mrs. Corbin and her sister had taken such alarm they were removed with the children to the home of a relative in another part of the city.

The "anesthetic prowler," as he was now being called, had won the first round by all counts. For whatever reason, he had at least succeeded in partially anesthetizing two victims without leaving a trace. Reporters speculated that the man was either a robber or a sex fiend who had been frustrated in his evil purposes by the untimely arrival of assistance. Lending support to the robbery hypothesis was the fact that the two women had a considerable sum of money in the house and were counting it just before they retired. Because the shades had not been drawn, it would have been possible for a prowler to have observed them from the street. Whatever the motive, there was little more the police could do but await further developments. Even the type of gas employed by the ghostly raider was uncertain. The prevalent opinions favored ether, chloroform or a mixture of both. Any of these would account for the sickening odor and the burned lips and throat of Mrs. Corbin, as well as the rapid disappearance of the fumes. Whatever his motive and whatever the chemistry of his gases, the anesthetist struck no more that night, at least as far as the authorities were aware.

On Saturday evening September 2nd a local newspaper, the *Daily Journal-Gazette*, headlined the attack on Mrs. Corbin in these prophetic words:

"ANESTHETIC PROWLER" ON THE LOOSE

Mrs. Corbin and Daughter First Victims

Perhaps the editor was displaying unusual prescience, or he may have been guilty of wishful thinking—hoping for additional material on what promised to be the local news story of the century. After all, an "anesthetic prowler" could scarcely be expected to come the way of a city editor more than once in his journalistic career. In any event, the editor got his implied additional victims in short order. In the next edition of the *Gazette* (which did not appear until Tuesday, September 5th, since on Sunday the 3rd, and Labor Day the 4th, no paper was published), it appeared the anesthetist had been far more active than anyone at first realized. Five other citizens had been felled by his powerful gases over the weekend, and the victims were just now making the facts public. It developed that Mrs. Corbin and her daughter could not even claim the dubious distinction of being the anesthetist's first victims, for he had visited the home of Mr. and Mrs. Harry Webb on Thursday night twenty-four hours prior to his gaseous invasion of the Corbin residence.

The Webbs were struck as they slept. Mr. Webb awoke choking at three o'clock in the morning. He felt ill and when he tried to get up discovered that he was partially paralyzed. "There was a peculiar heavy odor in the bedroom" which, at first, he thought might have emanated from the gas stove. He aroused his wife to inquire if she had turned off the gas. She assured him that she had. Shortly, she too was overcome by nausea accompanied by paralysis and remained sick for over an hour and a half. The Webb's visitors, who were sleeping in another part of the house, were unaffected by the malignant vapors. Apparently the Webbs did not attribute their illness to a marauding anesthetist since they failed to call the police at the time; but after reading of the attack on Mrs. Corbin, hindsight impelled them to make their harrowing experiences known to the public.

The same second sight brought to light other previously unreported victims. The first was a Mrs. Corey, who had been overcome late Friday night shortly after the Corbin attack. Mrs. Corey, who was at home with her son and daughter at the time, detected a peculiar odor in her bedroom and noticed that the children were unusually "restless." She became lightheaded as a result of inhaling the fumes, but did not notify the police, apparently attributing her symptoms to natural causes. Not satisfied with two depredations in one night, the gassing prowler struck still again. This time an unidentified woman and several children had been made ill by the fumes which he had apparently forced through their partly open window.

This new turn of events put an entirely different complexion on the case. No longer were the police dealing with an isolated prowler but a systematic wave of gas attacks occurring in scattered parts of the city. Moreover, the matter was no longer of purely local interest. The Chicago newspapers dispatched reporters to Mattoon, and soon state officials, chemists, and even agents of the Federal Bureau of Investigation were on their way to the besieged city. Perhaps if the weekend attacks had died then and there, they would have remained only an unhappy memory for the victims themselves and, for the police, nothing more important than unsolved prowler complaints. In fact, for a short time there were rumors that the prowler had "fled the city." But he struck again the next night and this time left a clue more tangible than gas fumes.

Mr. and Mrs. Harold Fraser returned home from their lunchroom about ten o'clock Tuesday evening, and according to custom, entered their home through the back door. Shortly after they had made themselves comfortable in the living room, Mrs. Fraser noticed a cloth resting against the front screen door. She went to the door, picked up the cloth, which was somewhat larger than a man's handkerchief, and unfolded it. She noticed a wet spot in the center. "Without thinking I brought the cloth to my face and smelled of it." Her curiosity proved to be her undoing. A sensation like a charge of electricity ran through her body. She started to collapse with numbness and paralysis, and Mr. Fraser had to assist his staggering wife to her bed. Meanwhile, her lips began to swell and her throat to burn. Subsequently this was all she could remember, since she was only semiconscious during the next four hours. It was when she began to spit blood that the alarmed husband summoned a physician. No record is available of the medical diagnosis, but Mrs. Fraser, at least, was convinced of the reality of the anesthetic prowler. The following day the Chicago *Herald-American* quoted her as follows: "I had believed all this talk of a crazy poisoner was nonsense. Now I know it is a real menace, and those who still scoff may look at my seared mouth." (Evidently some of the citizenry in Mattoon had been skeptical of the reality of a prowling gasser.)

But in this latest attack, at least, there was a concrete lead in the form of the chemically treated cloth. Moreover, a nearly empty lipstick case and a well-worn skeleton key were discovered the next morning on a sidewalk near the front of the Fraser home. Unfortunately, by the time the police had arrived the cloth had already lost its sickly-sweet odor. However, Chief Cole took it to headquarters where, according to the Chicago *Daily News,* University of Illinois scientists would analyze it for any residual chemicals which might account for the noxious fumes given off at the scene of the attack.

Though initial speculation had favored ether or chloroform. as the gas, there was by now a body of opinion which held it might be picric acid or chloropicrin, a gas employed by professional fumigators and also used in the Chemical Warfare Service of the armed forces. As to the gasser's motive, Chief Cole now entertained two alternative hypotheses. One possibility was that the phantom was a scientist gone berserk who manufactured gases in a basement laboratory and sprayed them through his victims' windows with some kind of high pressure gun. On the other hand there was a chance that he was a sex fiend attempting to overcome women in a novel manner for his own dark purposes. Some credence was lent to the latter viewpoint by the fact that women in their bedrooms had been his chief targets thus far.

While these clues and hypotheses were being investigated, the mad gasser raided two homes on Wednesday, September 6th, adding two more victims to his toll and raising the total to fifteen.

The new attacks followed the now well-established pattern. Both victims were women gassed in their homes late at night. Both inhaled the sickening vapors, then became nauseated, partially paralyzed, and subsequently suffered from swelling of the lips and mouth. Neither actually saw the poisoner. In addition to these attacks, there were several reports of the prowler in other parts of the city, but Chief Cole put these down to "nerves."

By this time, the city was under a state of siege. In the face of seeming official helplessness, citizens double-bolted their doors and wherever possible were sleeping in second-floor bedrooms. Persons whose custom had been to remain alone were now staying with friends; and, according to the Chicago *Daily News*, at least fifty persons slept with loaded shotguns by their beds. Volunteers began to patrol the streets along with the official police. Richard T. Piper of the State Crime Bureau expressed the prevailing official sentiment when he said, "This is one of the strangest cases I have ever encountered in many years of police work."

Then, unaccountably, the phantom took a one-night vacation. Perhaps the layoff was the result of fatigue brought on by his previous raids, or it may have been caused by fear of the vigilantes roaming the streets. Whatever his reasons, Mattoon felt somewhat relieved by the gasser's absence even though four belated victims of Wednesday night's activities were added to the mounting toll. Apparently some of the citizenry were reluctant to call the police when they detected the by now familiar odor. Meanwhile, the police investigation was being pushed forward. In fact, a "suspect" had been taken into custody. He was described only as a "youth," who, with the cooperation of Mr. Piper, had been given a lie detector test. According to the *Daily News* the young man was reported to have Peeping Tom tendencies, but the test nevertheless exonerated him of any implication in the gassings. The *Daily News* also reported that the police were "interested" in four Mattoon boys who had been recently discharged from military service, and who, significantly enough, had been assigned to Chemical Warfare during their tour of duty. Meanwhile, the cloth which had felled Mrs. Fraser was undergoing analysis by a chemist, but officials hinted that the tests might prove disappointing since the chemicals would have to evaporate rapidly in order to produce gases potent enough to account for the reported symptoms. To add to the spate of rumors, it was reported that a set of sample gases used in training air-raid wardens had disappeared under mysterious circumstances. The gases in question were harmless, but if inhaled were able to produce the same odors and physical discomforts as their real counterparts.

All of this proved to be a swell before the gale. The hysteria and terror which had been building up in a slow crescendo during the preceding week was to reach fortissimo during the approaching weekend. To start things off, on Friday evening, September 8th, after his Thursday layoff, the gasser added six new victims to his toll, five women and a boy. In the Mattoon *Daily Journal-Gazette*, the headlines for the gasser's victories now took precedence over those for Eisenhower's armies who were deploying for the critical battle along the Siegfred Line.

The anesthetist's most recent victims included the principal of a Mattoon grade school, Miss Rath, who with her sister and mother were attacked a total of three times. The first raid however, was unsuccessful. In fact, the ladies were reluctant to ascribe the noises heard outside their home to the gasser's spraying preparations but instead charged it to over-wrought nerves. But on Thursday it was neither imagination nor nerves, but gas. The first infiltrations caught them in their beds. They awoke gasping and choking and soon felt the characteristic partial paralysis creeping over their arms and legs. Later, while still awake and in considerable distress as a result of the previous attack, the other raids occurred. This time they saw a thin, blue, smoke-like vapor diffusing through the room. Just before the fumes entered, the terrified women detected a strange buzzing sound outside the window which they attributed to the anesthetist's spray gun in full operation.

Not satisfied with this triple assault on Miss Rath's home, the phantom anesthetist moved to the residence of Mr. and Mrs. R. H. Newton. Here he must have changed his tactics, since he sprayed the entire area so liberally that a taxi driver could smell the fumes as he rounded a corner near the Newton residence at the height of the attack. And here for the first time the phantom's activities drew a crowd.

It all began when Gloria Newton, a girl of eleven, raised the alarm. She heard a noise outside the house, and the edgy family rushed out to investigate. Neighbors, alerted by the commotion, came to assist, some armed with shotguns. There was no sign of the anesthetist, but the atmosphere was so charged with the paralyzing fumes that young Gloria became "severely ill." A Chicago *Daily News* reporter, Marie Hanson, who had rushed to the scene, described the attack this way:

> The gas had an odor like light perfume, and this reporter and other reporters and Mattoon policemen can testify first hand as to its violent effect. As we stood near the Newton home last night, the gas remaining in the yard struck at us. We became weak at the knees, our eyes lost focus; lips swelled. Headache and nausea followed.

Included among the "other reporters was Anne Holmes of the Chicago *Herald-American* who reported to her paper that seventy people at the scene felt the effects of the gas. She further testified that a "cloying, paralyzing cloud" lay over the street like a miasma. The "cloud" had a bittersweet odor that left her lightheaded and unable to shake off a feeling of unreality. Evidently the reporter (sex unidentified), for the Mattoon paper was made of sterner stuff. He (or she) came on the scene with the first contingent of police but could detect no odor and suffered no physical discomfort from the gas. Perhaps it is needless to add that no gasser was apprehended by the police.

Meanwhile, other phases of the investigation had turned up assorted facts, rumors and hypotheses. The chemical analysis of the cloth which had felled Mrs. Fraser revealed precisely nothing. Mr. Piper of the Illinois State Bureau of Criminal Investigation accounted for the negative results by suggesting that whatever chemicals might have been present at the time of the attack had long since evaporated. Piper added darkly, "The perpetrator of the attacks must be mentally unbalanced, possibly brilliant." When a reporter suggested the old Peeping Tom theory he brushed it off with these pungent words: "The man is a nut."

In the face of this less than satisfactory progress on the part of the police, rumors began to circulate that the citizens of Mattoon were planning a mass-meeting for Sunday, September 10th, whose purposes, according to the Chicago *Tribune*, were: first, to reassure townsmen that steps would be taken to stop the sttacks; and second, to protest the ineffectiveness of the local police force. In addition to this disquieting rumor, there were reports that Mayor Richardson would send a plea to Governor Green asking him to dispatch every available state trooper to Mattoon to aid in the search for the phantom. The Mattoon police, he added diplomatically, were worn out from working overtime during the preceding ten days.

Interest in the phantom had not only spread to the state level. The Federal Bureau of Investigation arrived in Mattoon to confer with local officials. However, much to the annoyance of reporters, the taciturn G-men refused to divulge why they were there. However, in newspaper jargon, "it was said" they had come chiefly to determine the type of gas the phantom was using and to investigate reports that he was a mad inventor who had concocted a new type of war gas which he was testing without authorization on his unwilling civilian guinea pigs. The authorities refused to comment one way or another on any of these rumors.

That same evening, Miss Holmes, the *Herald-American* reporter who had been poisoned by the phantom's fumes on the previous evening, dispatched a story to her paper cover-

109

ing the general state of affairs in Mattoon. She had strolled through the business district to collect her material and reported that the Saturday night appearance of the shopping district "presented a bizarre sight." Cars parked in the downtown area were veritable arsenals, equipped with rifles and shotguns. Small clusters of men and women huddled in doorways exchanging the latest information on the phantom's activities. Side streets were deserted. Nearby war plants had felt the gasser's effects in the form of absenteeism. Men were refusing to go to work and leave women and children to the mercies of the gasser. She concluded: "All skepticism has vanished and Mattoon grimly concedes it must fight haphazardly against a demented, phantom adversary. . . ."

Over the weekend, the terror and hysteria reached their height. On Saturday and Sunday the police received dozens of calls. There were, however, few authenticated attacks. Among the depredations recorded for Saturday evening was a new attempt on Miss Rath, the much-gassed principal. In addition, two women, one in her home and the other surrounded by people in a theater, were sprayed with the paralyzing fumes. Both women were taken to a hospital where they were examined by a physician. He could find no evidence of poison gas or other noxious chemicals, and attributed the symptoms to extreme nervous tension. However, he added that both victims had been nauseated and the stomach contents would be analyzed in an effort to find any foreign material which could account for their distress. After the doctor's report reached Police Commissioner Wright, he announced that all future complainants would be subjected to a similar medical examination immediately following an alleged attack.

On Sunday evening the gasser struck four miles south of the city. When the sheriff arrived at the scene of the assault, the house was deserted. "The Smiths and their guest, Frank Greene," reported the sheriff, "had all run wildly down the dark country roads." He found them at a neighbor's home a quarter of a mile away. This unprecedented countryside appearance encouraged Mattoon authorities to hope that the gasser had left the city. But such hopes were quickly shattered when he raided the Mattoon home of Mr. and Mrs. Harris, who were playing cards at the time in their living room. Mrs. Harris had gone into the kitchen on an errand, and her husband heard her scream: "The gas hit me!" Harris rushed to the aid of his stricken wife and fell prey himself to the powerful fumes. By assisting each other they managed to get out of the kitchen and call the police. By the time the officers arrived, Mrs Harris' lips and mouth were badly burned and swollen. An examination of the premises led the police to conclude that the gas had been sprayed through an ill-fitting rear door which led into the kitchen.

Shortly after the Harris invasion, a second call sent the police scurrying to another part of town where a family had been partially overcome by fumes reported to have an ether-like odor. The hard-driven officers found an open can of model airplane cement. It seemed clear that the "gas" had arisen from this source and no attack was officially recorded.

However few the assaults that could be laid at the phantom's door over the weekend, there were no dearth of other developments. To begin with, Police Commissioner Wright and Chief Cole, evidently not entirely appreciative of the citizen-volunteers, issued the following joint statement as reported in the Mattoon Daily *Journal-Gazette* for September 11, 1944:

To All Citizens of Mattoon

We want the public to know that everything possible is being done in this case, and we are grateful for the confidence of a majority of the citizens. However, we have a few points on which we hope to get 100 percent cooperation beginning tonight. They are:

1. Stay off the street in residential districts unless your business requires you to be there. There is no danger in the business districts.

2. Roving bands of men and boys should disband. They are in grave danger of being shot by some frightened property owner.

3. Put away the guns now in the hands of individuals, because some innocent person may get killed. The only time one should shoot is upon seeing a man peering into a window of one's home. Then extreme care should be used.

4. Don't follow the police car when it is speeding in answer to a call. Persons who persist in doing this will be arrested.

From Springfield, the state capital, five squads of state police had been dispatched in radio cars to lay a dragnet for the "mad Mattoon anesthetist." Each car was manned by a driver and an assistant armed with a shotgun. All units were under the control of a master-dispatcher stationed at the local police headquarters. The job assigned to this in-

111

domitable task force was that of patrolling the downtown area, leaving the less dangerous outskirts to the local police, who lacked the refined equipment of their state-appointed colleagues.

On the local level, Commissioner Wright and Chief Cole conferred with the States Attorney asking for a check on all patients recently discharged from Illinois mental institutions. Finally, by way of minor developments, there were newspaper reports attributed to no one in particular, that bloodhounds might be employed to track down the gasser and that fifty farmers, members of the "Anti-Thief Association," formerly the "Anti-Horse Thief Association," had pledged assistance to their urban brethren. All members of the Association had police experience in the form of "catching prowlers, livestock rustlers and chicken thieves." There is no record that this formidable organization's offer was accepted.

Tuesday's news bulletins revealed that no new attacks had been launched on Monday evening, September 11th, though fourteen abortive calls kept the radio-controlled task force out all night in a driving rain. One woman, thought to be a gasser victim, was rushed to the hospital in accordance with the recent police directive and was there pronounced a case of "extreme mental anguish." But in spite of the dearth of authentic attacks, the newspapers were not at a loss for material. The Chicago *Herald-American* claimed an exclusive release from Commissioner Wright to the effect that the authorities had narrowed down suspects in the case to a chemist. Certainly the chemist's living habits, if reported correctly, were enough to excite suspicion among the most skeptical. To begin with, he lived in the section of the city where most of the attacks had been perpetrated. Moreover, he was reputed to have inherited wealth from his parents and to have spent a considerable sum of money in fitting out a basement laboratory for the purpose of conducting chemical experiments. He had turned in a brilliant record in high school and college, but was now rumored to be "partially demented." Calculated to arouse further suspicion was the fact that a mysterious explosion in the laboratory had been called to the attention of authorities some time before the gassings, but the suspect refused to render any explanation when questioned. His sister, the only person to whom he spoke, was also unable to clarify matters. One wonders whether she had to live with unexplained explosions, or whether she happened to be away from home at the time. The record is silent on this point.

However enticing the chemist's qualifications for the role of the mad gasser, Commissioner Wright denied a rumor that the authorities had concentrated their investigation on any one person. Rather, there were four suspects whom he described in this laconic statement to the *Journal-Gazette*: "Two of the four are amateur chemists, and the others are crackpots." The Commissioner also told a meeting of seventy businessmen that the problem of combating mass hysteria was worse than dealing with the gas attacks. "Someone is going to get killed and it won't be from gas. The people here have lost control of themselves in a manner which is almost unbelievable in a modern world. I wouldn't walk through anyone's backyard for $10,000."

Chief Cole was also beginning to associate himself with the hysteria hypothesis. He suggested that nervous women might have smelled whiffs of carbon tetrachloride from a nearby war plant engaged in the manufacture of diesel engines, and then generated the rest of the symptoms themselves by autosuggestion. The manager of the plant laughed at the chief's theory and pointed out they had been using carbon tetrachloride at the plant for over four years. None of the plant's personnel had been adversely affected during this period.

By Wednesday, the 13th, the Mattoon Daily *Journal-Gazette* was able to headline the state of affairs in Mattoon as follows: "GAS CALLS AT THE VANISHING POINT." Only two false alarms had been reported during the previous night. One false was a prowler call that turned out to be a black cat on his legitimate nocturnal rounds. The other involved a doctor who had accidentally locked himself out of his office and was discovered by the patrolling task force in the act of climbing in through an open window. By now, the *Gazette* added, officials were openly charging the whole furor to mass hysteria. Meanwhile the only real skirmishes were in the carbon tetrachloride sector. Chief Cole insisted that fumes from *some* industrial plant must have been wafted over the city triggering the hysterical attacks. But spokesmen for the diesel engine company vehemently denied fumes were the sickening "gardenia gas," as it was now being called. So matters stood on Wednesday evening, September 13th. It seemed the Mattoon phantom had been dismissed as a will o' the wisp. But there was more to come.

The following day, Mattoon businessmen denounced the police as incompetent for concluding that the gassings were a combination of hysteria and carbon tetrachloride fumes. The manager of the diesel company, taking umbrage as a result of the chief's allegations about the fumes from his plant, joined in the criticism of the force. To make matters worse for the hard-pressed police, the States Attorney (with an eye no doubt on the political future), threw out dark hints about ordering the Grand Jury to investigate the case; and, at the same time, managed to get Captain Curtis, who had been in charge of the state police squads, recalled to Springfield and replaced by another man. He further let it be known that he would employ secret police, if necessary, and intended to base his future investigations on "scientific principles." This, he stated, he had already begun by sending the stomach contents of the two hospital cases to chemists for an analysis and by virtue of the fact that he was investigating the activities of eight persons recently released from mental hospitals.

On the gas front itself, the Chicago *Herald-American* belatedly reported an attack that had been perpetrated two nights previously. A widow, asleep in her front bedroom, heard a peculiar "whirring" noise outside her window which she attributed to the gassing machine. Suddenly she felt faint and nauseated. She summoned her three sons from another part of the house, and one of them ran out the back way to intercept the phantom, but only managed to see a shadowy form disappearing into the darkness. When the family searched the yard the next morning, several imprints of high heels were discovered under the widow's bedroom window. This discovery, coupled with the lipstick previously found at the scene of the Fraser attack, led the *Herald-American* to suggest that the phantom might be a woman. However, the *Herald-American's* hypothesis was destined to be disproved the following day when an "ape man" equipped with a gassing apparatus turned up in the kitchen of Mattoon's only fortune teller, whose more mundane means of existence was operating an inn. On the previous evening the lady in question had retired, but, upon smelling a strange odor, crept to the kitchen to investigate. There in the semidarkness stood the gasser: "He was like an ape standing there, crouched, his long arms reaching out as he held the spray gun in his hands." Before she could flee, three clouds of fumes enveloped the seer leaving her with the characteristic symptoms of nausea and paralysis.

But this was the end. The next night there were no calls, no gas, no prowlers and no ape men. The Chief of Police attributed the rapid decline and eventual cessation of the attacks to his order that all victims were to be examined by a physician or lodged in a cell. Thus, the phantom departed as quietly as he came, leaving his prey none the worse for their experiences but with what must have been embarrassing reflections on their own credulity. All that remained for the experts was to conduct post-mortem examinations over the phantom's absent body.

The Mattoon *Journal-Gazette* terminated its coverage of the case with an article consisting of humorous sidelights on the affair, several of which are worth summarizing. One item concerned the story of a woman who awakened her husband at the height of the terror and informed him that someone was lurking at their window ready to gas them. The husband slipped out of the house, crept through the darkness, and sure enough there at the bedroom window were two demon-like eyes glowing in the night. However, instead of belonging to a phantom, they were the property of a tomcat who, for some strange reason, had elected to climb the window screen. In another instance, a war widow got out her husband's shotgun intending to defend her home and person against the anesthetist, but as she was loading the weapon, it accidentally discharged blowing a gaping hole in the kitchen wall. Finally, there was the case of a young man who knocked on the door of a lady friend, and when she opened it, whispered out of the darkness, "May I leave my skull-cap and spray gun here for a while?" As the story was repeated and distorted, it ultimately led to the jokester's incarceration and submission to a lie detector test.

The Chicago *Herald-American* was not ready to give up a good thing without a struggle. The editor contracted for the services of a psychiatrist and dispatched him to Mattoon along with a feature writer to "psychoanalyze" the entire city. This psychiatric ledgerdemain provided the paper with another full week of feature articles the outcome of which was to prove the reign of terror was due to mass hysteria, which everyone knew by then anyway.

The Chicago *Tribune* ended its series on the gasser with the best climax of all. It carried a dispatch from Cedar Rapids, Iowa, to the effect that a woman (who had evidently been reading the Chicago papers), called the police alleging that a man had appeared at her window and had started pumping gas into her room. When the investigating officers arrived found no mad gasser—only a billy goat tied to a pole in the yard. The animal's caprylic aroma had blown in through an open window resulting in the false gas alarm.

The final post-mortem on the case was made by Donald M. Johnson, a professor of psychology at the University of Illinois, who shortly after the series of attacks launched a field study in Mattoon in order to assess the personality characteristics of persons subject to mass hysteria He was given a cold reception when he attempted to interview the victims, who by now were undoubtedly smarting under the

115

gibes of their more stalwart neighbors. In spite of these difficulties, he developed an interesting psycho-social study of Mattoon and the causes for the hysteria. His article appeared the following year in a technical journal.

Indeed, this case must interest any student of mass psychology or connoisseur of human credulity, for it probably represents one of the purest outbreaks of mass hysteria on record. In the first place, there was absolutely no basis in reality for the attacks. Secondly, the victims' symptoms (choking, swelling of mucous membranes and partial paralysis), are the classic symptoms of hysteria first observed over a generation ago by Janet, the famous French neurologist. Moreover, in keeping with hysterical phenomena in general, they were induced chiefly by verbal suggestion, just as similar manifestations can be produced in hypnotic subjects by means of the same technique.

In the case of the Mattoon gasser there were three such sources of verbal suggestion. The first and no doubt the most important, were the inflamatory newspaper accounts of the "attacks." Suggestive headlines were employed, reporters claimed to have been stricken in the streets, and there were strong hints of police incompetence, all of which was scarcely calculated to allay fears and dampen incipient hysteria. The second source of suggestion, in order of importance, must have been the telephone. There is, of course, no existing record of this, but it is difficult not to believe that Mattoon wires must have hummed every morning with the latest developments in the case, including lurid descriptions of personal attacks by those who were "victims." Finally, a good deal of old-fashioned back-fence gossip undoubtedly added to the verbal war of nerves.

A second major factor was the war. The atmosphere of excitement, greater public attention to radio and newspapers, the dislocations among families—with many women being left alone or with young children— though not in themselves causes of the hysteria, were instrumental in creating a conclusive atmosphere for the outbreak. We have already seen what an important part this factor played in the "Invasion from Mars." It may also be recalled in this same connection that reports of missing war gases and deranged ex-servicemen and chemists played a significant role in the Mattoon incident.

In concluding this study it is only fair to point out that the victims themselves actually suffered from the symptoms they so vividly described. Because hysterical symptoms are generated by unconscious mental processes, this makes them no less real and no less terrifying to the sufferer than symptoms resulting from true physical diseases. In no sense are the victims of hysteria merely malingering. Such individuals are just as truly blind, deaf, paralyzed or choked as those whose eyes, ears, nerves, or throats are organically diseased. No doubt the very genuinesses of the sufferings of the Mattoon victims made the hysterical foundation of their symptoms all the more difficult to detect. It is to the credit of the local police that they were the first to suspect the hysterical origin of the "Mad Gasser of Mattoon."

8: Celestial Crockery

I

THE TIME WAS 1:15 P.M.; the date January 7, 1948; the place, the control tower at Godman Air Force Base outside Louisville, Kentucky. A call had just come in from the Kentucky highway patrol. It seemed that several people in Marysville, a small town some eighty miles from Louisville, were concerned about a strange object they had seen in the sky. Quite naturally the police officers considered celestial problems outside of their jurisdiction and had turned the matter over to the Air Force. But Godman knew of no aircraft, mysterious or otherwise, that had not been accounted for in the vicinity. So Godman, in turn, inquired of Wright-Patterson Field in Ohio. Again, no Kentucky-bound flights had originated from that area.

At 1:35 the highway patrol called again. The strange denizen of the skies had passed to the west of Louisville, and by this time a number of people in two towns had seen it. The spotters were able to report that the mysterious object was circular in shape, some 260-300 feet in diameter, and moving westward at a good clip.

Ten minutes later the control tower personnel at Godman, along with other officers on the base, saw the unidentified object. Several of the airmen peered at it through binoculars, but none was able to hazard an identification.

About 2:30 P.M. four P-51's came within range of the control tower. It was a routine flight of National Guard airmen under the leadership of Captain Thomas F. Mantell, Jr. The tower radioed Mantell and asked him to look into the matter of the still-hovering unidentified object. The captain took two of his wingmen (the third was low on gas) in pursuit of the mysterious visitor. Since none of the pilots could see the object, the tower gave Mantell a bearing, and the airmen began to climb in the direction the tower had suggested.

By the time they reached 10,000 feet, Mantell had taken such a lead on his wingmen they could hardly see him. Shortly afterwards, the Captain called the tower and reported that at last he could see his target. Later there was some disagreement as to just how Mantell described the object, but according to the collective memory of those who were in the

118

tower that day he is supposed to have said the object was "metallic and tremendous in size . . . it appears like the reflection of sunlight on an airplane canopy." A little later he added, "It's bright and climbing away from me."

By now Mantell was at 15,000 feet and without oxygen, since the routine flight had not been planned for an excursion to such high elevations. When asked for a further report, Mantell replied he was going to 20,000 feet, and if he failed to close in, he would give up the chase.

This was the last anyone heard from Mantell. Neither the tower nor his wingmen could see him, and, after flying around for a while, the wingmen landed long enough to refuel and take on oxygen. They took off again to look for their leader but were unable to find any trace of him. A 3:53 P.M. the tower lost sight of the mysterious object, and a few minutes later word was received that Mantell had crashed and was dead. An eyewitness of the plane's final moments said the pilot acted as if he didn't know where he was going just before the plane went into a power dive towards the ground. The plane, according to the witness, exploded halfway down.

Since this was the sixth month of the first year of the age of flying saucers, wild stories about what had happened at Godman soon found their way into circulation. The plane, according to various reports, was said to have been "disintegrated," "shot full of holes," "magnetized," "made radioactive," and Mantell himself was rumored to have been reduced to primeval elements by his clash with the "flying saucer."

The more prosaic explanation of the accident given out by the Air Force was that Mantell had unwisely ascended to a height where he blacked out from oxygen deficiency, and in the resulting dive his out-of-control plane had lost a wing. The Air Force denied that either the wrecked plane or the body demonstrated any injuries of extraterrestial origin and concluded the report by suggesting that Mantell had been pursuing the planet Venus. This was the first casualty resulting from an attempted saucer interception.

II

The saucers first visited Earth a little over six months earlier on June 24, 1947, when Kenneth Arnold sighted nine odd-looking craft near Mt. Rainier while piloting his private plane from Chelais to Yakima, Washington. The weather was fine for flying, and he could see saucer-like objects clearly as they dipped in and out of the mountain peaks at terrific speeds, estimated by him to be over a thousand miles an hour. This was the beginning of a ten-year saucer-in-the-skies mania that is still going on, though much diminished in the last few years. It may well be the greatest mass-delusion in the history of the planet. It has resulted in thousands of sightings, several deaths and tens of thousands of wasted man hours spent in tracking down reports of unidentified celestial visitors. During the height of the hysteria, the President and members of Congress were deluged by letters demanding an "explanation." The Air Force came under heavy fire from the Believers who in books and magazine articles repeatedly charged the Pentagon with maintaining a conspiracy of secrecy about the nature and mission of the saucers. Among the Believers, some held that the saucers were secret weapons, some favored the space ship theory, and still others were inclined toward the possibility of unauthorized reconnaissance flights originating from the USSR.

It all began as a reaction to the Arnold sighting. Arnold, it has been claimed, never called the saucers "saucers," but described the unidentified craft over Mt. Rainier as "saucerlike." However, the newsmen who wrote up the incident christened them "flying saucers" and this was the name that stuck. Arnold was given a bad time by the newspapers. They reported his sighting with tongue far out in cheek, and Arnold was finally moved to comment on the possibility of future sightings to the effect that "even if it were a ten-story building flying through the air" he would disregard it.

The Air Force's reaction to Arnold's sighting was to send a search party of five P-51's on hunt over the Pacific Northwest, but the searchers found no trace of saucers, and, in view of the negative findings, announced there were insufficient facts to warrant any further investigation. Meanwhile, reports of saucers in the skies were originating as far east as New York and from as far around the world as Australia. However, it was rare for anyone to take the sightings seriously as yet. The New York *Times* on July 6th, 1947, came out with a hot weather editorial poking fun at the rash of saucer sightings. Along the same lines, an enterprising reporter asked Andrei Gromyko, who was representing Russia at Lake Success at that time, what he thought of the whole business; the Russian suggested the apparitions might be due to excessive importations of Scotch whiskey into the United States. More to the point, a professor of physiology in Sidney, Australia, had four hundred and fifty students go out and stare at the heavens and report back to him what, if anything, they were able to see. Within ten minutes some had returned with reports of discs in the sky. The professor charged the sightings to the students having seen blood corpuscles coursing across their retinas.

The citizenry in general were quick to react to Arnold's report and apparently took the saucers no more seriously than either the press or foreign commentators. *Life* magazine in its July 23, 1947 issue, published just a month after the Mt. Rainer incident, was able to summarize the situation across the Republic as follows: A rash of things have been seen. A woman in Seattle, Washington brushed the excitement aside with the blase statement, "Why they come through our yard all the time."

In Spokane, eight flying washtubs had been sighted. A dietary fanatic in Chicago believed the saucers were hallucinations brought on by bad dietetic practices. He thought the skies would clear if Americans would only eat fifty dandelion blooms every day. Earnest Hooten, the famous Harvard anthoropologist, had a different explanation: he believed the saucers were misplaced halos searching for persons who had been killed on the Fourth of July. Not only were saucers reported but chromium hub caps, dimes, teardrops, ice cream cones, and pie plates as well. The sky, it appeared, was becoming a veritable junk shop.

Of course, the hoaxters also got into stride shortly after the initial reports were published. In Shreveport, Louisiana, an aluminum disc with fake jet propulsion units crashed to the street, and when a portion of a buzz saw blade struck a church in Grafton, Wisconsin, the edgy priest called the F.B.I.

Such was the state of the skies in July. The New York *Times* had already put it all down to a mass delusion and believed the saucers would soon be consigned to the "limbo" reserved for such human vagaries. But the sightings continued, and in September of 1947, Project "Sign" was initiated by the Air Force to deal with the increasing flow of reports of unidentified airborne objects. At first the project employed only Air Force personnel, but these were soon augmented by astronomers, psychologists, physicians, physicists, meteorologists, and representatives of the dread Federal Bureau of Investigation.

It was early in 1948 that the death of Captain Mantell occurred; but curiously enough, 1948 did not prove to be a good saucer year. The only significant event aside from the Mantell incident occurred during the summer when there was a rash of sightings along the Eastern Seaboard, but these turned out to be released weather balloons. Scattered reports of sightings of unidentified flying objects, forwarded

121

to the Air Force throughout the year, were duly but unsuccessfully investigated.

By the early part of 1949, the Air Force was ready with a report. On the average they had been receiving twelve reports of unidentified flying objects every month. A dossier of two hundred and forty cases had been accumulated by April of 1949, and an analysis revealed that thirty percent were traceable to known phenomena such as meteorites, weather balloons, formations of ducks, and the like. Another thirty percent were probably of conventional origin, and the final forty percent remained a question mark. The big problem was a lack of accurate data; the witnesses had no way of making measurements of the speed, altitude, size and other characteristics of objects they had seen coursing through the skies. This problem was to continue to plague the analysts for years to come. Meanwhile, on February 11, 1949, Project Sign was dissolved and Project Grudge took its place as the official Air Force agency for investigating flying saucer reports. According to Captain Edward J. Ruppelt in his *Report on Unidentified Flying Objects* the whole policy of the Project was to "get rid" of flying saucers. It was, according to the Captain, "the Dark Ages" of the saucers. The Air Force did not believe in saucers but would grudgingly investigate further reports.

In April and May of 1949, two articles by Sidney Shalett appeared in the *Saturday Evening Post*. These accounts represent milestones in the history of the saucers, since they were published with the blessing of the Air Force and were definitely anti-saucer in their treatment of the subject. The Believers denounced the articles as following the "party line" of certain "Pentagonians" who, they alleged, were trying to hide the facts of the saucer menace from the American people. After the *Post* articles anything that was subsequently published under the imprimatur of the Air Force was immediately labeled by the Believers as part of a "conspiracy" of silence and misinformation they attributed to the Pentagon.

As spring wore into summer, reports continued to come in. In Seattle, Washington, a woman called the police when she discovered a flaming saucer on her roof. A hammer and sickle and the letters USSR had been crudely painted on the fiery missile. The device, however, turned out to be a homemade affair constructed of plywood; it was definitely *not* of Soviet origin. According to a UP report, some Texans saw flying bananas, saucers and a plate in the sky. This was the nearest thing to an entire airborne dinner reported up to that time. Up in New England, MIT sent up twenty-five research balloons which gave rise to a saucer scare in those conservative latitudes. Some of the New Englanders who had spotted the balloons excitedly reported there were "ghost riders in the sky."

In August, two old flying machines were discovered in a Maryland barn, and the Air Force thought these might be the answer to the saucer craze. The unconventional craft were the inventions of one Jonathan E. Caldwell who had disappeared in 1941, apparently abandoning his brain children to rust and decay. One was a kind of helicopter with a saucer-like body; the other looked more like a large wooden wash tub. The Baltimore *Sun* quoted the Air Force officer who investigated the strange craft to the effect that Caldwell might now be in another part of the country flying workable models of his "saucers" and that this might have resulted in the rash of saucer reports. Needless to say, the elusive inventor never showed up piloting a saucer.

By December, the Air Force was ready with its second report. After spending two years investigating the saucers, the Air Force announced that it was through. All the evidence indicated the airborne crockery was: (1) misinterpretations of conventional aircraft or celestial phenomena; (2) mass hysteria; (3) hoaxes. Thus ended the second year of the saucers.

In 1950, the Believers came into their own. It all began with an article in *U. S. News and World Report*, asserting the saucers were real. They were, in fact, United States Navy planes, still secret, and more or less saucer-like in general appearance. Henry J. Taylor, a radio network news commentator, seconded the notion that the saucers were top-secret United States inventions and newsmen immediately rushed to President Truman with the story. He denied that the Republic had any such aircraft and in a characteristic Trumanese said he was "just as puzzled as the next fellow."

It was also in the early part of the year that tales of captured "Saucerians" began to circulate. Up to this time one of the most puzzling features of the saucers was the fact that they never seemed to land or crash. Either event would have been most welcome from the Air Force's point of view, since the unprecedented machines could then be studied first hand. However, the Saucerians' lack of cooperation was soon made up for by Earthmen's imagination.

Out in Denver, Colorado, a mysterious "expert" on saucers, identified only as "Dr. Gee," gave a lecture at Denver University in which he stated that three saucers had been captured with thirty-four dead bodies aboard. If the Saucerians had been alive, they would have been from thirty-six to forty inches in height. Evidently the spacemen were more advanced in scientific matters than earthlings, since they had no cavities in their teeth and subsisted on food wafers, one of which put in a gallon of water caused such a plethora of mush that the vessel overflowed.

The saucers themselves were definitely not of earthly origin. The gears were unconventional in design, and there was no evidence of lubricants in the machinery. The metal defied classification, and in one case proved to be so hard that $35,000 worth of diamond drills were spoiled in trying to force an entry. Much was made of the saucers' measurements which always came out to be multiples of nine for all dimensions. The craft had no apparent motive power, but it was believed that they operated on a "magnetic principle." Just what this involved was not made clear.

"Dr. Gee," it turned out, was no expert at all but Leo GeBauer, the operator of a radio and television wholesale house in Phoenix, Arizona. Among his more terrestrial activities was the invention of an electronic dowser for locating oil deposits. He and an associate, Silas Newton, a Denver geophysicist, sold the device to a Denver businessman. The latter spent over a quarter of a million dollars on worthless oil land discovered by the "doodlebug." The two were convicted of a swindle when it turned out that the electronic dowser was a jumble of war surplus radio equipment worth approximately $3.50. In view of the circumstances, there seems to be little reason to put much credence in Dr. Gee's report.

In June, another saucer reached the earth. It had been shot down and was found to contain twenty capsules filled with little men. The saucerians were wrapped in aluminum foil for protection against cosmic rays.

Finally, there was the report of a space ship which had crashed in New Mexico with fifteen spacemen aboard. The latter were unable to talk, but one drew a map of the solar system and pointed to Venus—presumably their port of departure. A wise Earthman thereupon suggested that the Venusians be placed in a pressurized chamber containing carbon dioxide, since that gas abounds on Venus according to astronomic observations.

Understandably, the Air Force made no official comment on these reports. Something of this same skeptical attitude was revealed at a big airshow put on by the Air Force in San Antonio, Texas. It was announced over the loudspeakers that a top secret revelation about flying saucers would be given out as a climax to the affair. The excited spectators buzzed with anticipation, but the "revelation" turned out to be 30,000 paper plates released by planes flying overhead.

The year 1951 was not a good saucer year. It began with a Navy release which may have had a dampening effect on potential sighters. This was a statement released by the Office of Naval Research to the effect that during the past three years it was likely that the saucers seen by so many citizens were skyhook balloons the Office had been sending aloft for meteorological research but which up to that time had been kept secret. These research devices were huge plastic balloons capable of ascending to heights of 100,000 feet, and when they reached high altitudes, wind streams could move them about the skies at speeds up to two hundred miles an hour. Some remained visible for over thirty hours. All together a total of 270 skyhooks had been released up to the time of the report. It was considered probable that Captain Mantell had come to his death chasing one of these huge gas bags.

This revelation was received with mixed feelings. While it offered a convenient and credible explanation for the saucers, it made newspaper editors unhappy to think the whole thing had been kept in the dark for so long. What was so secret, they wanted to know, about oversized balloons? There were others who thought the explanation too pat. Among these was Dr. Anthony O. Mirarchi, a former Air Force scientist. He denounced the balloon theory as an oversimplification and implied the saucers might be enemy aircraft flying reconnaissance missions over our atomic installations.

Apparently the public in general must have given some credence to the balloon explanation, since all during the first part of 1951 there was a marked lull in sightings. However, toward the end of the year the number of saucer reports reached a "normal" level once again. In October the Air Force decided to use skyhooks and, before sending them aloft, appealed to the public not to report them as flying saucers.

However, the outstanding event of 1951, and possibly the most curious and controversial saucer incident of the entire decade was the so-called "Lubbock lights." Here was no isolated saucer report by an ordinary and possibly hysterical citizen, but a whole series of them turned in by two engineering professors, a physicist and a geologist. They were Dr. W. I. Robinson, Professor of Geology; Dr. A. G. Oberg, Professor of Chemical Engineering; Professor W. L. Ducker, Petroleum Engineering, and Dr. George, Professor of Physics, all of Texas Technological College at Lubbock. Better yet, several photographs of the lights had been taken by an amateur, but experienced, photographer.

The professors, all of whom were associated with Texas Technological College at Lubbock, first spotted the saucers by pure chance. They were enjoying an evening of academic discussion in the geologist's backyard. It is worth recording that the word fest was facilitated by nothing stronger than tea. Suddenly, they spotted a formation of lights moving across the sky. The lights were a bluish-green in color and spread out in semi-circular formation.

Naturally, the professors were unable to gather any details of the lights, altitude, speed, probable source, and so forth, since the visitation was both unexpected and over with in a matter of seconds. However, the academicians remained in the yard hoping for a return engagement, and fortunately the lights reappeared within an hour, this time not in formation. Their number was estimated to be thirty, and they crossed over the arch of the sky in several seconds. Hoping to establish precise measurements of altitude and speed, the professors kept a nightly vigil, and during the next two weeks were rewarded with a dozen additional transits. Unfortunately, the scientists were never able to determine the altitude of the lights; consequently, it was impossible for them to calculate their speed.

Many others living in and around Lubbock had also seen the strange lights. Their reports of both the times of appearance and the general characteristics of the lights agreed closely with the academician's observations. Thus, there could be no doubt of the existence of the lights; the question was what were they? The Air Force's investigator, Captain Ruppelt, hoped the answer might be found in an analysis of photographs which had been taken by a freshman at Texas Tech. The photographer in question was Carl Hart, Jr. who, though an amateur, was used to taking pictures at sporting events and therefore was not unacquainted with high speed photography. Moreover, he was prepared to snap the pictures, since he had first seen the lights by accident and, like the professors, thought they might recur. When they did he was ready for them and obtained five photographs which a friend developed for him.

Eventually, the Air Force obtained and analyzed four of Hart's photos. Unfortunately, the negatives had been badly treated and were scratched and marred from excessive handling. They showed only poor images of bright point sources of light. No objects were visible, and to make matters worse, the appearance of the lights did not tally with the professional reports. The professors went so far as to express doubt of the authenticity of the photographs. The Air Force's experimental attempts to duplicate Hart's photographic feat and thus settle the controversy ended inconclusively, and eventually nothing came of the photographic evidence.

In fact, nothing came of any phase of the Lubbock in-

126

vestigation. For a time it seemed the lights might be birds whose underparts were reflecting light from sodium-vapor street lamps below. But the estimated speed of the lights was too fast for birds. All other such hypotheses proved equally inconclusive at the time. Captain Ruppelt, in his *Report* published several years later, says he now knows what the lights were—some kind of natural phenomenon—but he was sworn to secrecy by the scientists who made the discovery. At any rate, while they lasted, the lights provided excellent grist for both the mills of Believers and Unbelievers. The pros took the apparitions as proof positive of visitations from outer space. The cons dismissed them as illusions caused by atmospheric refraction of city lights.

Aside from the lights, 1951 was only a calm before a storm that was gathering to break the following year when the hysteria reached its all time high. In fact, the year 1952 might well go down as the millennial year for the saucers. The Air Force was swamped with sightings. There are so many articles in newspapers and magazines published during that year, they defy reading except by the most Fortean-minded. There were reports sent in by the lunatic fringe. There were reports from reliable and highly trained pilots, both civilian and military. Unidentified objects were seen by radar operators, scientists, and plain, honest citizens. There were saucers in America; there were saucers in France, Britain, Italy and Japan. Some saucers stood still—some travelled at speeds estimated at 50,000 miles per hour. Some unidentified objects were saucer-shaped, some spherical and others resembled flying sausages. Some had green lights, others blue. Indeed, 1951 was a "blue year" as far as both the saucers and the Air Force were concerned. The saucers' lighting facilities were predominantly blue that year, and the Air Force had a bad case of the blues trying to keep up with both the saucers and its critics.

The mania was set off during the summer when the saucers put in an appearance over Washington, D. C. Naturally, any unexplained celestial visitors over the nerve center of the Republic was enough to put both civilians and the military on edge. But what was even more remarkable about the Washington reports, was the fact that the unidentified objects were tracked on radar as well as seen by the naked eye. This was not the first time flying saucers had been tracked by radar, but it was the first time that eyewitness sightings were confirmed by this means.

A radar scope is typically a twenty-four inch phosphor-coated glass tube not dissimilar in make-up to a television picture tube. But on the face of the radar tube, a sweep streak of light travels around at the rate of six revolutions per minute matched to corresponding rotations of the antenna. When blips appear, this means the antenna has picked up reflections of transmitted impulses which are bouncing back from some object. When such blips appear, they will be repeated every ten seconds. By calculation, using their distance apart as they appear on the scope on successive sweeps, the speed, distance from the station and compass bearing of the object causing them can be determined. For this reason radar sightings are far better than naked eye observations which give only crude estimates of such unknowns. But radar, too, has its limitations. It will reflect birds, balloons, and most important, "temperature inversions." These are isolated layers of heavy air hovering above the earth and which may be thick enough to send electrical impulses back to their source thus giving spurious sightings. In this way, by double reflections, objects on the ground may be picked up. If the latter are in motion, the effect as seen on radar is the same as if they were actually moving through the sky. Consequently, a double-check involving both eyewitness and radar sightings was most welcome in the case of the Washington apparitions.

The first of the main sightings occurred on July 19th, although there had been several previous reports of mysterious lights in the area. The latter had been seen by such trained sky-watchers as airline pilots and ground observers. However, the main force of saucers came over National Airport close to midnight on the 19th. There were eight in all which were picked up on the field's radar set. The objects were not airplanes, since they cruised along at 120 miles per hour for a while and then accelerated to supersonic speeds. Moreover, no planes were in the vicinity.

The targets were also picked up on radar by Andrews Air Force Base ten miles east of National Airport. Then, shortly after midnight, a Capital Airlines pilot spotted the lights. Still later, another pilot reported that a light was pursuing him. In view of this multiplicity of sightings and cross checks, Air Force interceptors were called out, but through unexplained delays did not arrive for hours, in fact, not until daylight when the lights had already disappeared. (One wonders what would have happened if a real enemy attack had been under way.)

During the following week the reaction among high moguls of the Pentagon was one of confusion. The attack had been unexpected; consequently no one was prepared, and the press was setting up an unholy clamor. The Believers, too, saw the most sinister portents in the Washington incident. An investigation was, of course, launched with the usual results; the radar operators swore by their sets, the pilots swore by their eyes, and the saucer debunkers blamed temperature inversions and refracted lights.

The Air Force, meanwhile, was beginning to get reports of saucer sightings at the rate of forty to fifty a day from all points in the United States. Evidently, the newspaper accounts of the Washington sightings either stimulated the mass hysteria or Saucerians were beginning to appear in force in their curious vehicles. Then, just a week after their first invasion of the Capital skies, the saucers returned.

Again, the mysterious targets were spotted by radar, and this time interceptors were ordered up after them at once. But again, by the time they reached the area, the lights had vanished. A little later a jet managed to get within range of one of the lights, but as the pilot tried to close in, his target appeared to speed away. Significantly enough, the radar operator in the pursuing plane was never able to get the target on his set. Still later another chase took place involving a different jet and saucer but wiith equally disappointing results. These investigations went on all through the hours of darkness; and when dawn broke, the skies were clear, and the Air Force had no more information about the saucers than before they had appeared.

Naturally, newspaper editors were delighted. All over the country headlines read as if the citadel of the Republic were under a state of seige. President Truman made firm inquiries down through channels as to what was going on. People wired the President asking that the Air Force be ordered not to shoot down the saucers. Any such stricture was, of course, wholly unnecessary. The Air Force would have been happy to get close enough just to look at a saucer from firing range.

In October, the Air Force decided to reveal the results of its investigation of the Capital invasions. A large and lengthy press conference was held in which General James A. Samford, Chief of Intelligence, speaking for the Air Force and aided by a radar expert, Captain Roy James, tried to debunk the sightings as due to natural phenomena, The Believers were left totally unsatisfied with the Air Force's explanation. Major Keyhoe in his *Flying Saucers from Outer Space* reports that he was allowed to attend the conference, and attributes the most sinister motives to the Air Force because of the military experts' general attitude of uncertainty about the cause of the Washington phenomena. Since Keyhoe was among the firm Believers, he argues that the Air Force also believed but was withholding information from the public in order to prevent panic among the populace. The New York *Times* appeared to accept the Air Force explanation at face value, as did most of the other responsible newspapers and magazines. Captain Ruppelt in his *Report* asserts the Air Force was simply trying to be objective and not jump to premature conclusions. Since the Capital has not subsequently been attacked by saucers, it seems the Air Force was vindicated in its attitude.

The other highlights of 1952 were the Sutton Monster and the Case of the Florida Scoutmaster.

The Monster appeared in Sutton, West Virginia on September 12, 1952. Presumably he arrived on a large, glowing object seen by thousands as it flashed across the sky. Among these was a Mrs. Kathleen May, her three young boys, and a visiting seventeen-year-old National Guardsman, Gene Lemon. They saw the glowing object appear to land on a nearby hill and courageously started off to investigate it. As they approached the probable site of the landing, the searchers noticed a suffocating odor but nevertheless pressed on. A little later they saw two shining objects reflected in the glow of the guardsman's flashlight—possibly the eyes of a raccoon. But upon closer inspection the reflections turned out to come from the eyes of a huge figure over nine feet tall with a glistening reddish face and protruding eyeballs set a foot apart. As the dumbfounded earthmen watched the monster's body glowed with a dull green light, and "he" omitted a peculiar hissing sound. When the appalling creature gave evidence of moviing in their direction, the guardsman decided the affair was beyond his military prowess, and the little group fled. After the refugees reached home, an examination revealed the boys' face and hands appeared to be covered with an oily substance which caused the affected parts to swell. The victims also complained of a burning sensation in their throats. A doctor who examined the boys described the symptons as consistent with a touch of mustard gas. However, no official explanation of the affair was even given out by the Air Force. Perhaps the flaming object was a meteorite and the rest imagination.

The case of the Florida scoutmaster was a more difficult nut to crack. The man in question was driving home on a country road with several of his charges from a scout meeting when he noticed a strange blue light off in the woods. A little distance further back he had seen lights, apparently descending from the sky, and putting the two facts together thought a plane might have crashed. Thinking that he might exercise his scouting knowledge and in the process render assistance to any survivors, he left the boys in the car and started off in the direction of the light. He left instructions with the scouts that should he fail to return within fifteen minutes, the boys were to go for help.

When he reached the general area of the light, the scout-master became aware of a rise in temperature as though he were in the vicinity of a brick kiln. There was also a peculiar odor in the area. Looking up to get his bearings from the stars he was amazed to find that none were visible. Shining his flashlight upward to investigate the cause of the blackout, he discovered that he was under a huge flying saucer hovering in the air directly above him. It was gray-metallic in appearance, with a turret—presumably for accommodating passengers—on its top. There were small portholes spaced at regular intervals around the perimeter of the saucer which suggested they might be exhausts of some kind that were associated with the vehicle's propulsion mechanism. He stepped back trying to collect his wits and shortly afterwards heard a sound as if a door were being opened. The next instant a ball of red fire emerged from the turret and began to drift in his direction. He was frozen to the spot but managed to throw his hands over his face just as he was enveloped in a gaseous mist. He lost consciousness and fell in the grass.

By this time the boys had taken alarm and had run to the nearest farmhouse to seek assistance for their beleaguered leader. The farmer summoned the sheriff, and the latter arrived just in time to see the now-recovered scoutmaster emerging from the woods. The sheriff accompanied the stricken man back to the scene of the attack, and there they discovered the scoutmaster's flashlight and machete which he had been carrying when he first entered the woods. The grass was pressed down where he had been lying while unconscious. There was, however, no sign of the saucer and no evidence of damage to the grass or brush from the powerful fire ball which had felled the scoutmaster. The latter was taken to the sheriff's office, and there it was discovered that his face, arms and hair were lightly burned—so lightly that the injuries might have been caused by a sunburn.

The Air Force carried out an elaborate investigation of the whole affair and eventually concluded it was a deliberate hoax perpetrated by the scoutmaster who was unwittingly aided and abetted in the affair by the scouts. The burns were probably self-inflicted by a few passes with a cigarette lighter and the mysterious light was caused by a farmer welding in the distance. The lights seen descending from the sky were actually airplanes landing at a nearby airport. The red fire ball and saucer existed only in the scoutmaster's imagination.

There were many other reports in 1952, some fantastic, others credible. Some were handed in by unreliable individuals. Others were simultaneous sightings made by hundreds of sober people, such as occurred when a huge glow raced across the sky in Indianapolis one weekend. There were more reports of saucers that had fallen into the clutches of the Air Force. There was even a report of a flying platter which came as a welcome variation on the saucer theme. During the year Dr. Donald Menzel was preparing articles and a book debunking the saucers. Major Keyhoe was writing articles and books denouncing the Pentagon and trying to convince his readers the saucers were from outer space. Menzel, incidentally, received an indignant letter from a Washington civil service girl as a result of one of his articles. She charged him with shattering her dreams of tall, dark and handsome Saucerians coming to Washington to take her away from it all. Along these same lines, a twelve-year-old girl asked the Air Force to "spare the Saucerians." A Catholic priest in an article prepared for a religious conference suggested the Saucerians might be celestial beings who had never fallen from grace as had their earthly brethren and would therefore be unkillable in any event. Finally, a minister of the Gospel wrote to Professor Einstein in desperation asking him to use his great powers to solve the mystery. The physicist's disconcerting reply was: "Those people have seen something. What it is I do not know and I am not curious to know. "

Somehow, during the succeeding years the saucers never came up to their previous performances. A glance at the New York *Times Index* reveals the number of articles on saucers took a nose dive during 1953 from which it never recovered. The Air Force continued to get reports, and the pros and cons of the saucer's reality were threshed out in books and articles, but much of this was a reboiling of old bones, and very little new material was added to what had already been said many times before. The report of reports came out in 1956 when Captain Edward Ruppelt got out his *Report on Unidentified Flying Objects*. It is a history of the affair during his tenure of office and was written more or less from the official Air Force point of view. Toward the close of the report he estimates there were something like forty-four thousand "UFO's" sighted since 1947, and a fairly detailed analysis by the Air Force of over fifteen hundred such sightings revealed about twenty-seven per cent remained as definite "unknowns." The rest were either known to be, or were at least "possible," balloons, aircraft, astronomical phenomena and such. All the Air Force was willing to conclude was that the saucers were *not* terrestrial vehicles. They were not *known* to be space ships, but the *possibility* that they might be interplanetary was not excluded.

III

There have been many theories to account for the flying saucers, and it is not within the province of this chapter to review them here. Rather, by way of concluding this study, a few suggestions will be offered to account for the hysteria resulting from whatever it was that was seen by thousands of Americans during the height of the hysteria. Naturally, this approach implies that the saucers existed only in the misperceptions and imaginations of those who saw them. Such is the author's belief. Those who wish to pursue the nature of the phenomena seen by the observers are referred to the books by Ruppelt and Menzel.

Clearly, the incredible spread and duration of the saucer mania is without precedent in American history. Long lasting delusions have plagued the human race before (such as the Loch Ness sea monster), but not in the United States and nowhere in our time with the advantage of our advanced scientific knowledge and sophisticated culture. But up to the onset of the saucers, people have never lived in an age of anxiety that has been so prolonged and about which they have been able to do so little. Cold wars do not provide the explosive catharsis of all-out hot wars. Moreover, never in our history were people so sky-conscious as they were during the decade of the saucers. This was the result partly of the tremendous strides in air power and partly because there was (and still is) good reason to believe that if war comes it will come from this quarter.

Aside from the atomic anxiety characteristic of our time, but related to it, is the factor of the incredible scientific and military discoveries made during the past twenty years. These, too, must be taken into account in any explanation of the saucer hysteria. With the invention of the Bomb, the breaking of the sound barrier, the formulation of plans for a space missile*, and the like, almost anything was believable. Moreover, the volume of science fiction produced during the two decades before the saucers must not be forgotten. It threatens to catch up with the detective story as the most popular genre of escape literature. The fact that it is fictional makes no difference. As the proponents of this kind of literature themselves point out, today's fiction is tomorrow's science. The end result of adding together all this scientific fact and fiction was

* One can only speculate on the effect of a Sputnik launching during the peak of the saucer scare. The Believers, at any rate, would have seen the most ominous portents in such an event.

an atmosphere saturated with mind-shaking accomplishments besides which flying saucers did not seem beyond the bounds of possibility. Putting this environmental factor with the first—the age of anxiety—we find that once again, as was true in every other instance of mass hysteria discussed in these studies, the *Zeitgeist* was partly to blame. In this case it was undoubtedly the major factor.

A third factor, which at first glance might seem trivial, was the felicitous name given to the objects after the first sightings. Had the apparitions that Arnold saw playing hop scotch on Mt. Rainier been labelled prosaically, they would never have started a chain-reaction. "Unidentified flying objects," the designation eventually adopted by the Air Force for such phenomena, is not only prosaic, it is non-committal. It may suggest any number of things—unidentified airplanes, ducks, balloons, scraps of airborne newspapers, meteorites, or other such flotsam and jetsam of the skies. But it does not immediately bring to mind a Buck Rogers' contrivance piloted by intelligent creatures from outer space. The very name "flying saucers" connotes a deliberately constructed device and one necessarily manned, since even a child knows saucers cannot fly by themselves. It was, then, the case of a rose by any other name not smelling as sweet. Or perhaps the philosopher, James' remark about getting the dog hanged by giving him a bad name is more appropos.

Finally, in this day and age, when a halfway credible report of unusual import gets into circulation it is certain to be swept into our highly developed mass-communication system. The Salem witchcraft remained localized partly because the means of spreading it were so slow. But in the case of the saucers, as was also true in the Invasion from Mars, the excellence of a communication system cuts both ways. A report of a saucer in Oregon will reach every city in the United States within a few hours, and a really menacing report within minutes. Since mass hysteria, like individual hysteria is largely a result of verbal suggestion, the report of one sighting generates additional sightings. Consequently, during the flowering of the saucers, unusual weather phenomena, astronomical quirks, balloons, balls of lightning, and such, became unidentified flying objects. Until the era of the saucers they were simply reported as celestial freaks and quickly forgotten.

In this connection, much has been made of the reliability of the sighters, since so many saucers were reported by pilots, ground observers, control tower operators, scientists, and others who are presumably sober men and specially trained in careful observation. Much of this is beside the point. Many years ago a convention of lawyers and jurists was held in a

European city, which at the same time, was also playing host to a circus. In the middle of a speech by the chairman of the legal convention, a clown (presumably from the circus) rushed onto the stage. Shortly afterwards another man entered and, after a brisk verbal exchange with the chairman, "shot" the clown. The chair, after restoring order, suggested that it would be helpful to the local authorities if all present jotted down their recollections of what had transpired. A subsequent analysis of the records showed that the lawyers were just as subject to errors and hysteria as ordinary mortals. Most of them fell victim to the very mistakes they so frequently deplore in courtroom witnesses. The experiment has since been repeated many times with the same results.

In conclusion, it's a pity in many ways that the saucers did not turn out to be manned by spacemen on a visit to planet Earth. Aside from fulfilling the romantic dreams of the Washington civil service girl, the saucerians might have been extremely interesting characters to have around, if for no other reason, for their broad perspective and astrophysical knowledge. Had the United States been made particularly attractive to the celestial visitors, it is possible we might be light years ahead of the Russians in missiles and space vehicles.

9: The Odyssey of Bridey Murphy with Notes on the Hysterical History of Hypnotism

IN THE SPRING OF 1956 hundreds of thousands of Americans were suddenly thrown into a state of violent spiritual agitation by the announcement that incontrovertible evidence of the immortality of the human spirit had at last been found. The realization of this age-old human dream had actually come to fruition several years previously in the living room of Morey Bernstein, a Pueblo, Colorado, man of business, who by avocation was a hypnotist of considerable prowess. Mr. Bernstein's intimations of immortality were withheld from the world, however, until published in a curious volume entitled *The Search for Bridey Murphy* which recorded, among other things, the life after death of an Irish lass. It was Bridey's adventures in ghostly realms which constituted the evidence for the persistence of the human shade following the death of the body. Not only did Mr. Bernstein's earthshaking volume promise immortality of the spirit, it also offered a concrete case history of human reincarnation in the form of a Colorado housewife who was the current re-embodiment of the departed Bridey.

The published account of Bridey's saga was given a remarkable reception by the American public. The publishers, according to *Life* magazine, hoped for a total sale of 10,000 copies, but during a ten-minute break at a salesmen's conference at the publisher's headquarters, orders for 17,000 copies came in. Bookstores sold out faster than they could be supplied, and the waiting lists at public libraries were a foot long. According to *Time,* in the first two months after its publication, the book had gone through eight printings for a total of 170,500 copies and was the number one non-fiction bestseller. In addition, the book was translated into five foreign languages, condensed by *True* magazine, and syndicated in forty newspapers.

The beginning of this remarkable chain of events took place one evening in November of 1952 when Mr. Bernstein succeeded in hypnotically "regressing" a young Colorado housewife whom he identified as "Mrs. Ruth Simmons" back "over the hump" to a prior existence as an early nineteenth century Irish girl, Bridey Murphy. Mrs. Simmons was a social acquaintance on whom Mr. Bernstein had been practicing his recently acquired hypnotic powers, and when he discovered that she was an extraordinarily good subject, had regressed her in a series of trances during which she gave credible performances of herself as a little girl in kindergarten. It was Mrs. Simmons' singular ability to regress during the hypnotic sleep that led Bernstein to try for the ultimate— a regression beyond birth. To Bernstein's surprise, the experiment was an overwhelming success. During this, her first prior-existence trance, Bridey reported to her amazed hypnotist that she was describing events when she was eight years old in 1806, in Cork, Ireland. Her first Irish memory had to do with girlish mischief; she was scratching the finish off her newly painted metal bed. She was, at that time, the daughter of a barrister. In subsequent sessions she went on to tell how she had grown up in a happy home, had been educated at a "Mrs. Strayne's Day School" and eventually married Brian MacCarthy, a barrister, who wrote occasional articles for the Belfast *News Letter,* and who also taught at Queen's University in Belfast where Bridey and Brian moved after their marriage. She described her life in that ciity, mentioning the names of several business establishments where she traded, the type of food she ate, journeys taken with her husband, the name of their church and parish priest, the books she read as a girl, and other such circumstantial details.

Most dramatic of all was her account of her own death and burial in 1864, and her "astral" life before her reincarnation in 1923, although her descriptions of the "astral state" make it sound like a dull kind of existence to have created such a pother in Mr. Bernstein's readers. Much was also made of the fact that she used certain Irish expressions such as "banshee"; "colleen"; "ditched" (buried), "tup" (a bounder or scoundrel); "lough" (lake); "brate" (a little cup), and on one occasion asked for a "linen" instead of a handkerchief. She also remembered hearing as a youngster in Ireland the tale of Cuchulain, the legendary Irish hero who defended his native Ulster against Ireland's armies. She also knew about the practice of lowering people head first by means of a rope around the feet so they might kiss the celebrated Blarney Stone. Finally, the re-incarnated Bridey could, at Mr. Bernstein's suggestion, dance a very passable Irish jig.

The elicitation of these essential facts took a great deal of time. Bridey's memory was often vague, and she frequently had to be questioned repeatedly on a single point before it could be fully developed. Moreover, Bernstein very naturally cross-questioned her from session to session as a check on the reliability of her memory for the Irish existence. All told he subjected Mrs. Simmons to six tape-recorded sessions, some in the presence of witnesses, before he was satisfied that he had established at least the possibility of his subject's prior existence. The last nine chapters of the book contain the literal transcriptions of the hypnotic sessions along with considerable interpolated comment and explanation by Bernstein. The first session was subsequently recorded on an LP record for commercial distribution, and it sold in the tens of thousands.

Unfortunately for the Believers, some factual checking by agents of *Life* magazine and the Denver *Post* soon cast grave doubt on the validity of Bridey's saga. No birth records, wills or obituary notices could be found testifying to either Bridey's or her husband's Irish existence. No record of the school she claimed to have attended could be discovered. Her description of the bridal journey from Cork to Belfast made by herself and Brian MacCarthy after their marriage was by a circuitous and improbable route. The so-called Irish words such as "tup," "brate," and "lough" were not Irish words at all, and even those that were genuine such as "colleen" and "banshee" are, of course, commonly heard in the United States today. Her husband's tenure of office at Queen's University, and that of two other faculty members she claimed to have known, could not be verified. She described her girlhood bed (1804) as metal, although metal beds were unknown in Ireland until 1850. Finally, she mispronounced Irish terms and used a considerable number of Americanisms in relating the events of her life in Erin.

What the independent investigators did turn up in the way of positive evidence was that Mrs. Simmons while a child had been closely associated with her Scotch-Irish aunt, and there was every reason to believe she had been regaled with many an Irish tale that was tucked away in her unconscious until resurrected by the hypnotic sessions. The exposé also turned up the fact that Mrs. Simmons had been talented in high school dramatics, could dance the jig, and was especially good at putting on Irish brogues. Moreover, at the time of the Colorado trances, a travel film about the Emerald Isle was being shown in Pueblo. Some items touched on by the movie were the Blarney Stone, descriptions of Irish lakes and seaside resorts, and at least one of the business establishments mentioned by Bridey. Whether or not Mrs. Simmons saw this film is not known, but it is an interesting coincidence in view of subsequent events. Finally, David Cort in an article in the *Nation* suggests that Mrs. Simmons must have had an imagination as powerful as that possessed by novelist Flaubert and could therefore make excellent use of the traces of her aunt's Irish lore. Thus, as *Time* summarized it so aptly, there was "more Blarney than Bridey" in the Colorado reincarnation experiments.

In general, Bridey's Gallic saga was not kindly received by newspapers and the more bookish journals, though some editors and reviewers took a fence-straddling position on the book's more metaphysical implications. The Chicago *Tribune*, for example, allowed that there was some question about the validity of the corroborative evidence touching on Bridey's Irish life, but did find the experiment a remarkable demonstration of the mind's creative ability under conditions of high concentration. Similarly, the San Francisco *Chronicle* took the position that the transcendental implications of the Bernstein research would find a warm reception among the Believers in occult phenomena but went on to suggest that "The sceptics might have the most interesting time of all." The New York *Times* attributed Mrs. Simmons' remarkable revelations to the strong suggestions given by hypnotist Bernstein during the regression sessions. The New York *Herald Tribune* took the attitude that if more were known about "Bridey's" current life the mystery of her pre-incarnation meanderings would evaporate.

Among the totally unkind comments was D. F. Malcolm's statement in the *New Republic* to the effect that he was convinced of Mr. Bernstein's prowess as a hypnotist, since the book had put him to sleep. Bennett Cerf in his Trade Winds column in the *Saturday Review of Literature* found Bridey's revelations as exciting "as a ninety-eight page speech reprinted in the *Congressional Record.*" Mr. Cerf also took the trouble to listen to the LP recording of Bridey's mesmeristic verbalisms which he compared to the "puffing of a donkey engine" or to the wheezing of "a patient struggling for breath in an oxygen tent." And, as might be expected, the conservative *Library Journal* found the book "badly written in the style of the worst press journeys to the moon." The public, obviously, either did not read the reviewers or, if it did, preferred to believe.

Aside from the book's fantastic reception by the public, there were a number of other curious developments as a result of its publication. Hypnotists were flooded with requests to take would-be Bridey's back to prior existences. *Time* reported that a west coast hypnotist offered to establish the previous lives of all comers at $25 an existence. In Shawnee, Oklahoma, a nineteen-year-old boy killed himself in order to investigate the theory of reincarnation in person. One psychiatrist in commenting on such developments, grumbled that the Bridey Murphy mania had set hypnotism back twenty-five years. Finally, along these same lines, was the report of experiments conducted by two Yale professors in which they had succeeded in "forwarding" subjects into the 1960's during the hypnotic sleep. Just how this what-you-will-be experiment compared with the what-you-were type was not recorded, but it did demonstrate hitherto unsuspected histrionic talents among hypnotic subjects.

Among the less-than-serious reactions to Bridey's tale were the experiments being carried on by amateur hypnotists around the country. They were regressing volunteer subjects back to an amazing variety of previous existences, and *Time* reported: "Ordinary Americans turned up as German leather merchants, French peasants, English princesses and in one case as a horse." One soldier turned out to be his own grandfather, and in Shreveport, Louisiana, a high school student took a woman back 10,000 years. Just what antedeluvian behavior patterns the subject exhibited while in the trance were not recorded, though they conceivably might have been of considerable interest to anthropologists.

Bridey also inspired three songs, a "reincarnation cocktail" and an "ectoplasmic punch." *Life* for March 19, 1956, in reporting these artistic and bibulous developments, also featured photographs of "come as you were" parties where reincarnated Cleopatras and Arab Sheiks turned up in full regalia. The *Saturday Review of Literature* printed a tongue-in-cheek review of the Bridey book in which the reviewer, Fred Grunfeld, suggested a "search" ought to be instituted for such historical characters as Louisa May Alcott, Richelieu and Columbus. The review ends with a mythical hypnotic interview with a reincarnated Leopold Bloom.

By summer, the reincarnation furor had pretty well died down. No doubt the lack of factual findings in Ireland had put a damper on the initial enthusiasm of the Believers. Their dreams of immortality had been dashed on the rocks of reality, and many who had been shaken to the depths of their being were shamefacedly confessing they had been badly taken in by their own lack of critical judgment.

The nationwide furor created by the book struck back at its creator and at "Bridey" herself. The devastating attacks on the metaphysical implications of Bridey's Odyssey in un-Believers, the exposé of the all too terrestrial sources of her Irish saga, and the tragic suicide of the nineteen-year-old Oklahoman, drove Mr. Bernstein to the verge of a nervous breakdown. He got away from it all by weathering the storm in a secret Florida retreat. When the worst was over, Mr. Bernstein took up residence, appropriately enough, in Greenwich Village, that celebrated haven for Bohemians in the heart of New York City. There he managed the Bernstein fortune, showing no signs of returning to the profession of amateur hypnotist.

Mrs. Simmons, her husband and their two daughters came to regret their association with Mr. Bernstein's supernatural researches. When a national news syndicate leaked out her real name, the deluge of reporters, crackpots and others interested in metaphysics and hypnotism disrupted their lives. They were forced to get an unlisted telephone number and became anxious over the safety of their children. Eventually, when the madness had died down, the Simmons' returned to normal living—sadder but wiser for their brush with mass hysteria.

The flash in the pan hysteria caused by Bridey's ghostly wanderings may be attributed in part to the superficial plausibility of the book itself. But such surface realism alone would not have been enough; in addition, *The Search for Bridey Murphy* appealed to two factors inherent to the psychological make-up of the average reader.

In regard to the book itself, it may be argued that it was plausible in the sense that it was written in the manner of an "experimental" report in which the "evidence" is laboriously but surely built up in the best scientific style. Indeed, Mr. Bernstein's first nine chapters have little or nothing to do with Bridey but are devoted to a rehash of other evidence for belief in immortality. To begin with, the reader is told of Mr. Bernstein's initial tough-minded agnosticism toward the theory of life after death. But after exploring the literature on extra-sensory perception and reading of the remarkable powers of on Edgar Cayce, an unlettered but skilled hypnotic healer, Mr. Bernstein became convinced that mind is free of matter and thus not necessarily liable to the fate of all flesh.

As Mr. Bernstein became more and more interested in strange mental phenomena, he decided to become a hypnotist himself. For reasons not entirely clear to professional psychologists, he underwent a series of harrowing experiences in order to make himself a better hypnotist. Among these were a course of electric shock treatments, the inhalation of carbon dioxide to the point of strangulation, and a bout with narcosynthesis induced by a "truth serum."

After lowering his reader's guard by establishing himself as something of an expert in the unconventional by ways of psychology, Mr. Bernstein introduced his *pièce de résistance* in the form of Bridey's hypnotic wheezes. At this stage the various lines of internal evidence in the story begin to operate on the reader's credulity. At first glance it seems unbelievable that a Colorado housewife would know Gaelic words, Irish geography, and the names of various obscure persons who lived in the early 1800's unless she had some personal knowledge of such matters. There was, of course, the possibility she had visited Ireland or was a student of Irish history, but earlier in the book Bernstein makes out a strong case that Mrs. Simmons was neither an Irish scholar nor had she ever been abroad. Thus, she had no personal knowledge of the Emerald Isle and certainly none from more than a century ago. Moreover, he argues the story she told was far too complex and circumstantial for an ordinary hypnotic subject to make up out of thin air. So, at first reading there seemed to be no alternative but to accept the reincarnation explanation of Bernstein's findings. Of course, when it was discovered that many of Bridey's "facts" could not be substantiated on the Old Sod, and that "Bridey" had been intimately associated as a little girl with her Scotch-Irish aunt, then the credibility of the findings rapidly reduces to zero. However, it must be remembered that these skeptical reports did not come out until after the book had been widely read and discussed. By that time the hysteria was well kindled.

The first psychological factor that played a part in the hysterical reaction to Bridey's meanderings, is the fact that the discoveries were made by means of hypnotism. Psychological phenomena have always been poorly understood by the average individual, and, because of this, are subject to abuse and misinterpretation. Of all such phenomena, hypnotism has been one of the most baffling. In the past, this is attributable to the fact that psychologists themselves have never been able to give a complete explanation of the process. For this reason, the hypnotic trance has been exploited by magicians, theater performers, and frauds.

Indeed, the modern systematic study and exploitation of hypnotism originated in the hands of a charlatan of the first water. The gentleman in question was Franz Anton Mesmer, a Viennese physician who, about the time of the American Revolution announced to the scientific world the theory and practice of "animal magnetism." Dr. Mesmer established a clinic in Paris for the treatment of patients suffering from various physical and mental disorders. Mesmer's hypnotic chambers boasted a large, dark hall in the midst of which stood a *baquet*, or large oaken tub. The receptacle was approximately a foot high and of sufficiently large diameter to accommodate thirty patients. Mesmer's ailing customers stood around the *baquet*, and each was assigned a jointed metal rod which projected out of the tub. The rods presumably conducted the "animal magnetism" generated by magnetized iron filings within the *baquet*. The treatment consisted of placing the rod against the afflicted member while Mesmer walked about in a brilliant silk robe creating the proper psychological atmosphere. Dr. Mesmer insisted on absolute silence on the part of his patients but provided soft background music to render the sufferers more amenable to the magnetism. In cases where the treatment was successful, the patient experienced a "crisis" and often collapesd, torn by convulsions. Mesmer reported that after several such psychic overhauls the patient experienced considerable improvement.

The more conservative members of the medical profession denounced Mesmer to the French government as an "avaricious charlatan." As is generally done in such cases, a commission was appointed to investigate the matter. Among those who served was the celebrated chemist Lavoisier, Benjamin Franklin, and the ambassador from the newly-created United States. It was Ben Franklin who struck the telling blow at Mesmer's theory of animal magnetism. Mesmer, it seemed, had branched out from the *baquet* and had been "magnetising" trees. Ailing French peasants found the trees' curative powers equal to those of the *baquet*. However, Franklin informd some peasants that certain trees had been magnetized when, in fact, they had not. Despite their lack of magnetism, the trees' curative powers appeared to be equal to those of the "hypnotized" trees. As a result of the exposé, Mesmer fled Paris.

The next significant event in the colorful history of hypnotism occurred in England, in 1843, when James Baird, a British surgeon discovered the true psychological nature of the hypnotic trance. We are indebted to Baird both for coining the term hypnotism and for more or less standardizing the technique for inducing the trance. Baird had his patients fixate a bright object in such a way that the eyes were under heavy strain. At the same time, the patient was given verbal suggestions to the effect that he was drowsy and was going to sleep. Baird used the trance as a technique for performing surgery painlessly—a use which is winning increasing recognition in recent years.

Despite the patently genuine nature of the phenomenon and its demonstrated usefulness as a form of anesthesia, doctors who dabbled in hypnosis were under heavy suspicion from their more conservative colleagues. As recently as the late 1880's when the great Dr. Freud began to practice hypnosis, he and his associate, Breuer, were considered treading on dangerous ground. However, as has been pointed out in the introduction to this book, Freud's studies of hysteria carried out by means of hypnotism led to the discovery of psychoanalysis. From the point of view of scientific progress, therefore, Freud was vindicated.

One final note on the development of hypnotism: in 1910 a young French pharmacist, Emile Coué established a "clinic" in his home for the purpose of mental healing. Coué became world-famous for his theory that all hypnotic suggestion was, in effect, autosuggestion or self-suggestion. As a result of Coué's teachings, millions of gullible people in the twenties were attempting self-cures by repeating to themselves the suggestion that they were getting better and better every day in every way.

Returning to the present case, a final word is in order regarding Mrs. Simmons' amazing ability to remember events from her childhood—events which it seems highly unlikely she could have remembered in a waking state. The technical term for this well-known hypnotic phenomenon is *hyper-amnesia*. It has been a well-established fact ever since Freud first began to unearth his patients' unconscious memories by means of hypnotherapy. Unfortunately, there has never been an adequate explanation of the process. In the case of unpleasant memories, it has been accounted for by the argument that during the hypnotic sleep, as is also true in dreams, the patient's guard is down allowing otherwise suppressed material to escape the censor. However, such an explanation fails to hold water when applied to the innocuous memories brought forth by Mr. Bernstein. Perhaps we all remember much more than we think we do but ordinarily are unable to call to mind many of our past experiences because of interference effects from the millions of competing memories that crowd consciousness. Somehow, in some as yet undiscovered way, the hypnotic sleep overcomes such interference effects allowing long "forgotten" memories to come forward. Why, we do not know.

The second inherent psychological factor that aided and abetted the Bridey mania was the average individual's subconscious belief in his own immortality. Most people, however well-adjusted they may be to life's exigencies, and however, reconciled they are to their eventual departure, would like to believe in survival after death. Most civilized religions subscribe to such a hypothesis, and even among primitive peoples belief in Valhalla or reincarnation is widespread. Thus, Bridey had a receptive audience to begin with and one that was predisposed to believe the events described in the book. But the significant thing about this particular volume was that it appeared to offer concrete or experimental evidence for such survival. If true, it would supplement one of man's oldest articles of faith with scientific fact and thus revolutionize life on this earth.

It was a nice dream while it lasted.

10: High Treason in the State Department

". . . I have here in my hand a list of two-hundred and five that were known to the Secretary of State as being members of the Communist Party and who nevertheless are still working and shaping policy in the State Department."

With these disquieting words addressed to a Republican Women's Club in Wheeling, West Virginia, on February 9, 1950, the late Senator Joseph Raymond McCarthy launched his ferocious attack on Communists in the United States Government. Within a few short weeks the Senator's startling revelations catapulted him into the limelight, where he remained during a four-year reign of hysterical witch-hunting which was without parallel in American history.

However, if the Senator expected an immediate wave of indignation as a result of his Wheeling exposé, he must have been disappointed. The Associated Press carried a few excerpts from the speech, but headlines there were none. It may have been that at this germinal stage of the McCarthy mania history hung in the balance while the Senator pondered the wisdom of pursuing the theme of "Communists in government" as a central issue for the 1952 campaign. But there were two more years to go—two years in which he could belabor the administration for coddling Communists and fellow travelers.

In keeping with his determination to bring home treason to Truman and his Administration, McCarthy reiterated his grave charges at Salt Lake City and at Reno, Nevada, that same Lincoln's Birthday weekend. On that memorable weekend the Senator was on a GOP-sponsored tour as part of the celebration of the most solemn high feast days of the Republican Party, and he intended to make the most of his first big opportunity.

But at Salt Lake City, and again at Reno, the 205 subversives in the State Department were unaccountably reduced to "57 card-carrying* Communists." Moreover, at the citadel of the Mormons the Senator offered to reveal the names of the disloyal 57 to Dean Acheson, then Secretary of State, if the latter would only telephone him at a Salt Lake City hotel.

---

* In this particular, at least, the Senator was wrong. Card-carrying had been abandoned by the Bolsheviki several years previously on a directive from the Kremlin.

145

Acheson, however, failed to pick up the gauntlet with the telephone.

While the Senator's denunciations fell short of banner headlines, there was sufficient publicity to enrage the Democrats to the point of challenging McCarthy to "put up or shut up," and he undertook to oblige them in a massive Senate speech on February 20, 1950 in which he exposed 81 anonymous cases of Communists associated with the State Department.

It is highly doubtful that the embattled Senator deliberately set out to make a numbers game out of Reds in government. Rather, he was hoisted by his own petard, in a manner of speaking. What had happened was this. To implement his charges of subversives in high office, McCarthy had resurrected an old letter of Jimmy Byrnes' dated July 26, 1946, in which the then Secretary of State had informed Congressman Sabath of Illinois that a preliminary screening of 3,000 government employees who had worked for various emergency war agencies revealed that 284 should receive "a recommendation against permanent employment." Of these, 79 had actually been dismissed from government service. Since 284 minus 79 leaves 205, the Byrnes letter was obviously the Senator's source of information for the Wheeling speech. It is, of course, equally obvious that McCarthy and McCarthy alone translated "recommendation against permanent employment" to "members of the Communist Party." Evidently a re-reading of the old files convinced the Senator that of the 205 cases only 57 were actually affiliated with the Reds. Then, at some point before the Senate revelations, he must have dredged up an additional 24 cases to make the final figure of 81.

As it turned out, the confusion in the number of Communists employed by Acheson worked in the Senator's favor, for the real issue was soon forgotten—namely, that it remained to be demonstrated that *one* "card-carrier" actually plied his trade in the State Department. Instead, it was tacitly assumed that *some* sizeable number of subversives enjoyed the emoluments of high government office and, at the same time, had a "big inch" pipeline for conveying secrets from Washington to Moscow.

The Senate speech itself began with a denunciation of President Truman, Dean Acheson, and the Majority Leader of the Senate. All three, according to the Senator, had ignored both his public alarms and private communiqués He then promised to discuss 81 cases of individuals employed by the State Department in which "there is a definite Communist connection." But many hours and thousands of words later it appeared that some were Communists and some were not. Some were employed by the State Department and others had never been. Four cases got omitted altogether adding still another total to the numbers game which now read 205 - 57 - 81 - 79. However, the true total might be 78, since one of the 79 turned out to be so virulently anti-Communist that he had to be dismissed from the State Department as a hopeless fanatic.

Moreover, there was a certain amount of confusion between subversion and sexual perversion in the Senator's allegations. Case number 62, he affirmed, was "unimportant as far as Communist connections were concerned." But since the file ". . . goes into some detail in regard to the peculiar—how can we put it?—the peculiar mental twists . . ." of certain individuals in the Department, he felt compelled to recommend it to "any Committee that cares to investigate it." Such individuals, the Senator added, were particularly subject to blackmail by subversive elements, and hence were poor security risks. There is no record of any Kinsey-like Congressional committee taking up the Senator's offer.

Then there was case 65 who, it appeared, was "very definitely communistically inclined." However, the Senator added, "it is entirely possible that this individual is merely a left-winger who has been dominated by No. 81, who will be covered later. . . ." Case No. 40 was especially interesting in revealing the Senator's thinking. The file in question referred to an individual employed in "Research" in the State Department since 1947. According to McCarthy, "there is nothing in the files to disprove his communistic connections." From this curious point of view anyone in the United States could have been a Communist in 1950, or at any other time for that matter.

While the denunciations were going on, McCarthy was constantly interrupted, especially by Senator Scott Lucas of Illinois, the Democratic Majority Leader, and Brien McMahon of Connecticut, in an attempt to reconcile his imprecise statistics and to determine whether the 81 (79?) cases were all presently employed by the Department. They were not. He was also urged to name names. He never did. Moreover, following the exposure of case No. 14, Senators Wherry and Dworshak requested and obtained a quorum call in view of the grave charges being presented by the junior Senator from Wisconsin. Because only twenty-four Senators were present—a number insufficient to constitute a quorum—the sergeant-at-arms was instructed by the presiding officer to "request" the attendance of the absent legislators. After two forays into the Capitol's social life, the sergeant managed to round up enough Senators to make a quorum, and the expose went on to end near midnight in these gracious, but not entirely accurate or grammatical phrases: "I wish to thank very much the Senators who very patiently have remained here and have listened to what may have been somewhat tedious during the last eight hours.

"I assure them that I have tried to keep my remarks as brief as possible, while at the same time giving Senators all the pertinent information from the files."

Since the cases discussed by McCarthy were mostly old (much of the information had been made public during the course of previous Congressional hearings) and were none too substantial in proving subversion in the State Department, the morning after official Washington reaction was largely negative. Dean Acheson ignored the charges, Truman testily denied them, and the Republican leaders in the Senate considered the affair a "reckless" and "disastrous" performance. Nevertheless, on a motion by Scott Lucas of Illinois, an investigations-conscious Senate ordered an inquiry by a subcommittee of the Foreign Relations Committee. Millard Tydings (Dem. Md.) was appointed chairman of the new subcommittee.

Despite the prosaic reaction from Capitol Hill, the fires of hysteria had been lighted. The public read the headlines and the public was disturbed. Just a month before the McCarthy revelations, Alger Hiss had been convicted on the evidence of the celebrated "pumpkin papers" secreted by Whittaker Chambers, the perfumed Communist turned informer. In the course of the same trial, Julian Wadleigh, another State Department employee, was exposed by Chambers as a spy. Wadleigh confessed his sins, joined the side of the angels and testified against Hiss. There *had* been Communists in high places; therefore, there was nothing intrinsically unbelievable about the possibility of a more extensive infiltration by Reds, provided one read only the headlines and ignored the fine print, as most Americans are wont to do.

And so the "crusade against Communists in government" had caught the ear of the people. At first the hysteria took root among the anti-New Dealers, the lunatic fringe, racists, violent reactionaries, and that curious breed of Texans, the oil millionaires or Cadillac cowboys. But soon the Senator's base of support broadened to include many honest though deluded Americans who were disturbed about our foreign policy, which was seemingly so inadequate in the face of the recent Communist gains in Europe and Asia. Others were afraid of Russia's military might and mistakenly took the Senator's crusade against Communists at home as the main bulwark of American defense against Communists abroad. Support, first in a trickle and then in a flood, came in the form of letters and telegrams of approbation—some laced with hard cash. McCarthy Clubs sprang up at scattered points around the country. The Minute Women, a kind of female KKK, lent militant support to the Senator's crusade. News commentators such as George Sokolsky, Fulton Lewis, Jr., Westbrook Pegler and Walter Winchell took up McCarthy's refrain. McCormick's *Tribune* and the Hearst apparatus lent friendly newspaper support* in the form of editorials and big black headlines. McCarthyism, though not yet born, was well into labor.

But not all went Joe's way. The Tydings' subcommittee, after a series of hearings extending over four mounths, decided that McCarthy's charges were "irresponsible" and "untruthful." The Senator was accused of perpetrating a "fraud" and a "hoax" on his colleagues. In its final report, the subcommittee exonerated all persons accused by the Senator of Communist affiliations. It seemed that during the course of the hearings the Wisconsinite gave the Committee names in closed sessions but no real evidence of their subversive affiliations. When asked to make specific charges backed up by concrete evidence, McCarthy countered with a statement to the effect that he was providing "information" against persons named, and that the evidence necessary to get them indicted was in the State Department files. Caught in a merry-go-round, the Committee requested President Truman to open the files to Committee inspection. After a two-week delay, Truman acquiesced. The dissatisfied Senator countered with the charge that the files were phony. They had been "raped," he said, of all unfavorable information supplied by the dread Federal Bureau of Investigation. In light of the Senator's countercharges, Chairman Tydings asked J. Edgard Hoover to examine the files. He pronounced them intact. The Senator's last word was to the effect that the critical information had been replaced by Acheson's agents before Hoover's men rechecked the files.

In the face of this heavy setback, the Senator offered to rest his entire case on the alleged subversion of Professor Owen Lattimore, whom he described as the "top Russian espionage agent in the United States." The Professor, then

---

* The Luce *Time-Life-Fortune* empire, to the Senator's considerable irritation, remained consistently anti-McCarthy throughout the four years of his reign. He frequently denounced *Time* in his public utterances, and devoted an entire Senate speech to its machinations against McCarthyism.

in the Far East, elected to return and testify in his own defense.

McCarthy managed to get Lattimore "identified" as a Communist by Louis Budenz, an ex-Communist turned Roman Catholic who had been elevated to a professorship at Fordham University. The gloomy Budenz enjoyed a "finger of doom" reputation during the late Forties as a reward for exposing Gerhardt Eisler and Sam Carr, both top-notch Communists. At the time of the Tydings hearings, however, he had degenerated into a second-rate, or "me-too" informer. But McCarthy also had Lattimore denounced by Freda Utley, another wandering minstrel, who, in her eagerness to convince the Committee of the Professor's subversive past, referred to him as a "Judas Cow" who led others of lesser intellectual prowess into the abyss of Communism. She also described him as a man who had "tried to influence Americans by quoting from people like Wendell Willkie."

The Professor was not, as McCarthy had hoped, proved a Communist during the course of the hearings, but eventually ended up in a series of inconclusive brushes with the Federal courts on perjury charges after considerable doubt had been cast on his veracity during the course of further loyalty hearings before the McCarran Committee.

After the Tydings hearings had thus ended inconclusively (as all hearings involving McCarthy were destined to end), the enraged Senator launched a "back street" campaign to defeat Senator Tydings, the Committee chairman, who was up for re-election in his home state. A Senate Committee which subsequently investigated the Maryland campaign found that a four-page tabloid entitled *From the Record* which had flooded the state during the campaign was partly the work of McCarthy and his staff. The tabloid, the committee reported, "contains misleading half truths, misrepresentations, and false innuendos that maliciously and without foundation attack the loyalty and patriotism not only of Sen. Millard Tydings, who won the Distinguished Service Cross for battlefield heroism in World War I, but also the entire membership of the Senate Service Committee in 1950." In addition, the committee found that a photograph in the tabloid showing Tydings in close and apparently friendly proximity to Earl Browder, the Communist leader, was an "infamous composite picture." Partly as a result of such tactics, Tydings was defeated by his Republican opponent by over 43,000 votes. McCarthyism in the last stages of labor was about to be born.

During the spring of 1951 the Senator continued to harass the administration with his allegations of Communists

150

in the State Department, and by midyear felt secure enough to strike at General George C. Marshall, the soldier-statesman, former Secretary of Defense, former Secretary of State, former Chief of Staff and subsequent winner of the Nobel Peace Prize in 1953. The attack took place in the hallowed halls of the Senate on June 14, 1951. Turning down a suggestion by Senator Wherry that a call for a quorum be voted in view of the small number of Senators present, McCarthy announced that the speech was approximately 60,000 words in length. He therefore felt it an imposition to require the legislators to sit and listen, but expressed the hope it would be studied in printed form by all concerned. In fact, the Senator read only a third of the speech; the rest was subsequently printed in the *Congressional Record*.

The speech, which McCarthy chose to call "America's Retreat from Victory: the Story of Gen. George C. Marshall," began with an analysis of America's role in World War II and in Korea. In effect, the Senator alleged that the Roosevelt-Truman administrations had engaged in "a conspiracy on a scale so immense as to dwarf any previous such venture in the history of man." The aim of the conspiracy was in essence, treason—the deliberate selling out of the United States to the forces of world Communism. More particularly, the American free-enterprise system had been undermined by creeping Federal controls and strangling corporation taxes during Roosevelt's administration. "Gutter intellectuals" were chosen to fill the roles of Presidential and military advisors. On the fighting fronts in pre-war China, in Europe and in Korea, the "pattern" conceived and implemented by the Marshall-Acheson apparatus was "collaboration" with the Communists. Indeed, Marshall and Acheson were but the "Kremlin's executioners" who, Macbeth-like were "steeped in blood." They sold out our allies and deliberately retreated from victory. But while Marshall and Acheson were joint leaders of the political conspiracy (with Truman their not-too-bright dupe), it was Marshall as head of the Armed Forces that excited the Senator's greatest ire and scorn. In a passage that was subsequently headlined around the world, McCarthy said, "Gen. Marshall is at the head of our Armed Services. Quite apart from the destructive nature of his public acts since the beginning of World War II, I ask in all gravity whether a man so steeped in falsehood who has recourse to the lie whenever it suits his convenience is fit to hold so exalted a place where he must be a model to the officers and men of our Armed Services." In another place McCarthy charged, "In all these attitudes, Eisenhower who had

151

been commander-in-chief in North Africa, was Marshall's firm supporter."

This bitter denunciation of Marshall, whom Truman had characterized as "the greatest living American," marked both the real emergence of McCarthyism and the beginning of the Senator's days of glory. Like his spiritual ancestors, the Salem witch-hunters, he became in Richard H. Rovere's words an "engine of denunciation." He cried out against virtually everyone in the Truman administration. He became a master of the Big Lie, the Smear, the Multiple Untruth, Character Assassination, Guilt by Association, Guilt by Collaboration, Guilt by Identification, and Guilt by Denunciation. In short, he employed every recipe in the pharmacopoeia of demagoguery to inflame the hysteria of the masses. Without the power of investigation that he was to wield under a Republican administration, the junior Senator became a Torquemada of the headlines—an accuser without portfolio. Shortly after his denunciations of Ambassador Jessup, John Paton Davies, Minister to Tangier, and John Carter Vincent, career foreign service diplomat, the usually gentle New York *Times* editorialized, "In making a political career of mud-slinging and Red-baiting, Sen. McCarthy has launched irresponsible, unprovable, and ridiculous charges against so many respected citizens that his attacks have become almost an accolade."

During the denunciation phase of McCarthy's career, Senator William Benton of Connecticut (Dem.), made the politically fatal mistake of attempting to unhorse his colleague on the grounds of political and financial corruption. Citing the Wisconsin Senator's unholy participation in the Tydings campaign, his below the board financial dealings with Pepsi Cola (the Senator was at one time known by the curious title of "the Pepsi Cola Kid"), the Lustron Corporation, and his handling of funds collected for "The Fight for America," Benton denounced McCarthy as unfit to hold office. The Senator counterattacked by challenging Benton to bring his charges outside the sanctuary of the Senate. Benton obliged and was sued by the Senator for $2,000,000 damages for libel.

Nothing came of the libel suit. Moreover, nothing came of the hearings by the Senate Privileges and Elections Committee on the Benton ouster motion. McCarthy went on in '52 to win a smashing victory in the Wisconsin primaries and a bare victory in the subsequent election. Benton, against whom McCarthy campaigned in Connecticut, was defeated by 40,000 votes. The Benton collapse signaled the end of any effective anti-McCarthy movements for a long time to come.

Senators and members of the executive had learned only too well that those who opposed Joe were verbally tarred and feathered and ultimately suffered political extinction.

During the 1952 campaign the Senator became the unofficial hatchet man of the Republican Party. He learned, moreover, how to play to mass credulity and mass hysteria—lessons that were to stand him in good stead at the height of his career in '53 and '54. He began by reiterating his oft-repeated charges against the Roosevelt-Truman administrations. He then lashed out at candidate Stevenson, offering early in the campaign to make a "good American" out of the silver-tongued Democrat by a few licks with "a slippery elm club," the treatment to be administered aboard Adlai's campaign train. By September, the Senator was "checking" the Governor's record. In it he found ". . . proof not of guilt by association but of guilt by collaboration." From then on there was a steady build-up of innuendos to dramatize what was to be McCarthy's greatest speech—the famous television attack on the Democratic candidate delivered in Chicago on October 27th.

The Senator began by announcing that "we are at war tonight." The war, of course, was against subversives in government. Since Stevenson was running on what the Senator called the "Truman-Acheson ticket," he proposed to "fit together the jig-saw puzzle of the man who wants to be President. . . ." The puzzle allegedly would prove Stevenson unfit for high office because of his questionable associations.

The Senator then presented the various pieces of the puzzle beginning with attacks on Stevenson's speech writers and associates. Writer Arthur Schlesinger, Jr., was suspect because both he and his wife had admitted to membership in the Young Communist League. Bernard DeVoto proved equally suspect because he had denounced the sacrosanct FBI as a group of "college trained flatfeet." Archibald MacLeish, the celebrated poet and friend of Stevenson, was under a cloud because of his long association with Communist fronts. But the real highlight of the speech was the famous "barn incident." It went like this:

"While you think, while you may think that there could be no connection between the debonair Democratic candidate and a dilapidated Massachusetts barn, I want to show you a picture of this barn and explain the connection. Here's the outside of a barn——Give me a picture showing the inside of the barn.

"Here's the outside of a barn up at Lee, Massachusetts. Looks like it couldn't house a farmer's cow or goat from the outside. Here's the inside. A beautifully panelled conference room with maps of the Soviet Union."

After interpolating a review of the Hiss case, the Senator went on to say that in the barn was a document "that shows that Alger Hiss and Frank Coe recommended Adlai Stevenson* to the Mont Tremblant conference which was called for the purpose of establishing foreign police—postwar foreign policy in Asia."

The attack then became more personal:

"In Detroit the other day the Democratic candidate made the statement, in condemning McCarthyism, that I had not convicted a single Communist.

"While his statement is technically correct, its implication is viciously untrue in that it was his clear intention to tell his audience that I had not exposed or gotten out of Government a single Communist or fellow-traveler. [sic]

"Of course, I have not convicted a single Communist.

"I am neither a judge, a jury, nor a prosecutor."

Finally, after more typical McCarthyisms, the speech ended in these words:

"How will your vote on Nov. 4 affect my fight? Up until now I have been fighting against tremendous odds—if I am chairman of that committee [the Senate investigating committee]—we will have the power to help Dwight Eisenhower scrub and flush and wash clean the foul mess of corruption and Communism in Washington."

It was a masterpiece of its kind. Twice during the speech the Senator said "Alger—I mean Adlai—" Perhaps the first was a slip-up, but the second occurred toward the end of the speech as recorded in the complete text printed in the New York *Times*. The Senator had been cut off television because of lack of time and did not deliver the final Freudian slip over the air. Again, the reader may have noted the reference to "foreign police" corrected to "foreign policy." Unintentional?

Reaction to the speech was, as usual, mixed. The GOP High Command was carefully noncommittal. The Democrats denounced it as a "typical McCarthy smear." Wechsler, DeVoto, Schlesinger *et al.*, naturally enough, denied subversive pasts. The *Times* reported over 200 phone calls and telegrams from vox populi which, without exception, were opposed to the speech. One man, when asked to wait for a line during the height of the rush said, "I will gladly wait an hour to say

---

* The Senator failed to point out that Stevenson was one of a number of individuals mentioned in the "document" as possible conferees.

what I have to say." Such was the power of the Senator in the fall of 1952.

Nineteen hundred and fifty-three was McCarthy's greatest year. Concomitantly it marked the height of the hysteria. Fortified by his re-election and given the most powerful post of his career, the chairmanship of the Permanent Investigations Committee, the junior Senator made the Congressional investigation the most feared and hated weapon in the annals of American politics. His targets were no longer defeated New Dealers and individuals employed in the State Department but leader-of-the-team Eisenhower, the United States Information Service, organized religion, the Foreign Operations Administration and, eventually, the United States Army. His committee, usurping the rights of the executive, "negotiated" with Greek ship owners who had been carrying cargo to Communist China. In short, the Senator became a symbol of power unlimited.

During the height of the hysteria, in 1953, McCarthyism began to permeate every department of thought. College professors openly admitted their fear of speaking freely in their classes lest they be subjected to an inquisition. The drama publisher, Samuel French, announced a contest in which the sponsor reserved the right to declare any writer ineligible if he became involved in a political controversy. Scientists were advised by Dr. Einstein to resort to noncooperation in the spirit of Mahatma Gandhi if hailed before Congressional committees. A member of the State Textbook Commission in Indiana charged that, "There is a Communist directive in education now to stress the story of Robin Hood. They want to stress it because he robbed the rich and gave to the poor." College students, in answer to the attack, launched a Green Feather movement in support of the legendary hero of Sherwood Forest. A psychiatrist in Chicago announced that one of his patients was under the delusion that he was G. David Schine. In the confusion of name-calling around the Capitol, both the newspaper reporters assigned to McCarthy and the Senator's troupe of twenty assistants were indiscriminately known as the "Goon Squad." *Common Sense*, published by Conde McGinley, one of the nation's leading racists, asked God to "Bless this man" [McCarthy] for taking the "lid off the sewer." The object of the paper's solicitude announced that the Eisenhower administration represented the twenty-first year of treason. All, it seemed, was lost.

The first of his famous investigations that year was directed at the State Department's United States Information Service. McCarthy, following the "team" concept of the new administration, began by acquiring a staff, two of whom eventually ran the Senator a close race in sowing the seeds of confusion and capturing headlines. First, there was Roy M. Cohn, an aggressive young lawyer from New York, whom the Senator appointed Chief Counsel to the subcommittee. Cohn had a hand in the conviction of Julius and Ethel Rosenberg, the atom spies, and had also taken part in the trial of the thirteen Communists convicted of conspiring to overthrow the government. In addition, he had had a role in the ordeals of Professor Lattimore following the McCarran hearings. With such a formidable record of Red-hunting, the young counselor came well recommended. Not so well recommended was G. David Schine, who, as the scion of the Schine Hotel family, disported in Cadillacs at Harvard University, served as a press agent for the Vaughn Monroe orchestra, and had by his own unaided efforts built up an enormous cigar collection in a private museum. Among his more intellectual activities was the fathering of a six-page pamphlet entitled *Definition of Communism*. This definitive work was printed by the thousands and deposited in the manner of Gideon Bibles in rooms of his father's hotels. The document, it might be noted, contained six gross mistakes in historical facts and interpretation, one for each of its six pages.

With this improbable combination the Senator laid siege to the "Voice of America," the radio branch of the State Department's Information Service. The inevitable public hearings began on February 16, 1953, and continued until March 19. For some days prior to the first hearings, the team of McCarthy, Cohn and Schine built up an appalling picture of subversion, espionage and Communist-inspired waste in the Voice. Essentially, four separate charges were levied at the broadcasting agency. First, that two giant radio transmitters, Baker East, to be located on Cape Hatteras, and Baker West, to be at Seattle, Washington, were liberately planned for such locations so as to render them ineffective, with an estimated waste in public revenue of $18,000,000. Second, that the Voice's broadcasts to Latin America showed a "pattern" betraying "sinister" influences that were suppressing anti-Communist propaganda in the broadcasting scripts. Third, the Hebrew language broadcasts had, the triumvirate alleged, been canceled as part of a "pattern" which gave aid and comfort to the Communist cause in Asia. Fourth, the head of the Voice's religious programs was identified as an atheist —atheists, of course, being Communists by definition.

The triumvirate, perhaps inadvertently, perhaps deliberately, had, in fact, picked a weak spot in the State Department. The Voice operated under serious handicaps from the very beginning. Many of its employees had been transferred from the

156

old Office of War Information without proper security clearance. As a result, some had dubious political pasts. Moreover, the whole concept of a propaganda agency was a novel idea in the United States, and because of wartime connotations, anything associated with propaganda carried an unpleasant aura. Finally, the agency had to justify its necessarily heavy expenditures to Congress once each year—a process that is difficult to accomplish in the case of a propaganda agency because it is almost impossible to evaluate objectively the effects of *any* type of psychological warfare. To make matters worse, a number of terrified employees formed a "Loyal American Underground" whose members fed the Senator information and denounced their colleagues to the subcommittee in the Schine suite at the Waldorf Towers, which had become the temporary offices of the McCarthy team. Eventually, the Underground spread beyond the Voice to people in the State Department, to the presumably top-secret FBI and to other government agencies. Giving "information" became so popular that Stuart Symington, the "sanctimonious Stu" of the Army-McCarthy hearings, was led to observe that the government was becoming "a bloody sieve."

The hearings followed the now familiar pattern. Conflicting "expert" opinion was educed from witnesses on both sides; no Communists were exposed; no evidence of willful waste could be proved; the "atheist" was no atheist after all but a true Christian—in short, the result was inconclusive as far as establishing proof of the charges of subversion was concerned. However, there was nothing inconclusive about the destruction of the Voice. The hysteria created among the agency's personnel brought about its defeat. It was a triumph of the Fifth Column. In the end Baker East and Baker West were never built. The cancellation of the contract resulted in a loss of eight million dollars. Yet in spite of all this bluster no formal charges were ever filed with the Attorney General against any of the Voice's personnel.

With the destruction of the Voice, McCarthy moved on to greener pastures. He sent his "Katzenjammer Kids," Cohn and Schine, on a ten-day whirlwind tour of Europe presumably to investigate overseas libraries under the jurisdiction of the State Department. Excluding traveling time, the two spent about 40 hours in Paris, 16 in Bonn, 20 in Berlin, 60 in Munich, 19 in Frankfurt, 40 in Vienna, 23 in Belgrade, 24 in Athens, a little over 20 in Rome and 6 in London. Questioned closely by newsmen and agency heads as to the purpose of their speedy safari, the Senate's boys gave varying accounts. Sometimes it was inefficiency, sometimes mismanagement, other times subversion. In Rome the most curious reason of all for the $8,500 trip came out. They were trying to determine how much tax money had been spent "in putting across the Truman Administration in the Old World."

Their personal capers, their endless but empty press conferences, and their cloak-and-dagger methods made them the laughing stock of Europe. Richard H. Rovere made a study of their Odyssey shortly afterwards which was published in the July 21, 1953 issue of the *Reporter*. He noted that a news story got widely circulated to the effect that Mr. Schine chased Mr. Cohn around a hotel lobby belaboring him with a rolled up magazine. Mr. Cohn labeled the story "a pack of lies . . . so fantastic it is really amusing." In the Hotel Excelsior in Munich they asked for adjoining but noncommunicating rooms, explaining to the bewildered hotel clerk that they did not work for the State Department.

They interviewed European wandering minstrels, cashiered spys and American embassy officials. They strolled through overseas libraries, sometimes barely glancing at the shelves. They were followed about by a squadron of reporters large enough, according to Rovere, to be worthy of "Kings, Presidents, Prime Ministers, and Rita Hayworth."

The result of the high-velocity hegira was precisely nil. No report of the investigations was ever made public; only a few scattered references to the trip came up during the subcommittee hearings. And, as usual, no Communists were uncovered. Its purpose, Rovere concluded, was simply catch-as-catch-can harassment of the administration.

Meanwhile, back home, the Senator was conducting public hearings anent the "appalling infiltration" of the State Department's overseas libraries by Communist personnel and pro-Communist literature. He hailed the authors of books on the shelves of overseas libraries before the committee. A number of the writers with pink pasts invoked the protection of the Fifth Amendment. Ignoring the fact that the political views of the author had nothing to do with a book's selection, the Senator was able to create the impression that such books had been deliberately selected *because* of their author's pro-Communist views.

Such an impression was strengthened when Karl Baarslag, formerly a member of the American Legions' National Americanism Commission testified that he failed to find the *American Legion Magazine*, the *Freeman* or the *National Republic* in either the Paris or Bonn libraries. "There were no anti-Communist magazines," he concluded. This was difficult to believe in view of the fact that the libraries subscribed to 520 publications, most of which were conservative and strongly anti-Communist. It is, perhaps, significant that Baarslag subsequently became a member of the McCarthy team.

Similarly, Miss Utley, the "me-too" witness, testified that she found it difficult to find anti-Communist books in the European libraries, whereas pro-Communist books were readily available.

With 10 pages of testimony from Baarslag and 6 from Miss Utley, plus 496 pages largely focused on alleged Communist or pro-Communist authors, who in the public mind were frequently confused with State Department employees, the hysteria reached its zenith. The State Department began to issue directives reversing the criterion of selection on the basis of content rather than the author's political views. Directive after directive confused the harassed librarians and officials in the overseas libraries. And, in June, a real Middle Ages-style book burning came to light. In a front-page story on June 16th the New York *Times* headlined the fiery affair as follows:

SOME BOOKS LITERALLY BURNED AFTER INQUIRY, DULLES REPORTS

In the body of the story it was reported that "John Foster Dulles, the Secretary of State, disclosed today that there had been a literal though small-scale burning of books after Congressional investigations as his department had moved to rid the shelves of its Information Service libraries abroad of works by Communist authors." Dulles, the report added, set the number of incinerated volumes at eleven.

A slight counterreaction set in as the real meaning of the book burning began to penetrate officialdom. President Eisenhower, at Dartmouth College for the commencement exercises, said, in earning his honorary degree, "Don't join the bookburners." About two weeks later he wrote the American Library Association, in convention assembled at Los Angeles, that only "zealots" with more "wrath than wisdom" sought to suppress information and ideas. With such support from the captain of the Republican team, the State Department again issued a new directive (its eleventh) reverting to its original stand to judge books by the contents rather than their authors' political convictions. The newly found courage of the Department was such that the directive termed book burning a "wicked symbolic act."

As the tide of opinion began to turn against McCarthy and his team, and as it became apparent that no Communists were employed by the Agency, the Senator managed to keep in the headlines by threatening to "investigate" anyone and everyone who crossed his path. Moreover, two unexpected developments kept the hysterical pot boiling.

The first involved Dr. Nathan Pusey, a little-known educational figure who was suddenly elevated to headline stature when he was appointed to the presidency of the grandfather of the Ivy League, Harvard University. Because Dr. Pusey was formerly a fellow townsman of the Senator's, the latter was asked for an opinion on the merits of the appointment. McCarthy replied, "I do not think Dr. Pusey is or has been a member of the Communist party." Since this backhanded exoneration of the recently honored Pusey left considerable latitude as to his political views, McCarthy went on to explain that Pusey "could well be compared to the undercover Communist who slaps at the Communist Party in general terms, cusses out the thoroughly well-known Communist, and then directs his energy toward attempting to destroy those who are really hurting the Communist party by digging out the dangerous undercover members of the party, who parade as loyal to the country which their conspiracy is attempting to destroy. What motivates Pusey I have no way of knowing. He is what could best be described as a rabid anti, anti-Communist."

This ferocious attack on Dr. Pusey was ill-taken, even by many of the Senator's long-time supporters. The uncalled-for assault drew especially strong criticism from Wisconsin newspapers, some of which had previously supported the Senator's crusade. Harvard University and Dr. Pusey remained silent. The enraged Senator subsequently referred to the University as a "sanctuary" for Communists. It might be noted that Harvard, along with other universities whose large endowments made them secure from the hysteria, refused to dismiss professors (most of whom were parlor pinks from the twenties and thirties) for invoking the Fifth Amendment. On the other hand, the presidents of many small private colleges and of the state-supported universities turned to jelly at the approach of the various Congressional committees that were seeking Communists during the height of the mania, and managed to dismiss allegedly subversive faculty members on one pretext or other.

The second instance which took place during the summer of 1953 that earned McCarthy headlines not of his own making was an attack on the reverend clergy by Dr. J. B. Matthews, another ex-wandering minstrel, a one-time Methodist missionary, who subsequently almost wrecked the McCarthy apparatus when he was appointed executive director of the Subcommittee on Investigations.

Dr. Matthews, following his conversion from fellow-traveling, became a violent anti-Communist. During the McCarthy furor, the enlightened Matthews used his position as a writer for *Mercury Magazine* to strike out at various professional groups which, he charged, were infiltrated by Communists. In fact, the *Mercury* made articles on Communist infiltration its special business that year. American doctors were infiltrated by Kremlin-directed "medicine men" who could be forced to perform illegal operations whose sinister nature, for reasons of delicacy, was not clearly brought out. Collegiate professorial ranks were hopelessly undermined, textbooks infiltrated, the administrators "powerless to punish" Fifth Amendment professors, and the principles of academic freedom of the American Association of University Professors "infused with hopeless ignorance." But according to the Matthews article of July, 1953, "The largest single group supporting the Communist apparatus in the United States today is composed of Protestant clergymen." So benighted were the clergy, Matthews went on, that they outnumbered the professors two to one in supporting the Communist cause as "party members, espionage agents, party-line adherents and unwitting dupes."

Matthews' awesome allegations were supported by authoritative statements made by Earl Browder, the great American Communist, and J. Edgar Hoover*—a pair of strange bedfellows, indeed! Matthews also thought it significant that many men of the cloth had either aligned themselves with the World Peace Offensive or had given it tacit approval. The Offensive was said by Matthews to be "Communist-instigated" according to the Congressional Committee on Un-American Activities.

A few days prior to the appearance of the Matthews article, the Senator's subcommittee had received notice of Matthews' appointment as its executive director. When the story of the *Mercury* article appeared in the newspapers, developments broke swiftly and with explosive force. The three Democratic members of the subcommittee, Senators Jackson, McClelland and Symington, denounced the article as a "shocking and unwarranted attack against the American clergy." They called on their chairman to convene the committee for "appropriate action." Protests came from

---

* What Hoover, a militant anti-Communist, actually said was: "I confess to a real apprehension so long as Communists are able to secure ministers of the Gospel to promote their evil work and espouse a cause that is alien to the religion of Christ and Judaism."

all over the country—from church leaders, educators, citizens, and clergymen. The three national co-chairmen of the Commission on Religious Organizations of the National Conference of Christians and Jews made a formal protest to President Eisenhower. Their communiqué alleged that "The sweeping attack on the loyalty of Protestant clergymen . . . is unjustified and unwarranted." Such wholesale condemnation, they added, could only "weaken the greatest American bulwark against atheistic materialism and communism." The President agreed with the Commission of Clergymen but took no specific action.

Meanwhile the subcommitte convened, and on a party-line vote of 4-3 granted the Senator sole authority to hire and fire staff members. The three Democrats resigned, announcing that they had been put in the impossible position of having to bear the responsibility of the Committee's activities without any "voice, right or authority." McCarthy, in accepting the resignations, replied in these not entirely relevant words: "If they don't want to take part in uncovering the graft and corruption of the old Truman-Acheson Administration, they are, of course, entitled to refuse." Precisely what this had to do with the Matthews issue was not made clear by the Senator.

After further deliberation, McCarthy—no doubt aware of the partisan make-up of the Committee—asked the Democrats to return to the fold. Again they refused, whereupon the Senator once more denounced the Truman-Acheson Administration and referred to the absent Democrats as "small, irresponsible boys."

Ultimately Matthews was forced to resign as a result of the continuing furor over his article; and after six months of wrangling, the Democrats finally returned to the subcommittee, but only after McCarthy surrendered his totalitarian powers over committee staff members. The Democrats also reserved the right to employ counsel. Perhaps they were less than satisfied with Mr. Cohn and his able assistant, Mr. Schine.

By the time the Matthews affair was leaving the headlines, the Senator had married his former secretary, Miss Jean F. Kerr, and was enjoying a honeymoon in the British West Indies. Unfortunately for the nuptial festivities, the Associated Press, on October 9, 1953, reported that a member of McCarthy's staff had uncovered "security leaks" in the U.S. Army's Signal Corps installation at Fort Monmouth, New Jersey. The Senator cut short his honeymoon and rushed back to take charge of the hysteria. On the 14th of October he began the first of a long series of "briefings" to newsmen on information he claimed was being extracted from reluctant witnesses at the Fort during closed hearings. To these we shall return presently.

At the same time that the Monmouth espionage situation was developing, G. David Schine, the Committee's expert on Communism, faced his own personal call to arms in the form of a draft notice. The Senator inquired of Major General Miles Reber, then Chief of Legislative Liaison for the Army, whether a direct Commission could be arranged for Schine to relieve him from the onerous duties of a private. Schine was invited to apply for a commission, but within three weeks the Army found him unqualified to be an officer and gentleman, by Act of Congress at any rate. After three more months of machinations (largely on Mr. Cohn's part) to keep Schine out of the Army's rear ranks, he was inducted as a private no November 3, 1953, and assigned to Fort Dix, New Jersey, for basic training. The failure to find favor for Schine among the Army brass was destined to have far-reaching effects on the current Monmouth "hearings," the subsequent Camp Kilmer affair, and the final great drama of the "Trial by Television" which took place the following year.

Meanwhile, back at Monmouth, McCarthy went on with his Star Chamber proceedings. For weeks witnesses trooped in and out. Some were Monmouth employees, some former employees, and some were not employees at all but persons working for firms under subcontract to the Signal Corps. Some witnesses, according to McCarthy, had pleaded the Fifth Amendment. Some had not. "Documents"—always a favorite subject with the Senator had disappeared only to reappear in Communist East Germany. A reluctant witness "broke down" and was going to expose a "spy ring." In short, the "pattern" was one of "espionage." Indeed, the Senator became enamoured with the "espionage" theme during his Monmouth days. In releases to the press on various occasions he worked the sinister term for all it was worth. "It has all the earmarks of extremely dangerous espionage." Again, "It appears to be a case of current espionage of an extremely dangerous nature." And, "It definitely involves espionage . . ." Finally, "We have uncovered very, very current espionage."

Despite the Senator's assurance, no espionage agents were found at Monmouth. In fact, neither the McCarthy investigations nor the Army's own inquiries turned up subversive activities of any kind. The report of the classified documents allegedly in Russian hands was ultimately traced to a technician evidently suffering from delusions of grandeur who boasted without foundation that "the Russians could get anything out of Monmouth." Needless to say the hearings petered out, and the Senator moved on to fresh fields. First, he pounced on the General Electric Company at Schenectady and later re-engaged the Army at Camp Kilmer. Of the two, the Camp Kilmer affair proved to be the more sensational.

The Army had admittedly promoted a dentist, Major Irving Peress, after the latter had been recommended for discharge on the grounds that he had refused to answer loyalty questions. The headlines quoting the Senator screamed "Who Promoted Peress?" and during January of 1954, McCarthy undertook an investigation to find out for himself.

Peress was hailed before the Committee, but the alarmed dentist again invoked the Fifth Amendment. McCarthy thereupon requested the Army to hold the Major for court-martial. Peress received an honorable discharge the following day. Beside himself with rage, the Senator summoned Brigadier General Zwicker to answer questions concerning the processing of the Peress case. Zwicker replied that a Presidential order forbade Army officers to reveal such information. The Senator shouted in reply, "You are a disgrace to the uniform. You're shielding Communist conspirators. You are going to be put on public display next Tuesday. You're not fit to be an officer. You're ignorant."

Robert Ten Broeck Stevens, Secretary of the Army, instructed Gen. Zwicker to ignore McCarthy's summons for the Tuesday session. He could not "permit the loyal officers of our Armed Forces to [undergo] such treatment." Four days later, at a luncheon with McCarthy and other committee members, the Secretary capitulated and agreed to withdraw his ban. The *Times* of London called the abdication of Stevens "the surrender of the American Army."

Gen. Eisenhower, appalled at the adverse public reaction to the Stevens collapse, gave approval to a statement in which the beleagured Secretary claimed not to have retreated from his principles. Thus shored up by the President, he promised not to accede to the "browbeating or humiliation of Army personnel." The Senator struck back by accusing Stevens of making "a completely false statement."

The degrading spectacle of the Zwicker-Stevens affair resulted in a front-page sensation throughout the world. Pro-McCarthyites and anti-McCarthyites joined forces in condemning the Senator's abuse of Zwicker and his attempt to overreach the Commander-in-Chief himself. The Chicago *Tribune* commented that he had become "an avenging angel" instead of an investigator. H. V. Kaltenborn, previously a defender of McCarthy, found it impossible to stomach the Senator any longer. "Power," said the venerable old commentator, "has corrupted him." Leonard Hall, chairman of the GOP National Committee and one-time McCarthyite, disassociated himself from the Senator and all his works. The President denounced his "disregard of the standards of fair play." The Senator tried to roll with the barrage of punches by referring to the furor as a "tempest in a teapot," as "mudslinging" and the work of "left-wing elements of the press and radio."

But with the coming of spring, the Senator's time was running out. Both in his home state of Wisconsin and in Washington the hysterical fear of McCarthy and McCarthyism was slowly ebbing. In Wisconsin, the famous "Joe Must Go" recall movement spearheaded the attack on the homefront. The indigenous effort to unseat the Senator was launched by Leroy Gore, a fifty year-old editor and publisher of the *Sauk-Prairie-Star* in Sauk City, Wisconsin. Gore initiated the recall petition in an editorial in his paper giving as his grounds that McCarthy had blackmailed Eisenhower and undermined his leadership, ruined the U.S. Army and ignored a Wisconsin dairy crisis. In the same editorial he suggested that McCarthy resign from the Senate and take up television wrestling. The campaign trademark for the recall movement was a picture of the Senator riding through a forest of Texas oil wells in a Cadillac.

The petition to recall did not succeed but was productive of considerable fireworks. On the streets of Wisconsin petitioners were spit at, called unprintable names, threatened with violence and had their cars damaged. Gore was alleged to be one of the "Red rats" and "dirty homosexuals" who made a practice of attacking the Senator. A "Give the Door to Gore" counteroffensive was started by a restaurateur whose lucrative avocation was mink-coat farming. Nevertheless, despite the opposition, the petitioners collected over 400,000 signatures, enough for a recall; but some 30,000 signatures had to be invalidated. If the recall movement had succeeded, McCarthy might well have ignored it with the odd result that it would have been up to the Senate to unseat him or, as an alternative, to have three Senators from Wisconsin following the special election with would have resulted from recall. As it turned out, the Senate had its own ideas on how to deal with the junior Senator from the Dairy State. But first he was to enjoy one last glorious round in the greatest television show on earth.

The Army-McCarthy hearings began after the Army, in a report prepared for some members of Congress and "leaked" to the press, charged that members of the Senator's staff had threatened "to wreck the Army" unless special treatment was given to their former associate and one-time expert on Communism, Pvt. Schine. McCarthy, in a counterblast, said that the Army tried to "blackmail" him into calling off his investigations of military installations. Since mediation appeared out of the question, the Senate Investigating Subcommittee voted to air the controversy in open hearings; and, after each party filed formal charges, the great debate was on.

The scene was the Senate Caucus Room, which, on the morning of April 22, 1954, resembled a television studio more than a legislative chamber. At 1 a.m., eight hundred people crowded into the room—the principals, Senators and their relatives, reporters, cameramen, Capitol policemen and bodyguards assigned by the friendly FBI to protect the Senator from possible assassination. When the "on-the-air" lights on the cameras glowed red, Senator Mundt, the chairman of the subcommittee for the investigation, rapped his gavel and delivered a precis of the charges and countercharges. He also promised that the hearings would be conducted "with a maximum degree of dignity, firmness and thoroughness." Ray Jenkins, the lawyer from Tennessee and counsel for the subcommittee, was then invited to call his first witness. But as Jenkins began to speak, the Senator's voice rang out loud and clear: "A point of order, Mr. Chairman; may I raise a point of order?"

The Senator, it seemed, objected to the charges being identified with the Army as a whole. Instead he felt they should be filed by the three civilians concerned, Stevens, Hensel and Adams. Eventually the chairman, Senator Mundt, ruled in favor of McCarthy. The Senator had found not only a battle cry but a successful formula for handling Chairman Mundt, and "point of order" reverberated across the nation for weeks to come.

When the initial skirmishes had crystallized into hard battle, it became apparent that Pvt. Schine had not taken kindly to life in the Army's rear ranks. He had been assigned to Company K at Fort Dix for basic training and marched off on the wrong foot by attempting to bribe his company commander. Testimony by Army personnel showed that the private had suggested that should the commander wish "to make a little trip to Florida he knew a Colonel. . . ." Moreover, the influential private had sought to evade kitchen-police duty, had obtained many passes on the plea of committee business, and generally engaged in behavior uncharacteristic of Army privates.

The military also charged that Mr. Cohn did, by means of "threats and abusive language," seek special treatment for Pvt. Schine. It was further alleged by the Army that the Senator's aides promised by implication to call off their investigative hounds if the Private could be given a special New York assignment where he could continue his valuable work with the subcommittee. (And, no doubt, live in Levantine luxury at the Waldorf.)

In response, the McCarthy team alleged that Schine would never have been drafted in the first place if the investigations at Monmouth had been called off. The Private, in McCarthy's words, had been a "hostage"; and he further charged that, as long as Schine was in the Army, the Committee would continue to be blackmailed and frustrated in its investigations.

As the days went on, 20,000,000 Americans found themselves fascinated by the show of the century. It had everything. First there was the senator himself—supposedly a witness but in reality the leading actor in the drama. The supporting role among the Senator's forces fell to Cohn, who could be angelic as a witness but sharp as a viper when he directed a question through counsel. Above all there was the gentle Welch, whose courteous language and pixie-like humor baffled and angered the Senator to the point of distraction—and ultimately, to disaster. There were others whose names became household words—John Adams, Counselor to the Department of the Army and the alleged target of Cohn's siege artillery in behalf of Pvt. Schine—Jenkins, Welch's lantern-jawed counterpart on the Committee's side—Francis Carr, the ex-FBI man who became executive director of the McCarthy team after the Rev. Matthews had to be cashiered. And among the Senators, Stuart Symington, or "Sanctimonious Stu," proved worthy of the dramatics that lay ahead.

As the days went on, 20,000,000 Americans watched, fascinated, as the drama unfolded—sometimes humorous, sometimes tragic, sometimes stormy, but never dull. In the early days of the hearings, the tragedy of a once proud Army browbeaten and conciliatory came out in painful passages such as this—

ADAMS. A great part of the luncheon was given over to conversation with reference to Schine. Mr. Carr stated to me as he had on numerous other occasions that he felt that I should understand that as long as the assignment for Schine was not satisfactory to Mr. Cohn the Army was in for continued trouble . . . He had no personal interest in Schine. He made that clear. But if he could give me advice in a friendly way his advice would be: You take care of this matter and we will get these investigations off your neck.

167

Then there were the frequent, angry interruptions by Senator McCarthy—

MCCARTHY: Mr. Chairman.

MUNDT: Do you have a point of order?

MCCARTHY: Call it a point of order or call it what you may, when counsel for Mr. Stevens and Mr. Hensel [Struve Hensel, counsel for the Department of Defense] and Mr. Adams makes a statement . . . do I have a right to correct it or do we find halfway through my statement that Mr. Welch should not have made his statement and therefore I cannot point out that he was lying?

And the gentle humor of Mr. Welch—

WELCH: Mr. Cohn, I assume you would like it understood that although I sit at the same table, I am not your counsel.

COHN: There is not a statement that has been made at this hearing with which I am in more complete agreement . . . Roy Cohn is here speaking for Roy Cohn, to give the facts. I have no counsel and I feel the need of none.

WELCH: In all modesty, sir, I am content that it should appear from my end that I am not your counsel.

And, toward the end, the dramatic and fascinatingly horrible moment when the Senator reached the depths of his career—

WELCH: Mr. Cohn, if I told you now that we had a bad situation at Monmouth, you'd want to cure it by sundown if you could, wouldn't you?

COHN: Yes, sir.

WELCH: May I add my small voice, sir, and say whenever you know about a subversive or a Communist or a spy, please hurry! Will you remember these words?

MCCARTHY: Mr. Chairman, in view of that question——

MUNDT: Have you a point of order?

MCCARTHY: Not exactly, Mr. Chairman, but in view of Mr. Welch's request that the information be given once we know of anyone who might be performing any work for the Communist Party, I think we should tell him that he has in his law firm a young man named Fisher . . . who has been for a number of years a member of an organization which was named, oh years and years ago, as the legal bulwark of the Communist Party, an organization which always swings to the defense of anyone who dares to expose Communists. I certainly assume that Mr. Welch did not know of this young man at the time he recommended him as the assistant counsel for this committee, but he has such terror and such a great desire to know where anyone is located who may be serving the Communist cause. . . . Knowing that, Mr. Welch, I just felt that I had a duty to respond to your urgent request that before sundown, when we know of anyone serving the Communist cause we let the agency know. . . . I have hesitated about bringing that up, but I have been rather bored with your phony requests to Mr. Cohn here that he personally get every Communist out of government before sundown. Therefore we will give you the information about the young man in your own organization. I am not asking you at this time to explain why you tried to foist him on this committee. Whether you knew he was a member of that Communist organization or not I don't know. I assume you did not, Mr. Welch, because I get the impression that while you are quite an actor, you play for a laugh, I don't think you have any conception of the danger of the Communist Party. I don't think you would ever knowingly aid the Communist cause. I think you are unknowingly aiding it when you try to burlesque this hearing in which we are trying to bring out the facts, however. . . .

WELCH: Mr. Chairman, under these circumstances I must have something approaching a personal privilege.

MUNDT: You may have it, sir. It will not be taken out of your time.

WELCH: Senator McCarthy, I did not know—(McCarthy had turned to speak to an assistant, Jim Juliana, and was apparently paying no attention to Mr. Welch) Senator, sometimes you say, "May I have your attention?"

McCARTHY: I am listening to you. I can listen with one ear.

WELCH: This time I want you to listen with both.

McCARTHY: Yes.

WELCH: Senator McCarthy, I think until this moment—(Again McCarthy turned to Juliana and in audible tones asked him to get the news story on Fisher so that it could be put into the record). You won't need anything in the record when I have finished telling you this. Until this moment, Senator, I think I never really gauged your cruelty or your recklessness. Fred Fisher is a young man who went to the Harvard Law School and came into my firm and is starting what looks to be a brilliant career with us.

When I decided to work for this committee I asked Jim St. Clair, who sits on my right, to be my first assistant. I said to Jim, "Pick somebody in the firm who works under you that you would like." He chose Fred Fisher and they came down on an afternoon plane. That night, when we had taken a little stab at trying to see what the case was about, Fred Fisher and Jim St. Clair and I went to dinner together. I then said to these two young men, "Boys, I don't know anything about you except that I have always liked you, but if there is anything funny in the life of either one of you that would hurt anybody in this case you speak up quick."

Fred Fisher said, "Mr. Welch, when I was in law school and for a period of months thereafter I belonged to the Lawyers' Guild . . ." I said, "Fred, I just don't think I am going to ask you to work on the case. If I do one of these days that will come out and go over national television and it will just hurt like the dickens."

So, Senator, I asked him to go back to Boston. Little did I dream you could be so reckless and so cruel as to do an injury to that lad. It is true he is still with Hale and Dorr. It is true that he will continue to be with Hale and Dorr. It is, I regret to say, equally true that I fear he shall always bear a scar needlessly inflicted by you. If it were in my power to forgive you for your reckless cruelty I would do so. I like to think that I am a gentle man, but your forgiveness will have to come from someone other than me.

MCCARTHY: Mr. Chairman.

MUNDT: Senator McCarthy?

MCCARTHY: May I say that Mr. Welch talks about this being cruel and reckless. He was just baiting Mr. Cohn, here for hours, requesting that Mr. Cohn, before sundown, get out of any department of Government anyone who is serving the Communist cause.

I just give this man's record, and I want to say, Mr. Welch, that it has been labeled long before he became a member, as early as 1944——

WELCH: Senator, may we not drop this? We know he belonged to the Lawyers' Guild, and Mr. Cohn nods his head at me. I did you, I think, no personal injury, Mr. Cohn.

COHN: No, sir.

WELCH: I meant to do you no personal injury and if I did I beg your pardon. Let us not assassinate this lad further, Senator. You have done enough. Have you no sense of decency, sir? At long last? Have you left no sense of decency? [Again McCarthy tried to interrupt.] Mr. McCarthy, I will not discuss this with you further. You have sat within six feet of me and could have asked me about Fred Fisher. You have brought it out. If there is a God in heaven it will do neither you nor your cause any good. I will not discuss it further. I will not ask Mr. Cohn any more questions. You, Mr. Chairman, may, if you will, call the next witness.

That day, when the hearings had ended, the Senator found it difficult to understand why no one had a kind look or a kind word for him. He spread his hands and said, "What did I do?" There was no one who could answer him.

At last, on June 17, the hearings ended—inconclusively, as all previous hearings had—yet this time with a difference. The mischief wreaked by the McCarthy team was exposed for all America to see. The Senator's fanaticism and paranoiac personality were brought home to the American people as they had never been before. And, of greatest importance, an effective opposition was formed. In the Senate, Ralph Flanders, who, in scorn, said of McCarthy, "He dons his warpaint. He goes into his war dance. He emits his war whoops. He goes forth to battle and proudly returns with the scalp of a pink Army dentist . . ." introduced a resolution of censure on July 30, 1954. The Senate, after considerable discussion, voted overwhelmingly to conduct an investigation. The Resolution stated: *"Resolved,* that the conduct of the Senator from Wisconsin, Mr. McCarthy, is unbecoming a member of the United States Senate, is contrary to Senatorial traditions, and tends to bring the Senate into disrepute."

The battle was finally joined. There was no Cohn to manufacture legal wizardry, no Schine to provide comic relief, no Mundt for the Senator to browbeat with points of order. The austere Arthur Watkins (Rep. Utah) conducted the hearings in a judicial manner and in a sober atmosphere—conditions which McCarthy could neither understand nor survive. The Senator was condemned by the Watkins' Committee, which the master of invective had called the "involuntary handmaiden" and "involuntary agent" of the Communist Party.

The condemned, meanwhile, had to be hospitalized, and Senate debate on the recommendation to censure had to be put off. The reason for his hospitalizaton was not entirely clear. One story had it that he was suffering from bursitis. But another, originating in Wisconsin, reported that the Senator's elbow had been violently shoved into a glass-topped table at a birthday rally by an admirer with an overly powerful handshake. However, during the delay the Senator was not without support. In New York a group calling themselves the Ten Million Americans Mobilizing for Social Justice undertook to get 10,000,000 signatures protesting censure. At the same time, the Ten Million denounced the findings of the Watkins Committee as "incredible" and the result of "subversive influences" in the Senate.

As the time for the Senate to reconvene drew near, the tempo of pro- and anti-censure movements picked up sharply. A giant rally was held on November 29th at Madison Square Garden. Thirteen thousand McCarthyites attended to hear speeches by Roy Cohn, Mrs. McCarthy and others. Roy alleged that "If the Senate votes to censure it will be committing the blackest act in our whole history." He was wildly cheered. The Senator, unable to be present, was applauded everytime his name was mentioned. So were Gen. MacArthur, Mr. Cohn, and Westbrook Pegler.

On the floor of the Garden, which resembled a political convention, various supporters bore placards supporting Joe and denouncing the censure motion. One Anton Coreth of Larchmont, N. Y., who had been active in the America First movement before the war, carried a sign reading, "Senator Joe McCarthy for President of our great Christian nation in 1956. Keep it Christian in the interest of America First."

Less sure of themselves were three delegates who were Catholic priests from the Passionist Order. When one was asked if he had signed the petition he replied, "I certainly did and plenty of us did. Aren't we American citizens?"

Not all present were favorably disposed toward the Senator, however. Lisa Larsen, a *Time* photographer, was evicted for snapping not entirely flattering photographs of the orgies. As she was being led out, a man shouted "Hang the Communist."

While the New York committee was succoring the Senator in his hour of trial a group of students at Harvard managed to get 3,000 signatures on a pro-censure motion. Evidently the Senator's jibes at the University were returning in the fashion of bread cast upon the waters.

On December 2nd, the great debate was finally held. It was productive of considerable invective, windy oratory, party-line maneuvering to get the terms of the censure softened, and, as is inevitable on all solemn occasions, humor. Just before the debate was scheduled to take place, a huge armored truck arrived in front of the Senate. Guards with drawn horse pistols dismounted from the vehicle and conveyed the signatures collected by the Ten Million into the building for presentation to Vice President Nixon. Because of the firearms, the Capitol police took a dim view of the proceedings, and when the matter was brought to the attention of the Senate, an "investigation" was ordered. The number of signatures, incidentally, was a little over a million. During the debate on the floor of the Senate, the Senator said little, leaving his defense to his supporters. He did at one point comment, "Let's get the dirty business over with," and when the vote was in and he stood condemned, he characterized the proceedings as a "circus" and promised now that it was over to get back to the job of "digging Communists out of the government."

But the days of glory were over. The Senator did make

a few attempts to recapture the old spirit and ignite the old fires, but with little effect. His colleagues in the Senate ignored his speeches. The administration no longer sought by devious ways to make peace with him. It was no longer necessary to do so. Newspapermen, once duty-bound to relay his every move back to their editors, now avoided him; the newspaper "goon" squad was disbanded. After four hectic years he was yesterday's news, discredited and defeated.

Senator McCarthy died May 2, 1957 at the age of 47 of a liver ailment, two and one-half years after his Senatorial censure. By one of those strange strokes of irony that make life unpredictable, the Senator was given a state funeral from the Senate Chamber following a solemn pontifical Requiem Mass at St. Matthews Roman Catholic Cathedral. This was the first Senate farewell awarded a departed colleague since William E. Borah of Idaho was so honored in 1940. It was a gesture of forgiveness, and politicians being what they are, a propitiary offering to the gods of guilt. The Senate chaplain, Rev. Frederick Harris, said of him that day, "This fallen warrior through death speaketh calling a nation of free men to be delivered from the complacency of a false security and from regarding those who loudly sound the trumpets of vigilance and alarm as mere disturbers of the peace."

To those words the Senator, if he had heard them, would have surely said, "Amen."

McCarthyism, like the feverish symptoms of an illness, rose and fell with the disease from which it sprang. That disease was fear. In the five years which preceded the Senator's rise to power, the American people were forced to realign their thinking with the swiftly changing course of world events. The comfortable isolationism of the prewar years was gone forever. The Grand Alliance of World War II had crumbled with the collapse of Hitler's armies. Our once great ally, Britain, had been reduced to a second-rate power—exhausted economically and spiritually by the long, hard years in which she had stood alone. Now *we* were alone, and face the potentially greatest enemy the world had ever seen—an enemy with virtually unlimited manpower; and, as developments in the atomic field were all too clearly showing, an enemy with considerable scientific skill. As Hiroshima and Nagasaki had already demonstrated (and as subsequent events have proved beyond possibility of a doubt), scientific skill was the kind needed to win.

In addition to the Russian threat, China had been lost to Communism, bringing over 600,000,000 of the world's people under the Red flag. Much of Eastern Europe had fallen into Soviet hands or had come under Soviet influence. Until the developments in Korea forced a containment policy, it seemed as if the Red specter were spreading over the entire continents of Europe and Asia. To make matters worse, there was a considerable body of opinion in the United States which assigned the blame for this tragic state of affairs on the State Department and the Executive branch. The "conspiracy theory" so ably defended by McCarthy, extreme anti-New Dealers, and the lunatic fringe, held that the Roosevelt and Truman Administrations had sold out the free world to the Soviet Union.

As has been said, strictly domestic developments were such as to increase Americans' fear of Communism rather than dispel it. There was first the minor league Soviet within the State Department that had been feeding classified information to the Kremlin. That its leaders, Hiss, Chambers and Wadleigh were no longer connected with the Department when the McCarthy charges hit the headlines made little difference. These men *had* been working for the Kremlin and *were* connected with the State Department. As has been pointed out, there was nothing intrinsically illogical or even improbable about the Senator's charges of an extensive infiltration. That his methods in attacking alleged subversives were unholy made little difference to a large segment of the American people. In defense of the Senator they pointed out that it was a question of fighting fire with fire. "Groin and eyeball" tactics were good enough for those who employed them.

It cannot be gainsaid that McCarthy the demagogue contributed to the hysteria of the first half of the fifties. But neither the demagogue nor the great humanitarian can flourish in an unfavorable culture medium. The Senator's strength was drawn largely from the rich soil of postwar fear. When the various brush fires had been put out or were dying out, and when it became apparent that the shooting was over, McCarthyism wilted on the vine. The containment policy had, it seemed, stopped the cancerous growth of Communism, at least for the time being.

It had also become apparent that the Senator with all his fuss and furor was more of a mischief-maker than a St. George come lately. McCarthy vs. the State Department was one thing. So long as he belabored the Truman administration he gave aid and comfort to the Republicans and to many Democrats who had "had enough." McCarthy vs. the Army gave aid and comfort to no one. And despite the fact that the Army's civilian leadership pandered to its own worst enemy, the McCarthy team sowed the seeds of its own defeat at Monmouth and Kilmer—seeds that grew into strangling vines under the television klieg lights during the Army-McCarthy hearings. At last the Giant-Killer had drawn too heavily on his own blood bank. The Senatorial censure amounted to little more than flogging the moribund Senator.

There have been demagogues since men first organized into social orders, and there will be demagogues as long as civilizations last. The Senator's place in this Satanic Hall of Fame is assured. But his position in the hierarchy is, as yet, uncertain. From the present perspective, it seems likely that he will take second or even third rank. He did much with what he had—which was little. But had he been a demagogue of shrewder mettle and one less dependent upon what chance threw in his way, he might have won all—even, some thought, the Presidency. There are many to give thanks that he was only a Prince among the Caesars.

11: On the Serious Side

ONE OF THE MOST DRAMATIC and terrifying incidents in George Orwell's *1984* takes place in Oceania's Ministry of Love where the hero, Winston Smith, is being "cured" of his unorthodox ideas. O'Brien, a party functionary, has explained to Smith that in the totalitarian Utopia in which they live party members who succumb to unorthodoxy are, in reality, mentally ill. They are a blot on the perfection of the party and state; consequently, they must be "squeezed empty" of all disaffection and refilled with love and conformity before being vaporized. As part of his treatment, Smith has just been given a dose of electro-shock therapy. O'Brien holds up his hand with the thumb concealed and asks Smith how many fingers he sees, at the same time suggesting that there are five. Smith sees five. It is the beginning of his total capitulation to the will of the party. He can be made to believe that two and two make five, that freedom is slavery, that war is peace.

Orwell's frightening picture of life in the world of the future all too realistically drives home the lesson that modern wars as envisioned by totalitarian states are fought as much on home grounds as they are abroad, using psychological weapons as well as bombs and guns. War for the dictator has become an all-pervasive ideological conflict which never ceases, whose battle grounds are men's minds and whose ultimate aim is absolute control over the human spirit. Whether atomic weapons are used or not in future wars, the real victory will already have been won. Once more——and possibly for the last time——man's tragic history of bloodshed hysteria, credulity and error will have prevailed over reason.

To understand the dynamics of psychological warfare, one must first know the dynamics of human nature, since propaganda or any other psychological technique that fails to take human nature into account cannot be effective. Propaganda, the chief weapon of the cold war, is based on precisely the same psychological processes that are in ascendance in hysteria or in the hypnotic trance. In each of these processes the aim is *to convince the subject by means of suggestion that he ought to believe certain things to be true and behave in accordance with those beliefs.* Just as one cannot make a hypnotized individual do anything of importance that goes contrary to his fundamental nature, so the propagandist cannot contravene the human nature which he seeks to mold to his will. Neither the hypnotist nor the propagandist *creates* needs; rather, both appeal to already existing motives and desires, and on this basis are able to modify beliefs, for we believe largely in accordance with our wishes and desires.

The mainsprings of human action which psychologists call motives seem at first impression to be myriad and beyond comprehension. There are literally thousands of terms in the language which refer to those human wants, needs, desires and emotions which impel us to action. But if we consider only the fundamental human motives, we find that they can be grouped into five simple classes: creature needs, security needs, belongingness, prestige and self-realization. It is to these basic motives that the Communist program is directed.

In order to appreciate the connection between the basic human motives and Communist psychological warfare, let us exemplify the relationship by examining the ultimate in the manipulation of the human mind—brain washing—since brain washing is but an extreme logical extension of cold war propaganda. Our example will be based on the actual methods employed by the Chinese Communists in the Korean conflict. In each case, parallels will be drawn between individual brain washing and the *en masse* technique which is the stock in trade of the propagandist.

Because human motives fall into a hierarchical order beginning with the lower order motives or "animal needs," the first step in brain washing consists in exaggerating such needs by depriving the victim of all creature comforts and putting him on a semistarvation diet. Every human being demands and has a right to food, drink, adequate shelter, sleep and proper medical care. The captive soldier who is being slowly starved to death, who is illclothed and housed, who is allowed insufficient rest, and whose bodily machine is slowly deteriorating, is on the way to capitulating to the will of his captors. Perhaps during the initial stages of the "treatment," when he is "rewarded" with a cigarette or a candy bar for having performed "intelligently" during an interrogation, the captive is deliberately "falling in line" to trick his captors, trying, as it were, to beat them at their own game. But they have tricked him. As General Dean reported in describing his experiences in the hands of the Chinese Communists, the weakened brain after hours of interrogation without sleep becomes unable to discriminate the razor's edge that separates the false from the true. The General, incidentally, believes the only sure defense against such treatment is a suicide tablet.

The reader at this point may object that all this has

nothing to do with propaganda and psychological warfare in general. The Communists, after all, cannot deprive a free nation of its food or other creature-comforts. The answer is simply that they do not have to. Most of the peoples of the world are undernourished to begin with because of economic impoverishment or underdevelopment. In Egypt, India, in pre-communist China and in the numerous countries of Southeast Asia, starvation, inadequate shelter and disease are the common lot of the common man. If we bear in mind that one of the entering wedges of Communist psychological warfare is "agrarian reform," and that once in power the Communists heavily emphasize increased agricultural production as part of their communal farm programs and periodical "plans," the importance of the most primary of all human motives in the battle for men's minds becomes obvious.

The United States and her Allies, are, of course, fully aware of the importance of economic aid to impoverished nations. The United Nations' Point Four Program was instituted in recognition of the desirability of improving living standards throughout the world. Russia and Red China also have their economic and military "aid" programs. However, there are two insurmountable difficulties which stand in the way of *either* the West or East rendering any substantial aid to the world's starving masses. First, to adequately feed the undernourished people of Southeast Asia alone would take the entire annual farm production of the United States and Canada. Secondly, the population bomb would make any such program obsolete within a year, since in India alone the population is increasing at the rate of 5,000,000 people every year. Incidentally, if Communist dominated countries maintain their present rate of population increase for the next ten years, approximately two-thirds of the world's people will be under Communist control—nearly twice as many as now are.

The Communist answer to the insoluable problem of food supply is lies. Because they are in no better position than the West to solve the agricultural difficulties of those they seek to enslave, their technique is to make promises which they have no intention of keeping. Once in power, they are more likely to bleed rather than feed their victims, and with impunity, since once under Communist control there is no way to fight back. But from the psychological point of view, a promise of food is a good as food in the basket in the hunger-weakened mind of the starving man. The Communist propagandists, as well as the specialists in individual brain washing, are fully aware of this principle. It is perhaps the single greatest problem that the West must contend with in the war of nerves.

The second step in brain washing involves an appeal to the safety or security motives of the intended victim. The same appeal is an equally important ingredient of Russian and Chinese political propaganda. In the case of the captive soldier, the technique is to keep him in uncertainty as to his ultimate fate. He is charged with "crimes" but never told precisely what crimes. He is not informed of the date of his trial. He is continually threatened with fearful punishments; and is, in fact, punished often enough to make the threats effective. One especially ingenious technique used by the Chinese in dealing with American prisoners of war ought to be singled out for special mention. The captives were frequently awakened in the middle of the night and told that they were to be executed by a firing squad. They were then marched to the place of execution which was the edge of their own graves previously prepared by the G.I.'s themselves. While there is no evidence that such threats were ever carried out in fact, the prisoners could never be sure but that each night might be their last.

In appealing to the security motive on the international level, the Communists first build up a vivid picture of the war-mad West in the minds of their targets. They then promise to protect the alleged victims of capitalistic warmongering by sending in military aid, "technicians," and eventually troops. If necessary, "internal disorders" are arranged which provide an excuse for the latter, and, incidentally, aid and abet any fifth columnists who may be taking part in the "civil war."

It has always been difficult for Americans to realize that anyone could possibly believe that we are warmongers, power mad capitalists, enslavers of inferior races, and so on down the Communist list of hate-inspired Western characteristics. But we forget that millions of Americans in the twenties believed that the United States was virtually at the mercy of a "Bolshevik Army." We forget that during the reign of the late Senator McCarthy millions believed that our government was hopelessly in the grip of a "monstrous Communist conspiracy." We forget that one Halloween in 1938 millions of our fellow countrymen believed that the world was under invasion by Martians. In short, we forget the power of hysteria and credulity. Bearing in mind that Communist propaganda is directed at millions of insecure, undernourished people, many of whom wear dark skins, the lies seem less fantastic, indeed, almost mild by comparison.

The appeal to creature needs and to the universal desire

for security is largely based on negative motives. Deficiencies exist or are deliberately created which the Communists then promise to fulfill. But man does not live by bread alone. He looks to life for more than security in the face of life's exigencies. From the very beginning the Communists have been fully aware that human nature is impelled forward by positive goals. Marx and Engels recognized this fundamental truth in the *Communist Manifesto* when they wrote of the brotherhood of man and of the international scope of the labor movement. In essence, the appeal is to man's desire for belongingness. It is the same motive which, in part, underlies the lure of religious and fraternal orders. There is no normal human being who does not need to belong to some group, however small. But what could be more satisfying to the downtrodden masses than to ally themselves with a supra-national group—a group, moreover, that promises security, relief from oppression and the material rewards so conspicuously consumed by the idle rich?

The brain washers, too, are fully aware of the force of this motive. The captive G.I.'s were informed that they were the pawns of the capitalists, the victims of a kind of mental disease imposed upon them by industrialists, war lords and munitions makers—a disease whose chief symptom was the monstrous delusion that they were fighting for democracy and freedom when in reality they had risked their lives to preserve the interests of corrupt capitalists and profiteers. They were informed that the Communists are the true champions of the downtrodden; and that once the G.I.'s had been "cured" of their "disease," they, too, could join the World Brotherhood movement. Like Winston Smith in *1984*, the G.I.'s were told they must suffer pain and degradation before they could be returned to sanity. However, the suffering was imposed in the spirit of love, not hate. Such were the childlike rationalizations that some Americans believed.

We must not forget that less than two dozen American captives did actually succumb to brain washing. For the most part these were ignorant, weak young men who had been hand-picked by Chinese psychologists for character defects. Nevertheless, it remains an incontrovertible fact that the thing was possible, however small the number. Moreover, we must bear in mind that even the lowliest G.I. has enjoyed a standard of living and a measure of status far superior to those experienced by the Asiatic masses. For the world's untouchables and shirtless ones, a World Brotherhood, however inspired, may be the only brotherhood their poor lives have ever been offered.

Similarly, and perhaps more obviously, brain washers and

propagandists alike appeal directly to the positive motives for power and prestige. In part, the international scope and brotherhood aspect of the Communist movement are directed as much toward the status motives as to the need for belongingness. But more particularly, the victim of brain washing, whether individual or en masse, is promised a place in the sun. The captive G.I. private with his recent memories of not-always-gentle army discipline and his lack of status in civilian life was told that he would be sent to a Chinese university for special leadership training and upon graduation would take over a cell or block in the International Communist movement. The peasant-class Asiatic, often the victim of an avaricious landlord, the low caste Indian, the starving Egyptian are similarly offered a brave new world where they will be the masters, just as Marx and Engels promised the workers of the world that they would become the lords instead of the tools of the capitalists. Again, that much of the rosy picture of the new order promised by the Communists is lies makes little difference. Those to whom the appeal is directed are in no position to discriminate. They have, in a manner of speaking, nothing to lose and everything to gain by believing.

The fifth class of human motives recognized by modern psychologists has been variously called "self-realization," "self-actualization," "self-expression" or "self-fulfillment." Whatever the name, the impulse is real enough. We all have talents, skills and potentialities that we strive to realize in the course of our lives. For the creative artist, the accomplishment of his inner potentialities may be the paramount *raison d'être*. But to some degree, even the lowliest human being experiences a restlessness and an urge to come to grips with a deeper meaning for living than can be found in merely existing to stay alive, work and procreate. Perhaps this vague yearning is what the ancient Chinese called Tao, or it may be what underlies the current interest in existentialism. Let us simply call it self-realization.

In the main the Communists have not found it necessary to appeal to this motive. But for us the basic assumption underlying the democratic form of government is that human beings can best realize their potentialities in an atmosphere of political and religious freedom. The best government is the least government. Because Americans in general do have at least the freedom of opportunity to realize whatever talents, skills and ambitions they may possess, our propaganda line has tended to emphasize freedom, equality and the right to self-determination for all the peoples of the world. In effect we are saying that the democratic way of life offers the individual the best opportunity to realize the self, since under democratic government a minimum of restrictions are imposed upon the individual. But we tend to forget that freedom, equality and self-determination are meaningless to the man who is hungry, and whose needs for security, belongingness and a little status are unfulfilled. Thus, a great deal of American propaganda has been beside the point. You cannot begin with the top of the hierarchy of human motives and work down. You must begin at the bottom and work up.

What effective weapon is there for us in our defense against this psychological warfare? If we were to use the propaganda techniques of our opponents we would be in a much more favorable position to wage the war of nerves on even terms. But this would mean placing ourselves in the same false position as those we condemn. Our only weapon is reason, which up to this time in the United States has been sadly at the mercy of emotion. We cannot claim that we ourselves have not been victims of hysteria or mass hypnosis, in which our subjection to various delusions has done us no credit.

During the closing years of the depression, millions of Americans were badly taken in by "dictator appeal" and a starry-eyed acceptance of the then respectable Communist philosophy. During the thirties, Mussolini was cheered by American audiences when he appeared in newsreels. There were many who admired the Führrer's "business-like" methods of getting things done during the rise of Nazi Germany.

Our reactions to events since World War II have been hardly more creditable. The "spy scare" launched by the revelations of Elizabeth Bentley and Whittaker Chambers gave the late Senator McCarthy ample opportunity to show the gullibility of the American People. The fear generated by his investigations of Harvard College, government agencies and defense plants approached the proportions of mass hysteria. More important, this fear was and still is reflected in our conduct of foreign policy, foreign aid programs, our attitude toward the United Nations and our handling of such brush-fire crises as the Suez Canal incident and the Quemoy-Matsu emergency. The bold, new policies and the dynamic new psychological approach to world problems envisioned during the closing days of the war—the policies that promised a sophisticated, reasoned, long term foreign policy commensurate with our new position as a world leader—degenerated into a kind of hysterical philosophy of living from one day to the next, hoping that somehow each new crisis would be the last.

The question before us now is—can we free ourselves from this emotional-hysterical approach to the world as it is today? Can we recognize what must be done to secure our very existence in the world in the path of spreading Communism?

The key to world problems lies in understanding human nature and helping the free peoples of the world to meet their needs. We and our Western allies have come a long way in the past half-century by recognizing the principle that the smaller nations of the earth, however insignificant they may be, are not the pawns of larger powers to be exploited at will and played against each other in the game of power politics. But the more fundamental problem of winning allies by helping people to meet their needs—creature needs, security, belongingness, prestige, and self-realization—is, as yet, only dimly recognized. The appalling lack of knowledge on the part of the average American about such basic matters as the language, folkways, mores, religion, and political institutions of even the relatively familiar European nations is indicative of our unsophisticated provincialism. It is sad to report that many of our diplomats and foreign aid technicians are equally ignorant of the language and psychology of the peoples with whom they must deal. Human nature may be the same all over the world, but it expresses itself in a variety of ways according to the environment and culture in which it is nourished.

If the argument in the preceding paragraphs is sound, a clear thinking, realistic approach to the greatest problem that human beings have ever had to face can only be resolved when we fully accept the principle that only through knowledge and sympathetic understanding of our fellow men can we help them to achieve the way of life that leads to self-realization through the fulfillment of basic motives. Admittedly, the problems are appalling. There are the obvious barriers of language, religion, race and custom. Even more formidable are the problems of limited food supply, birth control, *lebensraum,* and the world-wide rising tide of nationalism. But however great the difficulties, there is no real alternative. The Russians and Red Chinese *are* actively engaged in mastering these problems. That we must face up to the task is scarcely to be questioned. The only serious consideration is whether we will be in time.

It is far beyond the scope of any single individual to attempt to formulate the complex and detailed programs basic to a reformulation of our approach to our foreign friends. However, by way of conclusion, it seems evident that the first basic step ought to involve the appointment of commissions of experts in the social sciences of anthropology, psychology, sociology, and others as indicated to carry out objective studies of India, Pakistan, Turkey, and the small nations of Southeast Asia. Such commissions would act in an advisory capacity to the State Department furnishing the latter with the necessary information upon which to base both a foreign policy and propaganda offensive that are congruent with the dynamics of human nature. Until we have the key to the understanding of human nature, our programs will continue to be dictated by expediency; war hysteria and credulity, not reason, will hold sway as they often have.

NOTES

CHAPTER 1

BOOKS

Beecher, Lyman. *The Works of the Reverend Lyman Beecher.* Boston: 1852.

Billington, Ray Allen. *The Protestant Crusade 1800-1860.* New York: Macmillan, 1938. A scholarly history of anti-Catholic prejudice in the United States. It contains a description of the burning of the convent.

Fenwick, Benedict J. "The Destruction of the Ursuline Convent at Charlestown, Mass." *U. S. Catholic Historical Society, Records and Studies,* Vol. IX. New York: 1916. This is a brief account of the convent's destruction in the form of a letter written by Bishop Fenwick.

Frothingham, Charles W. *The Convent's Doom; a Tale of Charlestown in 1834.* Boston: Graves and Weston, 1854. This fictitious account was written after the event. It is of interest today only as an example of the kind of fantasy people were willing to believe at the time. It centers around the story of a young girl kept in a convent against her will and eventually released by her lover.

Leahy, William. *The Catholic Church in New England.* Boston: Hurd and Everts, 1899.

Ricci, Scipio. *Female Convents: The Secrets of Nunneries Disclosed.* New York: Appleton, 1834. This volume was originally published in London in 1829.

Shea, John. *History of the Catholic Church in the United States,* Vol. III. New York: John Shea, 1890

Spofford, Harriet E. P. *New England Legends.* Boston: James R. Osgood Co., 1871.

Whitney, Louisa. *The Burning of the Convent.* Cambridge: Welch Bigelow and Co., 1877. This was the primary source for the description of those events in the present study that took place in the convent on the days preceding the burning.

PAMPHLETS AND OTHER DOCUMENTS

"The Charlestown Convent; its Destruction by a Mob on the Night of August 11, 1834." Boston: Patrick Donahue. This is the best secondary source for the accounts of the trials.

"Report of the Committee Relating to the Destruction of the Ursuline Convent." Boston: J. H. Eastburn, 1934. This is the document quoted at the end of the study.

"An Account of the Conflagration of the Ursuline Convent—by a Friend of Religious Toleration." Boston: 1834. This is a collection of newspaper clippings, letters to editors, etc., about the affair.

Boston Morning *Post*, August 11 and 12, 1834.

CHAPTER 2

Bernhard, H. J., Bennet D. A., and Rice, H. S. *Handbook of the Heavens.* New York: Mentor Books, 1950.

Busch, George. *Treatise on the Millennium.* New York: J. J. Harper, 1832. A history of the subject from ancient times up to the 1830's. Miller is not included among those discussed.

Dictionary of American Biography, 1933 edition.

Haynes, Carlyle B. *The Return of Jesus.* Atlanta: Southern Publishing Association, 1917. Contains an easy to understand explanation of the various Biblical prophecies on the Millennium. Also predicts the imminence of the end in 1917.

Ludlum, David M. *Social Ferment in Vermont. 1791-1850.* Montpelier: Vermont Historical Society, 1948. Valuable for the social background of the times.

Mackay, Charles. *Extraordinary Popular Delusions and the Madness of Crowds.* Boston: Page, 1932. Chapter 5 contains an account of similar panics in the Middle Ages.

Miller, William. "Evidence from Scripture and History of the Second Coming of Christ . . ." (Pamphlet) 1833.

Priest, Josiah. *A View of the Expected Christian Millennium.* Albany: Loomis Press, 1827. This book undoubtedly influenced Miller. Like Miller, Priest attempted to prove the end of the world was near, and in its time the volume was widely read and discussed.

Sears, Clara Endicott. *Days of Delusion.* Boston: Houghton Mifflin Co., 1924. This is the best book on the Millerites. It contains many amusing incidents of the resurrection eve taken from personal recollections.

Skinner, Rev. Otis. *Miller's Theory Utterly Exploded.* Boston: Thomas Whittemore, 1840. A blow-by-blow refutation of Miller's calculations.

White, James. *The Life of William Miller.* Battle Creek: Steam Press, 1875. This is actually a reprint of Sylvester's *Life of Miller,* the classic autobiography of the prophet, but is more readily available than the latter.

CHAPTER 3

The accounts of the sightings were taken from contemporary newspapers, chiefly the New York *Herald,* which carried a day-by-day report of the airship's activities gathered from all points in the Midwest. Some of the introductory material for this chapter was suggested by Herbert Lyon's article "The Not-So-Gay Nineties . . ." published in the New York *Times Magazine,* April 20, 1941. The advertisements described or quoted were published in the Burlington (Vt.) *Free Press* in January of 1897.

CHAPTER 4

The literature on the red menace of the twenties is very extensive. Much of it is repetitious or devoted to special aspects of the problem, such as the Red infiltration of labor. The following articles and books were used in the preparation of the present study.

BOOKS

Allen, Frederick Lewis. *Only Yesterday.* New York: Harper and Brothers, 1931.

Bailey, Thomas A. *America Faces Russia.* Ithaca: Cornell University Press, 1950.

Chaffee, Zechariah. *Free Speech in the United States.* Cambridge: Harvard University Press, 1946.

Schriftgiesser, Karl. *This Was Normalcy.* Boston: Atlantic, Little Brown, 1948.

Slosson, Preston W. *The Great Crusade and After.* New York: Macmillan Co., 1930.

Swisher, Carl B. *American Constitutional Development.* Boston: Houghton Mifflin Co., 1943.

ARTICLES

Literary Digest: July 5, Oct. 25, Nov. 22, Dec. 27, 1919; Sept. 8, 1923. The *Digest* took great alarm at the Bolsheviks, and the 1919 issues are full of reprinted newspaper cartoons and editorials denouncing the Reds.

Nation: Feb. 14, May 1, May 15, July 12, 1920; May 9, 1923.

New Republic: Jan. and Sept., 1920. In 1924 this journal ran a series of articles by Swinburne Hale on "Professional Patriots . . ." The latter were a kind of aftermath of the Red scare.

Outlook: Aug. 4, 1920.

In addition to these book and magazine accounts, contemporary newspapers were full of the scare. Descriptions of the bombing incidents in the present study were taken from this source.

CHAPTER 5

The chronological account of events was taken chiefly from contemporary newspapers. In addition, the following were helpful.
Allen, Frederick Lewis. *Only Yesterday.* New York: Harper & Brothers, 1931.

MacDougal, Curtis D. *Hoaxes.* New York: Macmillan Co., 1940.
Mencken, H. L. *A Mencken Chrestomathy.* New York: Alfred
A. Knopf, 1949.
Literary Digest: Sept. 11, 1926; Aug. 20, 1927, and Feb. 7, 1931.

CHAPTER 6

Most of the reactions to the broadcast that are described in
this study were gleaned from contemporary newspapers from
representative sections of the United States. Those published in
the East carried the most detailed accounts. In addition, the following sources were used:

Cantril, Hadley. *The Invasion from Mars.* Princeton: Princeton
University Press, 1940. This is a psychological analysis of the
scare and contains a full reprint of the script used in the broad-
cast.
Klein, Alexander (ed.), *Grand Deception.* New York: J. B.
Lippincott Co., 1955. The quotation on page 97 is from this
volume and was taken from the article by John Houseman
entitled, "Panic: The Men from Mars."
Newsweek, Nov. 7, 1938.
Time, Nov. 7, 1938.

CHAPTER 7

Mattoon (Ill.) *Daily Journal-Gazette,* Sept. 2-11, 1944.
Chicago *Herald-American,* Sept. 8-12, 1944.
Chicago *Tribune,* Sept. 6-15, 1944.
Time, Sept. 18, 1944.
Newsweek, Sept. 18, 1944.
Journal of Abnormal and Social Psychology, Vol. XL, 175-186.

CHAPTER 8

The following bibliography is highly selective and includes only
the more important books and articles on the saucers by both Believers and Unbelievers. A complete list of articles would extend to
hundreds of references. These are readily available in the *Readers'
Guide.* The New York *Times Index* serves as a good chronology
for the mania as well as a valuable source of reference on saucer
articles printed in that newspaper.

BOOKS
Arnold, Kenneth and Palmer, Ray, *The Coming of the Saucers.*
(Privately printed): Boise, Idaho and Amherst, Wisconsin, 1952.
This is the first eyewitness account; the last 30 pages are a

portfolio of photographs of saucers. The book is very difficult to obtain.

Heard, Gerald. *Is Another World Watching?* New York: Harper & Brothers, 1950. Heard believes the saucers are Martian in origin and manned by "super-bees." Only creatures such as these could withstand the inertia of blast-offs and sudden turns at saucer-speeds. Heard also thinks Phobos and Demos are space platforms for launching Martian saucers.

Keyhoe, Major Donald. *Flying Saucers from Outer Space.* New York: Henry Holt, 1953.

———. *The Flying Saucers Are Real.* New York: Gold Medal Book No. 107. Fawcett Publications, 1950. This book may be difficult to obtain. It is an out-of-print paperbound publication.

———. *The Flying Saucer Conspiracy.* New York: Henry Holt, 1955.

Menzel, Donald H. *Flying Saucers.* Cambridge: Harvard University Press, 1952. Menzel is a professor of astrophysics at Harvard. He is a strong Unbeliever, and his book is an attempt to account for the saucers in terms of natural phenomena and optical illusions.

Ruppelt, Edward J. *The Report on Unidentified Flying Objects.* New York: Doubleday & Co., 1956. This is the best single source on the saucers. It contains detailed analyses of the more important incidents.

Scully, Frank. *Behind the Flying Saucers.* New York: Henry Holt, 1950. Contains accounts of captured saucers and Saucerians.

ARTICLES

Life, July 23, 1947. An early summary of the first rash of sightings.

Saturday Evening Post, April 30 and May 7, 1949. These are the important articles by Shalett mentioned in the present study.

U. S. News and World Report, April 10, 1950.

New Yorker, Sept. 6, 1952. An excellent and objective summary of the main events up to that time.

True, Dec. 1949. One of the early Keyhoe articles which stirred up a considerable pother at the time.

CHAPTER 9

Bernstein, Morey. *The Search for Bridey Murphy.* New York: Doubleday & Co., 1956.

Gardner, Martin. *Fads and Fallacies in the Name of Science.* Dover Publication T-394, 1957. Contains a chapter on the Bridey mania.

Murphy, Gardner. *Historical Introduction to Modern Psychology.*

New York: Harcourt, Brace & Co., 1949. Chapter 9 includes a brief history of hypnotism.

Life, March 19, 1956. The best magazine account of the "Hypnotizzy" caused by the book's publication.

Newsweek, April 9, and *Time,* March 19, 1956. Both magazines contain feature articles on Bridey and hypnotism.

Saturday Review of Literature, April 28, 1956.

Nation, March 24, 1956.

Commonweal, April 27, 1956.

The last three magazines cited published reviews of the Bernstein book and LP record along with commentaries on the entire affair.

CHAPTER 10

Printed material on the life and times of Senator McCarthy would fill a fair-sized library. The following is intended only as a guide to the more important bibliographic sources which were used in the preparation of this study.

BOOKS

Rovere, Richard. *Senator Joe McCarthy.* New York: Harcourt, Brace & Co., 1959. The most definitive study on McCarthy the man that has been published to date.

Rorty, James and Decter, Moshe. *McCarthy and the Communists.* Boston: Beacon Press, 1954. A reasonably objective analysis of McCarthy and his methods from the liberal point of view.

Straight, Michael. *Trial by Television.* Boston: Beacon Press, 1954. A highly readable account of the Army-McCarthy hearings.

Gore, Leroy. *Joe Must Go.* New York: Julian Messner, 1954. Chiefly of importance as a record of the recall movement initiated by the author.

Buckley, William and Bozell, L. Brent. *McCarthy and His Enemies.* Chicago: Henry Regnery, 1954. An analysis of the Senator's methods from the pro-McCarthy viewpoint with special emphasis on the Tydings investigation.

Goldman, Eric F. *The Crucial Decade.* New York: Alfred A. Knopf, 1956. A social history of the decade, 1945-1955. The material on the Senator is scattered through the second half of the book. Chapter VI is devoted to the "conspiracy theory" of the Roosevelt-Truman administration's foreign policy.

Lattimore, Owen. *Ordeal by Slander.* Boston: Little Brown & Co., 1950. Lattimore's account of his appearance before the Tydings Committee. The Professor's protestations of innocence must, of course, be evaluated in the light of his subsequent indictment for perjury.

Davis, Elmer. *But We Were Born Free.* Indianapolis: The Bobbs-Merrill Co., 1954. Interesting as representative of the liberal news commentator's attitude toward the Senator.

McCarthy, Joe. *McCarthyism: The Fight for America*. New York: Devin-Adair Co., 1952. An autobiographical account of the Senator's career from the time of the Wheeling speech through the Tydings hearings. Also contains sections on "documented answers to questions asked by friend and foe."

McCarthy, Joe. *Major Speeches and Debates of Senator Joe McCarthy 1950-1951*. Washington, D. C.: U. S. Government Printing Office. The speeches are reprinted from the *Congressional Record*. The two most important are the first (the "81 cases" speech) and the 11th (the Marshall speech).

PERIODICALS

The best analysis of McCarthy and McCarthyism to appear in a journal was published by the *Progressive* magazine in a special edition in April, 1954. The Rovere article on Cohn and Schine cited in the text also contains a general analysis of McCarthyism and its effects on government agencies. The *Mercury* articles referred to in the text may be found in the following issues: May, July, Oct. and Nov. of 1953.

OTHER SOURCES

The direct quotations from speeches, hearings, etc., were taken from contemporary newspaper accounts, the *Congressional Record*, and government documents. The syndicated column by Joseph and Stewart Alsop is valuable for a contemporary running commentary on McCarthyism.

ABOUT THE AUTHOR

J(AMES) P. CHAPLIN was a member of the faculty of the University of Vermont, where he was professor of psychology and chairman of his department. Born in 1919 in Santa Monica, California, he spent most of his boyhood in Albuquerque, New Mexico. He held bachelor's and master's degrees in psychology from the University of New Mexico, and served during World War II as a psychologist in the Aviation Cadet Program. He was the author of a number of technical papers in psychological journals, co-author of a textbook in *Theories and Systems of Psychology,* and author of the *Dictionary of Psychology,* the *Dictionary of the Occult and Paranormal,* and the *Primer of Neurology and Neurophysiology.* James died in 2010.